THE
BLUEPRINT

THE
BLUEPRINT

OBAMA'S PLAN
to Subvert the Constitution
and Build an Imperial Presidency

KEN BLACKWELL
KEN KLUKOWSKI

LYONS PRESS
Guilford, Connecticut
An imprint of Globe Pequot Press

From Ken Blackwell:
To my best friend and wife Rosa, and our children, and my mother Dana, who passed on to me a reverence for life and a passion for freedom.

From Ken Klukowski:
To my loving wife Amanda, and our children, Chase Everett and Caleb Augustine, who are our daily reminders that we must faithfully protect liberty for the next generation.

To buy books in quantity for corporate use
or incentives, call **(800) 962–0973**
or e-mail **premiums@GlobePequot.com**.

Lyons Press is an imprint of Globe Pequot Press.

Library of Congress Cataloging-in-Publication Data is available on file.

ISBN 978-0-7627-6134-0

Printed in the United States of America

10 9 8 7 6 5 4 3 2 1

CONTENTS

INTRODUCTION:
Freedom in Crisis

We are five days away from fundamentally transforming the United States of America.
                        —BARACK OBAMA, OCTOBER 30, 2008

sub • vert v. 1. To undermine or erode, especially with regards to the character of, principles of, or allegiance to; 2. To ruin or corrupt

Barack Obama promised to "fundamentally transform" America as our nation's president. That's not surprising, because in various ways most presidential candidates say they will do just that.

But it's different with President Obama, because his plans, dreams, and vision for the United States are irreconcilably at odds with the most important thing our nation's Founders gave us and hoped for us to keep safe forever: our Constitution. The Constitution of the United States stands in the way of what Barack Obama wants to do.

For Obama to remake our country into what he wants it to be, he must subvert the Supreme Law of the Land.

Key parts of the Constitution are designed to protect us from our own government. Obama knows he must execute an aggressive strategy to disarm those constitutional safeguards, to free himself from its constraints so that he can truly "fundamentally transform" this nation.

And that's what he's doing.

Fundamental Change Means Subverting the Constitution

Barack Obama ran on just two words: *hope* and *change*. But those are just a couple of words; they're not a plan for governing a nation. For those who were paying attention, he promised to "fundamentally transform" the United States of America. That's his plan, and he's working on it every day.

Those who listened to more than *hope 'n' change* started to hear things that didn't sound quite so "hopey." Obama talked about the "wealthy" paying their "fair share." He spoke about ditching traditional energy sources like coal and oil. He crooned about giving away trillions of dollars' worth of free stuff—health care, education . . . everything you might ask for except guns. (Because he says that people only cling to guns—or religion—out of "bitterness.")

But everyone knows that such things don't come for free. If he wants to spend trillions of dollars, then those dollars have to come from somewhere. So people who listened past the slogans knew there was more to the Obama plan than just hope 'n' change.

Once President Obama took office, we saw our worst fears realized. Legions of powerful officials, not confirmed by the Senate and not subject to congressional oversight, have been installed in key positions. The government is taking over massive corporations and attempting to take over entire sectors of our economy. To maximize the number of people who see things his way, the president is working to silence dissenting voices, shut down media outlets that expose the truth, and co-opt the rest of the media to parrot his daily messages. To make sure these changes outlast him, Obama's blueprint calls for changing the way Americans think about government, and even the way Americans think about themselves.

To keep the Obama plan moving forward in the face of certain opposition, the president's blueprint calls for changing the way democracy works in this country so that he and his supporters can continue holding on to their offices and their power. And to keep these things in place and advance them even further, Obama plans on remaking our courts so that he will have judges who will decide constitutional cases in his favor.

Barack Obama does indeed plan on giving us "change." He plans on changing our government, our families, our property, and our private lives.

He also plans to change our Constitution. Not changing it by literally rewriting it; instead, he's changing it by ignoring the limits it imposes on government, disregarding the parts of the Bill of Rights that forbid his agenda, changing the way democracy works in this country so that he and his supporters can't be voted out of power, and creating a Supreme Court that will simply rubber-stamp and uphold everything he wants to do.

The Constitution is what gives us limited government, protecting our states from an all-powerful government. Indeed, it protects each of us as American citizens from *any* government—federal or state—having too much power over our lives.

The Constitution is a problem for Barack Obama. Through its words, the Framers declare much of his blueprint to be unlawful. That's why that same Obama blueprint calls for him to subvert our Constitution. President Obama needs to overcome the Constitution so that he can give us something that he genuinely believes to be better than our current form of government. He thinks he's doing us all a great service by amassing unchecked power to give us things that he believes are for our own good.

Barack Obama's blueprint would create the ultimate imperial presidency. It would be the end of our constitutional republic, and the beginning of a government with unlimited power over all our lives.

He promised us "change." He promised that if elected to the most powerful office in the world, he would start executing his blueprint for "fundamentally transforming the United States of America."

And he is.

Obama Told Us He Would Do This

The amazing thing about Barack Obama's far-left liberalism is that so many of us seem amazed by it. Look—he told us he would do this.

It's true that some of his rhetoric was moderate. He promised to be a post-partisan president, just as he also promised to be post-racial. It seems his favorite line on the campaign trail was that we need to get past red states and blue states to be the *United* States of America.

Good words, but also empty ones.

Ironically, those words could have been uttered in all honesty by John McCain. To the perpetual frustration of the GOP base, McCain was often moderate. On some issues, such as cutting wasteful spending, ending earmarks, or strengthening national security, McCain was a reliably conservative vote. But on other issues, from tax cuts to the environment to campaign finance, McCain struck toward the middle. If McCain had used such moderate rhetoric, it might have rung true.

But it rang false from Obama.

First, his record gave him away. He was the single most liberal senator in the U.S. Senate. On everything—including the Supreme Court, taxes, spending, the environment, defense, abortion, health care, education, earmarks, terrorism, the military, foreign diplomacy, and national security—he was a purely knee-jerk, doctrinaire liberal.

National Journal, the well-respected and moderately liberal publication that rates senators every cycle according to where their votes place them on the political spectrum, rated Barack Obama the most liberal senator in America going into the 2008 election. That means Obama was to the left of the late Ted Kennedy, Barbara Boxer, and avowed socialist Bernie Sanders. You know that you're a radical when those people look conservative when compared to you.

Second, although he tried to maintain moderate rhetoric, occasionally his mask would slip, and there would be Obama's very telling and anything-but-moderate words. We need only to look at some of the highlights of statements he made either during the campaign or that came to light during the election season:

First, Obama said this to the editorial board of the *San Francisco Chronicle:*

What I've said is that we would put a cap-and-trade system in place that is as aggressive, if not more aggressive, than anybody else's out there. I was the first to call for a 100 percent auction on the cap-and-trade system, which means that every unit of carbon or greenhouse gases emitted would be charged to the polluter . . . So if someone wants to build a coal-power plant, they can; it's just that it will bankrupt them. . . .[1]

Pair that with Obama's campaign speech where he said, "We can't drive our SUVs and eat as much as we want and keep our homes on 72 degrees at all times . . . and then just expect that other countries are going to say okay. . . . That's not leadership. That's not going to happen."[2]

Really? Who cares if countries like China and Venezuela approve of what we eat or what temperatures we set on our thermostats? We don't need foreign approval to drive an SUV.

But the mentality here is the terrifying part. First, his statements show that he thinks we should tailor our lives for the approval of foreign countries. Second, and far more troubling, is that he responds to the notion that we will live as we want by declaring, "That's not going to happen." In other words, if we don't live as *he* wants us to, he thinks the federal government should have the power to force us to obey.

This imperial attitude goes beyond economics, extending into social issues. Regarding the need for teenagers to have the right to get an abortion, Obama said, "I've got two daughters . . . I am going to teach them first of all about values and morals. But if they make a mistake, I don't want them punished with a baby."[3]

Since the right to abortion was the product of a judicial activist decision of the U.S. Supreme Court in 1973 (*Roe v. Wade*), that brings to mind another statement Obama made about the Supreme Court. Talking about the Supreme Court during a 2001 radio interview when he was an Illinois state senator, Barack Obama said:

The Supreme Court never ventured into the issues of redistri-bution of wealth and served more basic issues of political and economic justice in this society . . . I think one of the tragedies of the civil rights movement was because the civil rights movement became so court-focused . . . there was a tendency to lose track of . . . the actual coalitions of power through which you bring about redistributive change. And in some ways we still suffer from that.[4]

What's scary about that statement is this is the language of the Ultra Left. Not the Left or even Far Left; it's the language of the Radical Left Fringe. Most of us have never used the terms *economic justice* or *redistributive change*, but these terms are common among radical leftists when discussing how government should redistribute wealth to create a society that is more "just" and "fair" in how it allocates economic resources to make sure the poor get their "fair share" of what is now held by the rich, and even the middle class.

This Obama opinion is pure socialism, possibly to the point of sounding Marxist. It presupposes that it's the role of government to redistribute wealth, taking it from some and giving it to others. According to this mind-set, the government is entitled to decide how much of your hard-earned money you should keep, versus how much you'll be forced to give up so government can give it to others. It's a denial of the basic American concept of private property ownership.

For those skeptics who think such a characterization of Obama's views isn't completely fair, all you have to do is take those statements above, together with Barack Obama's now-infamous exchange with Joe the Plumber. When walking through a neighborhood in Ohio, Obama passed a resident named Samuel Joseph Wurzelbacher who was playing football in the yard with his son. Joe the Plumber approached then-Senator Obama, saying he wanted to buy his own plumbing business, and asked, "Your new tax plan is going to tax me more, isn't it?"

After Obama answered that it would, Joe the Plumber protested, "I've worked hard . . . I work ten to twelve hours a day and I'm buying this company and I'm going to continue working that way. I'm getting taxed more and more while fulfilling the American Dream."[5]

Obama responded, "My attitude is that if the economy's good for folks from the bottom up, it's gonna be good for everybody. I think that when you spread the wealth around, it's good for everybody."[6]

There you have one of the most revealing quotes in all of the 2008 campaign season. Barack Obama believes that "when you spread the wealth around, it's good for everybody." This is the core philosophy of socialism: When the government takes over the means of economic production and redistributes wealth according to the government's judgment as to what a "fair" allocation is of economic assets among the population, it makes for a better society.

It's the antithesis of free-market capitalism, where everyone has their fair shot and government gets out of the way. In capitalism, government levels the field at the beginning and provides equal opportunity. In socialism, government levels the field at the end and provides equal outcomes; government picks the winners and losers, removing the incentive to succeed because the more you make, the more government takes, and the less you make, the more government gives you.

Barack Obama told us all of these things before Election Day. Millions were outraged. But those millions were not enough, as America was unhappy at the moment with the incumbent Republican president, and thus with the Republican Party. (This outrage was fueled, however, through a Republican administration and congressional members that had abandoned conservative principles in favor of "big-government conservatism"—which is a contradiction in terms. In other words, voters were mad at the Republican Party for not acting like Republicans.)

Even so, the reality is that the McCain-Palin ticket took the lead over the Obama-Biden ticket in the polls starting September

7, 2008.[7] After both party conventions were over and the VP selections were considered by the public, John McCain and Sarah Palin were ahead in the polls. Then the markets crashed and panic set in. People blamed George W. Bush, and the McCain campaign did not manage to separate itself from the Bush administration. Obama ran against the "Bush-McCain" economic policy, and won the White House.

But none of this changes one simple fact: We were given all the information we needed to understand exactly what Barack Obama planned to do. And now he's doing it.

Methods of Deception

In carrying out their plan to remake our country, Team Obama has a clear method of convincing the public and moving Congress. There are four techniques Barack Obama, his White House staff, and his allies use to package and sell their agenda. These four techniques pop up repeatedly in our analysis of the topics you'll read about in this book.

1. Crisis

Almost everything the Obama White House demands is an "emergency" response to some "crisis." The crisis is always so pressing, and the consequences of not blindly following Obama so dire, that immediate action is called for every single time.

No one read the disgraceful $787 billion "stimulus" bill. Why? Because everyone was told there was no time. The bill was not released until after midnight in the early morning hours of Friday, February 13, 2009 (Friday the 13th—very appropriate). Despite the fact that the bill was 1,071 pages long—a monster that was over eight inches thick—Speaker Nancy Pelosi forced a vote on it just a few hours later on Friday, before a single member of Congress had had time to read it.[8] The stimulus bill must be passed *immediately*, and if it was, unemployment wouldn't exceed 8 percent.[9] (It's over 10 percent at the time of this writing. Change we can believe in? Keep the change.)

So it is with everything from this Obama White House. A calamity will befall us if we don't obey Obama right this moment without delay. So Congress obeyed, and calamity befell us anyway.

2. Straw Man

A "straw man" is a false argument, in which you characterize your opponent's position as something other than what it truly is when you're communicating with your audience. You then defeat this fabricated position and claim to have overcome your opponent's position in doing so. In other words, you erect a straw man (like a scarecrow in a field), and then you knock the straw man to the ground, call it your opponent and his position, and claim victory. Of course you haven't beaten your opponent, because the argument you defeated was never what your opponent supported. But that's the deceptiveness involved in straw-man arguments.

Barack Obama loves to knock down straw men.

The perfect example is health care. President Obama says that Republicans oppose health-care reform. That's absurd. Republicans and conservative groups have put forward innovative health-care ideas—which Democrats have opposed for almost twenty years, and Obama has rejected since he entered public life (which wasn't all that long ago). For example, as you'll read in chapter 4, Republicans have (a) argued for tort reform to try to save more than $100 billion a year in "defensive medicine"; (b) called for allowing small businesses to join together as associations to get the same large-group discounts that big corporations and unions get; and (c) called for allowing people to buy insurance across state lines in order to get the lowest-priced plan that best suits their needs.

One example from the campaign trail shows that this has long been a favorite tactic of Barack Obama. In 2007, one of your authors (Klukowski) went with his wife (who is an emergency room doctor) and a friend to hear then-Senator Obama speak. This was early in the campaign, and we wanted to hear for ourselves the person who was causing Hillary Clinton such headaches on the campaign trail, just to get some sense of what was going on within the Democratic Party.

We went to an event on the main campus of George Mason University in Fairfax, Virginia, on February 2. In a room with hundreds of college students who were ecstatic with joy, we listened to Obama make his pitch. During the speech, he said he would fight to change health care, saying, "I dream of an ER where you can go and you won't be turned away because you don't have the right insurance."

Suddenly, I heard a feminine voice I know very well shout out, "That's a lie!" I turned, eyes wide, to see my usually friendly and happy wife with anger in her eyes and her fists clenched. My wife, who almost always avoids political debates when she can help it, chose to dive in with both feet on this occasion. I looked around, realizing that at least a hundred people were giving us looks that, if looks could kill, would have killed us dozens of times over. Wondering if the three of us might involuntarily be visiting an emergency room later that afternoon, I moved us to a different section of the crowd.

Fortunately for us, most of the crowd didn't hear my wife. Obama kept speaking, the crowd kept hollering, mesmerized as if in a euphoric trance as they gazed upon their Anointed One, and we went unnoticed except for the people who had been standing around us when my wife had decided to contribute to the discussion.

But my wife was right. Barack Obama's statement was, in fact, a lie. Federal law requires that every person who shows up at an emergency room be treated regardless of whether they have insurance or not. Under EMTALA (the Emergency Medical Treatment and Active Labor Act), if any person shows up at an emergency room in a hospital that receives federal Medicare dollars (which is essentially every hospital in the country), the doctors and staff there will immediately give full treatment to a person regardless of whether they have any insurance, or even whether they are legally in the country.[10] The federal government openly acknowledges that the whole purpose of the law is "to ensure public access to emergency services regardless of ability to pay."[11]

I can attest to that based on real-life knowledge. My wife told me that at the hospital where she did her residency after medical school, an estimated 70 percent of her patients—more than two out of three—were uninsured.

So no one is turned away from an ER for not having insurance. Barack Obama is too intelligent not to know that, yet he said it anyway to get a reaction out of the crowd (that cheered wildly at his vow to end the nonexistent, cold-hearted refusal to treat uninsured people in emergency rooms). It's the worst form of demagoguery. Obama set up a straw man and then knocked it to the ground to the adoring cheers of his onlookers.

We've seen this technique used in other issues, ranging from the automaker bailouts to stimulus bills. President Obama says that Republicans don't want to stimulate the economy. That's not true, and the president knows it. The truth is, Republicans don't believe that a decade-long spending bill filled with hundreds of billions of dollars of wasteful, pork-barrel spending will stimulate anything. Instead, many Republicans proposed an alternative bill that was largely based on across-the-board tax cuts for all people and all businesses, to surge fresh money into the economy.

President Obama's statement that Republicans opposed stimulating the economy was just one more straw man, and it's par for the course.

3. Bogeyman

The next trick used for each of the White House's agenda items is Team Obama's creation of a bogeyman to vilify the opposition.

It makes sense, doesn't it? If what President Obama and his henchmen want is so good and beneficial, then those who oppose it can't all just be thinking about it all wrong; some of them must actually be acting from reprehensible motives. They must be bad people. Thus, Team Obama must cast such an opposition figure as a bogeyman.

We saw this with health care, where insurance companies and pharmaceutical companies were cast as the bad guys. We also saw this with the cap-and-trade battles, in which oil and gas companies were cast as villains. In card check, it was business owners who were portrayed as not caring about their employees, exploiting their workers out of greed. And it was corporate executives who were portrayed as devils during the takeover of the financial industry and corporate crackdown, where materialistic, cigar-smoking robber barons were seen as erecting luxury palaces on a foundation of deceit. Every time Team Obama goes after an issue, they always assign the worst motives to those private-sector actors who are engaged in that issue. Each time, the message is that this private-sector person (or opposition politician in government) cannot be trusted and is harming ordinary people, and the Obama administration must step in to make things right.

In President Obama's America, opponents are rarely simply wrong. Often, they are also evil.

We even saw this with a media outlet: Fox News. When the rest of the media was swooning over Obama, Fox was giving airtime to opposition voices. So White House brass, from the chief of staff to the senior advisor to the communications director, started saying that Fox was not a true media outlet and should instead be treated as a twenty-four-hour talk radio–style opinion show.

The coordinated attempt by Rahm Emanuel and other top Obama advisors to recast Fox as being anything other than a bona fide media outlet failed (more on that in chapter 8). But it shows that there is no one person or entity that Team Obama will not try to characterize as dishonest and conniving in order to demonize that opposition voice.

But on at least one occasion, the president overreached. In discussing health care, the president accused doctors of lining their pockets by making decisions out of greed and self-interest instead of the best interests of their patients. He used the example of a child with a sore throat going to the doctor, saying that oftentimes a doctor would order the child's tonsils removed rather than a less-drastic treatment because the doctor would make more money by making the child undergo surgery.[12]

First, let us remove the appalling Obama bogeyman label from doctors. As a group, doctors are among the finest Americans. They have to perform at top academic levels all the way through college to get into medical school, where they spend four brutal years. Then they do a multiyear training program in residency, officially not exceeding eighty-five hours per week but which sometimes tops one hundred hours a week. After all this, and often with $100,000 or more (often far more) in student loans, they're qualified to save lives on their own. These people are passionately dedicated to helping others. They deserve our thanks and our respect, not the scorn of an opportunistic politician who can't seem to refrain from insulting doctors as greedy, lazy, and self-serving.

Secondly, it's a flat-out lie, as any doctor in the country can explain to you. (We can hear Congressman Joe Wilson shouting, "You lie!" somewhere.) The family doctor who diagnoses the need for a tonsillectomy is not the ENT specialist who actually performs the removal surgery.

And third, it was a huge mistake. Doctors are one of the most-respected groups of people in our society, and rightly so. Politicians and lawyers (Obama is both), however, are among the most despised and reviled of professions, and often—though not always—rightly so. This hyperpartisan swipe coincided with the accelerating plummet of Obamacare in the polls, showing that the American people were siding with their trusted doctors over their smooth-talking president.

4. Victims
Fourth of President Obama's tactics is to always create a victim. He'll always tell a group of people that there's someone to blame, and that

someone is never Barack Obama (or his friends, such as the ever-popular Nancy Pelosi).

And whoever President Obama says should lay the blame, those are the victims. For health care, it's the uninsured or those with pre-existing conditions. For wages or business issues, the victims are blue-collar workers. For affirmative action, the victims are blacks or Hispanics. (We can't say all minorities, because the tremendous over-all success of Asians and Indians proves that there's no systemic racism that keeps all minorities down.) For school choice, the victims are teachers and public-school students. For cap and trade, the victims are our children and the apocalypse that Obama says they will inherit.

Whoever you are and whatever you do, if you are not a wealthy white male with a great education and a great career, a stable family, and in fine health, then Barack Obama says you are a victim of something and will tell you who to blame.

The politician who promised to bring us all together instead couches almost everything he does in terms of us-against-them, with "us" always being some sort of victim, who should blame "them" because "they" are somehow responsible for "our" lot in life.

The Pattern Is the Point
Some might be surprised at the widespread focus of this book. The sections of the various chapters in this book cover what seem like a lot of topics, even though we keep most of those chapters short enough to be read in one sitting and to avoid getting too far in the weeds on any one issue.

But covering that number of issues is essential, because the pattern is the point. For each of these chapters and the sections within each chapter, we show how what President Obama is attempting is not only bad policy, but it's also unconstitutional; it violates our supreme law, time and time again.

If this were two or three or five issues, then one could wonder if it's just coincidence. But when you have over twenty separate issues around which the president violates our Constitution's safeguards, which are particularly designed to protect our liberty by restraining the power of government, then a terrifying truth emerges:

He's doing this deliberately. He seeks to remake our nation, violating our supreme law, and to abuse the levers of power to permanently change this country into a big-government collectivist society that our Founders would abhor.

This is not to say he's evil. Obama thinks that what he's doing is right. He thinks government really *does* have all the answers, and he paternalistically thinks he's helping ignorant people who don't know enough to run their own lives, and instead need the wisdom and direction of an all-powerful government to make decisions for them and their children. A government full of the best and brightest, led by a brilliant and eloquent leader. Him.

It's insulting. It's appalling. But that's how he thinks.

The Blueprint's Architects
Others share President Obama's values, priorities, and thinking. They are the architects of his blueprint, the people whom he's brought to the table to devise the details of the blueprint to achieve his vision.

For all his intelligence, Barack Obama was elected as perhaps the least-experienced and least-prepared president in more than a century. He was a U.S. senator for merely two years before he started running for president. Before that, he was only a state senator, representing a far-left city in a liberal state, and lecturing at the University of Chicago. Before that, as we all know, he was a community organizer working with groups such as ACORN.

Barack Obama had a vision for America. He knew the broad strokes of what he wanted. But lacking any experience or background with high office or the countless policy issues handled by the federal government, he needed others to devise strategies and policies to realize his vision.

Three such assistants fill the most senior positions in his White House. They are Chief of Staff Rahm Emanuel, Senior Advisor David Axelrod, and Assistant for Intergovernmental Relations Valerie Jarrett. These three form the execution half of President Obama's inner circle, responsible for passing and implementing Obama's programs and priorities.

Behind them are three more individuals, who actually think up the programs and policies. They are John Podesta, chairman of the Center for American Progress, top lobbyist and Democratic operative Harold Ickes, and Andy Stern, president of the Service Employees International Union (SEIU).

While others play a role in the blueprint, these six are perhaps the most important figures in designing the details to create the imperial presidency that the Far Left has dreamt of for decades.

But make no mistake: This blueprint is Barack Obama's blueprint. It's his vision. It's his agenda. And if he succeeds, the power will be his as well.

Conservatives Must Unite

For President Obama's power grab to be stopped, everyone who opposes his collectivist quasi-socialism, anti-sovereign globalism, social engineering, centralization of power, and court packing must unite. We cannot allow differences on one or two issues—even important ones—to keep us from working together for our common goal of stopping the most radical leftist president in America's history. And, needless to say, if we cannot allow policy differences to divide us, then we certainly cannot allow egos, personality conflicts, and old grudges to stand in the way. It's true that Washington, D.C., is full of prima donnas and control freaks, and that some of these people are as intolerably arrogant as they are self-serving.

But Barack Obama is counting on those divisions to keep us from working together. He believes that these issues and feuds—many legitimate, but some not—will prevent us from working together to stop him from permanently changing the United States, moving it away from our Founding Fathers' ideals of limited government, personal responsibility, Judeo-Christian morality, and economic opportunity. We must prove him wrong.

At the signing of the Declaration of Independence, one of the most revered Founders uttered words that are as true today as they were then. Benjamin Franklin admonished all those present that, "We must all hang together, or assuredly we shall all hang separately."[13]

The final clause of the Declaration concludes, "with a firm reliance on the protection of divine providence, we mutually pledge to each other our lives, our fortunes, and our sacred honor." They meant those words, because they knew that their lives were on the line. If they failed in the Revolutionary War and Britain reestablished control in America, then all the names we've grown up revering—Thomas Jefferson, John Adams, James Madison, Patrick Henry, George Mason, and the father of our country, George Washington—would all have been executed as traitors. Their lands and wealth would have been confiscated, and they would have been vilified for all time in British history.

We do not face times such as those. But as you'll read in this book, Barack Obama and his team seek not to cooperate and collaborate with any Republicans or other non-Democrats. Instead, they plan to divide opposition forces, and beat conservative interest groups one at a time, until none are left. In President Obama's America, dissent will not be tolerated.

The only solution is to unite. As the president's numbers remain consistently under 50 percent, there are more who disapprove of what he is doing than those who do approve. By marshaling resources and educating our fellow citizens, this unconstitutional power grab can be stopped, and this ultra-left ideologue can be defeated in 2012.

Many conservatives are starting to come to the same conclusion. On February 17, 2010, more than one hundred conservative leaders (including both of your humble authors) gathered to sign the "Mount Vernon Statement," also titled "Constitutional Conservatism: A Statement for the 21st Century." This document makes the case that all three types of conservative Americans—social, economic, and national security conservatives—need to act as one. It makes the case that a prosperous society requires ethical citizens; that an overspending big government is dangerous to personal morality; and that national security requires both brave and virtuous citizens and a thriving, robust economy.[14]

Conservatives are starting to understand that we're all in it together. The Constitution that serves as the Supreme Law of the Land also mandates conservative policies in all three of these areas.

The Constitution's Promise: A Federal Government of Limited Powers

There are plenty of books out there on why what Barack Obama is doing is wrong. What's different about this book is that we show how President Obama's actions are not just wrong; they are *illegal*. More precisely, they are *unconstitutional*—they violate our country's supreme law.

It's impossible to overstate how important this distinction is. Our Constitution isn't just some random collection of do's and don'ts. It lays out the charter of our government, but what's truly important here is why those charter provisions design the government the way that they do.

The Constitution creates a federal government of limited powers. After the American colonies declared independence in 1776, there was a reason that the Constitution wasn't written until 1787 (and not ratified until 1789). The Continental Congress, operating under the Articles of Confederation that were adopted in 1777, was a weak and disorganized entity that had almost no power, and the states were entirely sovereign entities that were essentially small countries unto themselves.

The American nation was a disorganized mess as a result; people may have been free, but the way they did things differed so much from state to state that it was impossible to organize a national defense, or conduct diplomacy with other countries, or for a thriving national economy to develop.

Yet for more than a decade there was no Constitution. The Founders were so concerned about the danger of replacing the British king with an American king that they didn't want much at all by way of a national government. Every year made clear, however, that the country could not survive without a stronger, unifying government. How could America have both a viable national government and still make sure that such a government wouldn't threaten the freedom of the people and the states?

The solution was to adopt a Constitution that established a government of strictly limited powers and a federal system with sovereign states.

A new national government would be created primarily to handle three areas of governing: military and national security, diplomacy with foreign countries, and regulating interstate and international commerce. The new government would have all the necessary powers to handle those three areas, such as raising and equipping an army and navy, and making a national currency. Beyond these, the only other federal powers would be those necessary for carrying out those express powers, which were thus implied in the Constitution.[15] Any powers not explicitly granted to this federal government, nor implicit in performing those express powers, nor explicitly denied to the states, would be reserved to the states or the people.[16] It's the perfect definition of a limited government.

This is one of the biggest differences between the federal government and state government in America's federalist system. The legal terms are "general jurisdiction" versus "limited jurisdiction."

The states are governments of *general jurisdiction*, meaning they have the authority to make laws in every area of life as explained in their state constitutions, except for those few areas that the U.S. Constitution expressly reserves to the federal government. This general jurisdiction includes a government power called the police power, which is the authority to make laws for public health, public safety, public welfare, and social morality.[17] States have this police power.[18]

The federal government, by contrast, is a government of *limited jurisdiction*. As a government of "enumerated powers," it only has those powers specifically granted to it in the Constitution.[19] The federal government has no police power.[20] This means more than the fact that the government cannot violate any of your constitutional rights. It means that beyond protecting your individual rights, if any federal law is not authorized by at least one specific provision of the Constitution, then that law is unconstitutional.

Unconstitutional laws are a nullity. Any Act of Congress "contrary to the Constitution is not law," as the Supreme Court explained in its most consequential case, *Marbury v. Madison*, adding that any action of the federal government "repugnant to the Constitution is void."[21] Anything done by the federal government that violates the Constitution is irredeemably illegal, with no rightful authority over any American citizen. Such unconstitutional laws must be recognized as such and struck down by the federal courts, and the voters should expel from office those officials who enact such illegal measures.

Conclusion

Freedom itself is in danger under the administration of President Barack Obama, aided and abetted by a far-left Congress led by Speaker Nancy Pelosi and Senate Majority Leader Harry Reid. Our supreme law is being ignored and at times even trampled underfoot, and the government is running rampant over the liberties of American citizens. The concept of limited government is on the verge of disappearing. That's what is at stake in America today.

Barack Obama is waging a war against the U.S. Constitution. He made his beliefs clear on a Chicago radio show (years before he became president), saying that the courts have not done their job in terms of bringing about "redistributive change" (i.e., government- and court-ordered "spreading the wealth") and "economic justice."[22] These are (easily deciphered) code words for the Radical Ultra Left when speaking about government redistribution of wealth through cradle-to-grave government entitlement programs, paid for through crippling taxes and regulations.

These things are not simply the opposite of America's free-market economy and our concepts of personal liberty. They violate critical provisions of the Constitution that are designed to keep government at bay so that we may live free and happy lives, raising our children as we see fit, keeping most of what we earn, and living in a society where we can defend ourselves, each other, and our way of life.

President Barack Obama has a different vision for America than that of our Founders. It is one that is radically different in terms of social values, economic prosperity, the role of families, and the role of government. To get to his vision of America, he must violate critical parts of the Constitution, relying either on political allies to support him, or shaping a judiciary that will agree with him. Such changes would be so sweeping that they would forever change our nation.

Remember—we should not be surprised by what President Obama is doing. As we've already shown, he told us he would do it. And now you know the basic techniques he's employing to sell specific parts of his plan to the American people. What you are about to read is a breakdown of the staggering number of changes Obama is attempting to make to our country, and the shockingly unconstitutional ways he will make them. The first step in preventing the current president from "fundamentally transforming the United States of America" is to inform ourselves of all the steps he's taking to make it happen.

Without further ado, here's President Obama's blueprint for building a permanent liberal nation upon the ruins of American exceptionalism.

Chapter 1

ALL THE PRESIDENT'S MEN: THE CZARS

The biggest problems we're facing right now have to do with George Bush trying to bring more and more power into the executive branch and not go through Congress at all. And that's what I intend to reverse when I'm president of the United States.
—Senator Barack Obama, March 31, 2008

We're *Star Wars* fans—and not at all ashamed of it. In fact, we think an argument could be made that liking *Star Wars* might make you a better American. Case in point: In the final blockbuster installment of the six-part *Star Wars* movie series, the evil Chancellor Palpatine, citing an "emergency," makes his move to abolish the Constitution that has kept the Galactic Republic free for a thousand years. "In order to ensure security and continuing stability," proclaimed the wrinkly chancellor, "the Republic will be reorganized into the first Galactic Empire! For a safe and secure society!" The chamber leaps to its feet, clapping and cheering their new emperor, a supreme leader with a unified government devoted to realizing his agenda.

All were cheering except for a few statesmen in one booth, who had fought tirelessly to protect the Constitution and keep the Republic free. Looking on with despair and disbelief as the crowd showered their praise and adoration on their emperor, one said to the others, "So this is how liberty dies . . . with thunderous applause."

* * * * *

The cheers and applause from his inauguration ceremony had barely faded when Barack Obama made the opening moves in his strategy to transform our republic.

As soon as he was elected, Barack Obama began naming his senior political appointees. Like every president-elect, he announced his nominees for secretaries of State, Treasury, and Defense, for attorney general, and for all the various departments and agencies in the executive branch: Hillary Clinton to State, Janet Reno's old deputy Eric Holder to the Justice Department, Robert Gates to the Pentagon. Also as expected, he named various White House staffers, such as his chief of staff, national security advisor, and press secretary. Such appointments were routine at the time, though Obama may have had second thoughts about them since then. (Watching press secretary Robert Gibbs try to give a press briefing on any given day illustrates this point nicely.)

All of these appointments were normal, the actions of any new president. But unlike other new presidents, Obama also started naming a new type of political appointee. These people would have the powers of Senate-confirmed government officials without ever having to undergo Senate confirmation. They would have budgetary power over vast sums, but would not have to submit to the congressional appropriations process. They would have dozens answering to them, throughout government agencies. But they would answer to no one—except the president.

They are the czars.

There is no more blatant aspect of President Barack Obama's power grab than his czar strategy. Obama has appointed a number of "czars"—executive officials named by this president to wield vast power, often in secret, and answerable only to him. They enable him to avoid congressional oversight and public accountability.

And they are unconstitutional.

What the Heck Is a "Czar"?
President Obama's czars—a key element of the imperial presi-

dency—have centralized unprecedented power in the White House, creating a shadow government. Considering the transparency that Obama promised when running for the White House, the hypocrisy associated with these czars is simply stunning.

Barack Obama's czars come in three types, of varying threat levels to our democracy.

The first—and least dangerous—are Senate-confirmed officials in certain departments in the executive branch, exercising intrusive power into private industry or people's lives. They must testify before Congress, and they hold offices that were lawfully created, but use government power to interfere in the private sector, meddling with the business decisions made by corporate experts and co-opting private companies into extensions of the government.

The second kind consists of certain presidential appointees in various White House offices invented by Congress. These offices are authorized by Congress and have a mission defined by statute. Some are even Senate-confirmed. But these officials are part of the Executive Office of the President (EOP), and some are part of the White House Office (WHO), which primarily consists of those directly answering to the president or his immediate staff. As such, these czars in EOP, and especially those listed as part of WHO, are shielded from all sorts of congressional accountability and oversight, even while shaping major aspects of national policy.

The third—and most dangerous—are officials named by President Obama to certain posts that Obama fashions out of thin air. Almost all are White House staff officials exercising the sort of power found in Cabinet secretaries or undersecretaries (which are Senate-confirmed positions), but were simply named to these brand-new positions by President Obama. These officials, and even the offices they fill, were simply created by executive fiat.

Each of these czars is dangerous. Most, if not all, are illegal—for several reasons. All of them must go, and the republic is not safe until they're gone.

No One's Had Czars like Obama

President Obama's defenders love to trot out the line that previous presidents have had czars. It's only fair to acknowledge that other presidents have, in fact, had appointees that were *called* czars. For example, George H. W. Bush appointed Bill Bennett (Ronald Reagan's education secretary) as America's "drug czar."[1] The real title for that position is the director of the White House Office of National Drug Control Policy.[2] That office was created by Congress, and everyone refers to its director as the drug czar because it's easy to

---

CZAR ART

Let's be fair: Not everyone called a czar is in fact a czar. For example, some list Dennis Blair, the director of national intelligence (DNI), as the "intelligence czar." But the DNI position is a Cabinet-level post, created by Congress in the Intelligence Reform and Terrorism Prevention Act of 2004.[3] It is a Senate-confirmed post with supervisory authority over all the country's intelligence agencies, and DNI is fully subject to congressional oversight. All intelligence activities continue to flow through the congressional appropriations process. The DNI is not a "czar."

It's important to note the distinction so that everyone is on the same page as to what poses a problem and what does not. Otherwise, the White House can point to officials such as the DNI, point out that some call him a czar, and then ask why anyone has a problem with it. This is a red herring used to distract people from the fact that many of the decisions impacting hundreds of millions of Americans are now being made by unauthorized, unaccountable power brokers.

---

remember and the title is not such a mouthful. And Bill Clinton appointed an AIDS czar.[4] So sure, there have been czars before.

But not like this.

While other presidents have had one or two appointees nick-named "czars," Barack Obama is using dozens of czars to actually run much of the federal government. Few people object to the idea of someone in the White House focused on finding policies to keep drugs away from kids. But now whole areas of national policy have been taken inside the White House and vested in these czars, removed from the democratic process and input from the people's elected representatives in Congress. Worse still, some of these czars are specifically overseeing vitally important matters for this country.

At the moment of this writing, there is only one of the first types of czar (the least-dangerous type, from a constitutional standpoint). He is Herb Allison, the Troubled Asset Relief Program (TARP) czar. His official title is the assistant secretary of the Treasury for financial stability.[5] This person has the power to direct the hundreds of billions of dollars in the financial bailout (the TARP program) to stabilize the American financial sector.[6] He has enormous power that interferes with the private sector and injects politics into corporate America, but at least we have some safeguards against too much abuse from this office. It's terrible policy, but not inherently illegal.

Another czar that may fall into this category is Mark Lloyd, the diversity czar whose official title is the chief diversity officer of the Federal Communications Commission.[7] As part of the FCC, Lloyd is not part of the White House staff, and his position is not Senate-confirmed, either. Lloyd is discussed in detail in chapter 8, as he is the White House's point man on banning conservative talk radio.

The other czars, all of whom belong to the two most dangerous varieties, are listed below. They operate entirely within the White House.

The Shadow Government

1.	Ron Bloom	Car czar	Director, White House Auto Task Force
2.	John Brennan	Terrorism czar	Deputy National Security Advisor
3.	Carol Browner	Energy czar	Assistant to the President for Energy and Climate Change
4.	Adolfo Carrion	Urban czar	Director, White House Office of Urban Affairs
5.	Aneesh Chopra	Tech czar	Chief technology officer
6.	Jeffrey Crowley	AIDS czar	Director, Office of National AIDS Policy
7.	Nancy-Ann DeParle	Health czar	Director, White House Office of Health Reform
8.	Earl Devaney	Stimulus czar	Chair, Recovery Act Transparency and Accountability Board
9.	Joshua DuBois	Faith czar	Director, Office of Faith-Based and Neighborhood Partnerships
10.	Kenneth Feinberg	Pay czar	Special Master on Executive Pay
11.	Danny Fried	Gitmo czar	Special Envoy to Oversee the Closure of the Detention Center at Guantanamo Bay
12.	J. Scott Gration	Sudan czar	Special Envoy to Sudan
13.	Melissa Hathaway	Cyber czar	Director, White House Office of Cybersecurity
14.	Richard Holbrooke	Afghan czar	Special Representative for Afghanistan and Pakistan
15.	John Holdren	Science czar	Director, White House Office of Science and Technology Policy
16.	Van Jones*	Green jobs czar	Special Advisor for Green Jobs, Enterprise and Innovation
17.	Gil Kerlikowske	Drug czar	Director, White House Office of National Drug Control Policy

---

*   It should be noted that Van Jones has already been booted from the White House because his radicalism was publicly exposed in 2009. But he's not going away; he's still publicly speaking.

18. Vivek Kundra	Info czar	Federal chief informational officer
19. George Mitchell	Mideast peace czar	Special Envoy to the Middle East
20. Ed Montgomery	Autoworker czar	Director, Recovery for Auto Communities and Workers
21. Dennis Ross	Mideast policy czar	Special Advisor for the Persian Gulf and Southwest Asia
22. Gary Samore	WMD czar	Coordinator for the Prevention of WMD Proliferation and Terrorism
23. Todd Stern	Climate czar	Special Envoy for Climate Change
24. Cass Sunstein	Regulatory czar	Administrator, White House Office of Information and Regulatory Affairs
25. Paul Volcker	Economic czar	Chairman, Economic Recovery Advisory Board

There are other czars as well, some even created by George W. Bush: the terrorism czar, and the war czar who coordinates the wars in Iraq and Afghanistan. But while Bush and previous presidents had five or fewer czars, *President Obama has more than thirty.* The issue is not so much that any such czars exist, but that the president has enough of them, holding exactly the right positions of power, to run much of the government completely outside the constitutional framework.

Together, these czars form a shadow government. Whole swaths of federal power, both policymaking (i.e., lawmaking) and enforcement, have been concentrated in the White House under President Obama's exclusive control. Power that once was vested in agencies, or determined to be outside the proper scope of government, has now been seized by the White House. We are witnessing a massive, unconstitutional power grab.

These Czars Are Unconstitutional
Quick review: The Constitution of the United States is a remarkable document. Article I of the Constitution creates the legislative

branch and establishes the offices of House and Senate members. Article II sets forth the executive branch and establishes the offices of the president and vice president. And Article III maps out the judicial branch, with the offices of Supreme Court justices and the judges of any lower federal courts Congress creates by statute. Just like that, in three articles, our Founding Fathers created the most stable government in history.

It's a strong framework—one that allows *Congress* to fill in the blanks by creating new offices when needed. Why is congressional power to create new offices a big deal? Three reasons:

First, if an office is a creation of Congress, then Congress has a right to exercise oversight, and so the person holding that office can be required to appear before Congress and testify under oath about his actions.

Second, offices created by Congress are covered by the Administrative Procedure Act,[8] which requires public hearings and records when decisions are made, leaving a paper trail. The APA also empowers people or companies affected by these decisions to sue in federal court, allowing a judge to see if the evidence supports what the agency did. The APA makes government transparent.

And third, all of these offices have separate lines in Congress's annual appropriations bills. This gives Congress the power of the purse, meaning legislators can get information about activities to decide whether to continue funding them.

These three safeguards help make government work for the people. But the Obama presidency has decided they're simply in the way, and have exempted themselves from each of them.

How has Obama been accomplishing this? By ignoring the law. The Constitution's framework lays out two types of positions in the executive branch: principal officers and inferior officers. The first of these are nominated by the president and confirmed by the U.S. Senate.[9] For less-important government officers, called inferior officers, Congress decides whether they are appointed either by the president, agency heads, or the courts, and they do not require Senate confirmation. (Congress can never authorize itself to appoint officers, however.[10] Our Founding Fathers didn't trust government. For separation-of-powers reasons, the only branch that can create a federal office—Congress—is the only one that can't fill those offices. Brilliant, right?)

It's a fuzzy line separating principal officers from inferior officers. Courts consider several factors in distinguishing between the two types of executive officers, like whether the officer is subject to removal by another officer, the nature of the officer's duties, the scope of his jurisdiction, and how long he serves.[11] But principal officers go all the way down the governmental food chain to assistant secretaries and deputy undersecretaries. If the assistant secretary of agriculture for civil rights and the deputy undersecretary of commerce for intellectual property must be confirmed by the U.S. Senate, then it doesn't really pass the laugh test that a government official running General Motors or overseeing the national economy doesn't need to be Senate-confirmed.

But whether such positions require Senate confirmation or not, the important fact remains that all these offices *must be created by Congress.* Congress never created a car czar to run the nation's largest automakers. Yet Ron Bloom (a former union official) now controls General Motors, dictating what cars GM will make and wielding the power to fire its executives.[12] And one CEO has already been canned because Automaker in Chief Obama didn't approve of him.[13] Congress never established an office to regulate executive compensation, yet pay czar Kenneth Feinberg has the power to dictate how much any senior employee at any company taking bailout funds can make.[14] And they're now talking about regulating all companies, whether they took bailout funds or not.

Two key constitutional principles protect our republic:

- **Separation of powers:** The Constitution divides government power between the legislative, executive, and judicial branches to keep any one branch—or one person—from having too much power.

- **Checks and balances:** The Constitution gives each of the three branches a check over the power of the other two, to use government power to keep other government power in check.

Both principles protect the liberty of the American people from an overreaching, all-powerful government. And both are thrown out the window by the existence of President Obama's czars.

Need an Example? Just Look at Ambassadors

If this all seems a bit theoretical, there's one type of czar that perfectly shows how this whole system is constitutionally illegal. The president's apologists can bicker over what sort of appointees need Senate confirmation, but there's at least one office that's beyond doubt: In Article II, the Constitution says that all ambassadors must be confirmed by the Senate.[15] On that point, President Obama is clearly in violation.

An ambassador is appointed by the president to represent the United States to foreign nations. While the White House or State Department often sends higher-ranking officers to handle especially dicey situations or weighty matters, sometimes even sending the secretary of state, all those individuals whose full-time, permanent duties are to represent America are ambassadors. Yet Obama has named Richard Holbrooke (the Afghanistan czar) as Special Representative for Afghanistan and Pakistan, George Mitchell (the Mideast peace czar) as Special Envoy to the Middle East, and J. Scott Gration (the Sudan czar) as Special Envoy to Sudan.

These men are not "special envoys"; they're ambassadors. They speak for our country, representing the president and his foreign policy, with the power to represent our nation in deliberations and negotiations with the foreign nations they're visiting. We cannot have one man assigning such power to anyone he wants. The Founding Fathers knew that, and so they put a constitutional check on the president with Senate confirmation of ambassadors.

So why haven't these three men stood for confirmation? Just look at their assignments: Afghanistan, Pakistan, the Middle East. That's about as important as it gets; those are among the hottest spots around the globe where our vital interests are at stake. If the U.S. ambassadors to Micronesia, Sri Lanka, and Belgium (countries that most people can't even find on a map) require Senate confirmation, then why is that constitutional check not in play when it comes to delicate relations with areas that could lead us all to a nuclear war?

Because President Obama wants to completely control the foreign policy concerning those countries *without having to consult with the Senate* or without having any of his lieutenants be subject to oversight. So he calls them "special envoys" instead of ambassadors to avoid the confirmation process. But if these guys aren't ambassadors, then we don't know what an ambassador is. And since one of your authors served as an ambassador to the United Nations (Blackwell—and yes, I had to be confirmed by the Senate), we think we know an ambassador when we see one. And we're pretty sure Obama does too.

Even Democrats Admit These Czars Are Unconstitutional

Even some of President Obama's own Democrats acknowledge that his czars are unconstitutional. Senator Robert Byrd is a Democrat from West Virginia, the longest-serving senator in U.S. history, having held his Senate seat since 1959 (two years before Barack Obama was even born). During that time Byrd has served as the Senate majority leader (the person who wields most of the power in the Senate), and currently is the president pro tempore of the Senate, which means that he is third in line to take the powers of the presidency if something should happen to the president, vice president, and Speaker of the House. With an institutional memory like no other, Senator Byrd carries extraordinary clout when speaking on constitutional issues involving the roles of the three branches of government.

Senator Byrd sent a letter to President Obama on February 25, 2009, taking the unusual step of blasting a sitting president of his own Democratic Party. Byrd wrote that these czars, "threaten the Constitutional system of checks and balances. At the worst, White House staff has taken direction and control of programmatic areas that are the statutory responsibility of Senate-confirmed officials."[16] Byrd warns of these dangers because, "As presidential assistants and advisers, these White House staffers are not accountable for their actions to the Congress, to Cabinet officials, and to virtually anyone but the president."[17]

Senator Byrd understands that public accountability is essential for democracy, and with this letter sounded an alarm as to how dangerous these czars are. Far from any right-wing rant, these words from the longest-serving Democrat in Senate history are a somber warning to all of us about President Obama's imperial approach to government.

Some on the Far Left also acknowledge the danger posed by these czars. Ron Bloom is the czar heading a task force to remake the auto industry and make business decisions for the car companies. Perennial presidential candidate Ralph Nader, formerly of the Green Party, condemned the White House automotive task force. Nader argues that it is Congress that should be making decisions on cutting Chrysler dealerships, not a "secretive" task force.[18]

These two gentlemen aren't conservatives. Between Byrd (moderate liberal) and Nader (ultra-liberal), you have a broad cross section of the people who are Obama's base, not his opposition. Even they oppose President Obama's unconfirmed czars. But as you'll see below, the president's czars, confirmed or unconfirmed, are dangerous either way.

Four Case Studies:

Here, drink this!: Czar Holdren

One great example of a dangerous Obama czar who will have to testify before Congress and did undergo Senate confirmation hearings is John P. Holdren. Dr. Holdren is President Obama's "science czar," meaning he is the director of the White House Office of Science and Technology Policy. A former professor at Harvard, Holdren is an environmental zealot. He supports radical measures to save the environment, including a "Planetary Regime" (world government) to regulate the world's population and allocation of resources.[19] He supports putting chemicals in the drinking water or requiring devices to be implanted to limit or neutralize fertility as a form of permanent birth control.

In a book he coauthored, Holdren shows the extreme lengths of his fanaticism when he considers how "population-control laws, even including laws requiring compulsory abortion, could be sustained under the existing Constitution."[20] In Holdren's world, such authoritarian laws might be needed to save the earth from you and me.

The question is: Who's going to save us from Holdren?

Yet surprisingly, Holdren's office is a Senate-confirmed position, and he was confirmed without a single "no" vote on March 19, 2009.[21] This is absolutely stunning, given this man's radicalism. This shows, however, that if President Obama throws legions of far-left activists at us, then some of them will slip through the cracks because there are only so many hours in a day. It seems that few if any got wind of Holdren's extremist views before his confirmation. Now it's too late.

If it moves, regulate it. If it stops, take its organs: Czar Sunstein

Take Cass Sunstein, the regulatory czar, as another example. His official title is the administrator of the Office of Information and Regulatory Affairs, which is a division of the White House Office of Management and Budget.[22] Although that office may not sound terribly important, nothing could be further from the truth. Thousands of federal statutes are interpreted and applied to countless Americans and different situations through regulations. These are found in the Code of Federal Regulations (CFR). There are tens of thousands of pages in the CFR.

All of those regulations are issued by executive officials such as Cabinet secretaries. But all of those officials are appointed by the president, and so everything they do must be approved by the White House. The regulatory czar reviews all draft regulations.[23] The regulatory czar thus has the final word on all of these regulations, and can impact every area of your life.

Consider Cass Sunstein's positions over the years. We have a lot of material, given that he worked for years as a top professor at the University of Chicago Law School and Harvard Law School, and is a prolific writer and frequent speaker.

Take a few of his more-extreme positions: He believes that animals should have legal rights like human beings, including the right to sue in federal court.[24] Because they lack the ability to speak English (or the intelligence to formulate any abstract thought), he believes that lawyers should be appointed to speak on behalf of animals. Naturally, he believes that hunting should be completely banned, something that will not go over well with NRA members. Speaking of the National Rifle Association, those who would seek to assert that they have some Second Amendment rights associated with hunting are out of luck, because Sunstein believes that even if the Second Amendment secures an individual right for private citizens, it's a right providing such minimal protection that almost no gun-control law violates it.[25]

We could go on and on about Sunstein's positions. For example, he weighs human lives according to their economic value to society. He writes in one of America's most-respected legal journals:

If a program would prevent fifty deaths of people who are twenty, should it be treated the same way as a program that would prevent fifty deaths of people who are seventy? Other things being equal, a program that protects young people seems far better than one that protects old people, because it delivers greater benefits.[26]

Those benefits Sunstein refers to are benefits to society. In other words, the value of a human life varies according to its usefulness to the state and the government. That's consistent with Sunstein's other belief that when people die, the government should have the right to all of their organs automatically; we all become organ donors, whether we want to be or not.[27]

The most alarming thing about Cass Sunstein, however, is what he's using this regulatory czar job as a stepping-stone for. He's on the short list to be appointed by Obama to be a federal appeals judge, and is even mentioned as a possible nominee to the U.S. Supreme Court. He is a brilliant and well-accomplished legal scholar, and if put on the Court he could become the most liberal justice in the history of the United States.

But Sunstein is well on his way. In August of 2009, he was confirmed to the regulatory post by the Senate with a 57–40 vote.[28] Sunstein may not be as far beyond the pale as Holdren, but he's close. And given his top-notch standing in the legal profession, he could do far more lasting damage as a federal appeals judge or a Supreme Court justice.

It only gets worse
And if someone like Holdren or Sunstein—a perfect example of someone on the fringe—can actually make it through Senate confirmation, then just imagine what sort of skeletons are in the closets of some of these other czars that don't need to be confirmed.

A communist in the White House: Czar Van Jones
But we don't have to imagine. Just take a look at what we already know about some of these other czars.

President Obama's "green jobs czar," Van Jones, would never make it through Senate confirmation hearings. This man openly declares that he is a communist.[29] He also calls himself a Black Nationalist,[30] someone who holds a militant belief that blacks should separate themselves from whites in this country and establish their own self-governing areas. No avowed communist or Black Nationalist would ever be confirmed as a dogcatcher by the U.S. Senate. Good thing for Van Jones that he didn't have to go through that process, and doesn't need to ever testify before Congress.

Van Jones advocates creating an entirely new economic system. He says we must transform our agriculture into a system where illegal aliens are not exposed to any fertilizers or pesticides when working in the fields. Regarding Native Americans, Van Jones said that we should give them the wealth that Americans reap from the land that was once held by them before colonization.[31]

And he says plenty to clarify what he believes as a communist. As Van Jones said on tape, "I'm willing to forego the cheap satisfaction of the radical pose for the deep satisfaction of the radical ends."[32] More telling, he supports "reparations for slavery . . . We want redistribution of all wealth."[33]

Beyond all that, Van Jones is a 9/11 "truther." That means he's one of the people who believes that the Bush administration was somehow complicit with the terrorist attacks of 9/11. He signed a petition calling for an immediate investigation, a petition that said there was compelling evidence that top officials in the Bush administration had knowledge about 9/11, and that an investigation must be done to find out exactly who was involved so that appropriate action can be taken.[34]

That turned out to be too much embarrassment for Team Obama. The weekend after the story broke that Van Jones was a truther, Van Jones resigned from the White House. But the fact remains that for a couple of months, this radical extremist worked in the White House, advising the president of the United States.

Is it possible that President Obama was unaware of these frightening and sometimes appalling statements? Could his vetting team be that incompetent? Not at all. Valerie Jarrett, Obama's senior advisor—one of the architect's of Obama's blueprint mentioned in the introduction—said, "Van Jones, we were so delighted to be able to recruit him into the White House. We've been watching him, really for . . . as long as he's been active . . . the creative ideas that he has, and so now we have captured that, and we have all that energy and enthusiasm."[35]

Okay. Enough said.

Even with Van Jones gone, however, there are still plenty of czars to consider—more lunatics running the asylum.

With socialism for all: Czar Browner

Finally, take the example of Carol Browner, the energy czar. Her official title is Assistant to the President for Energy and Climate Change. It's a position that has never existed before and is not subject to Senate confirmation or congressional oversight.

In her position as energy czar, Browner has complete control over the Department of Energy and the Environmental Protection Agency (EPA). These agencies are supposed to be Cabinet-level departments, headed by Level I presidential appointees (which are Cabinet secretaries). Browner the energy czar has enormous power for an unconfirmed, unaccountable person to hold, so much so that Republican members of Congress are pushing a bill introduced by Congressman Patrick McHenry, calling for the president to give an account of all these czars. Browner is McHenry's chief talking point in pressing the need for this legislation.

Why should we worry about Carol Browner? Because she's a socialist. Until June of 2009 (when this became a political problem for the White House), Browner was on the board of the Commission for a Sustainable Society, which is the action arm for Socialist International. Given that socialists do not believe in capitalism and that the primary focus of Obama's Energy Department and EPA is developing a new green economy that would fundamentally restructure the United States' entire capitalistic economic system, it's more than a little alarming that the president's point person on that front is a socialist (which would have kept her from ever being confirmed by the U.S. Senate).

A whole book could be written on Obama's czars (and it's a safe bet that such books are being written), but you get the point. They're all like this. There are plenty of them, and they're running your life in ways you don't even realize right now.

Even If They Were Legal, Czars Are a Really Bad Idea

This is about legality, not policy. Under the rule of law, we don't ask whether we like the law; we simply must follow it. If the law is wrong, we change it—through the proper channels. But we never ask whether the law benefits us to decide if we should follow it; that would be lawlessness. The chief problem with President Obama's czars—what makes their existence wrong—is their very unconstitutionality.

But setting aside that problem for a moment, these czars aren't a good idea even if they were legal. From a policy perspective, they're a terrible idea. Czars are illegal *because* they're a terrible idea. The Constitution is designed to provide our democratic republic with transparency and accountability. Czar-creation violations of the separation of powers and the system of checks and balances give more power to the president than the Constitution allows. Such vast power without accountability or oversight, power exercised in secret, is what you expect by an absolute ruler, not a democratic one. It's just bad government.

Wisdom from Someone Who Knows

For perspective, wisdom, and insight on the czars, we can learn from a master: Ed Meese.

Former Attorney General Edwin Meese III is one of the most powerful, influential, and respected leaders in Washington, D.C. With the sole exception of U.S. presidents, General Meese has done as much as anyone to shape the law in this country in the past century. A graduate of Yale who then earned his law degree from the prestigious University of California at Berkeley, Meese was a law professor in California and an officer in the U.S. Army, retiring from the Reserves at the rank of colonel. He became part of Governor Ronald Reagan's team, and worked on the campaign as Reagan ran for national office. Once Reagan was sworn in as America's fortieth president in 1981, Meese served in the White House as Counselor to the President, one of Reagan's three closest advisors during his first term. When Reagan was reelected, Meese then led the Department of Justice from 1985 to 1989 as the seventy-fifth attorney general of the United States.

During the eight years of Ronald Reagan's presidency, General Meese was President Reagan's top advisor on shaping our nation's courts, including the Supreme Court. A constitutional scholar, Meese focused tremendous efforts on finding the right people for Reagan to nominate as judges. Supreme Court Justices Antonin Scalia, Anthony Kennedy, and Clarence Thomas, as well as top federal circuit judges such as Douglas Ginsburg, Robert Bork, David Sentelle, Ken Starr, and Laurence Silberman, owe their positions to this titan of constitutional conservatism.

Since the end of the Reagan administration, General Meese has continued to work in leading positions in America's corridors of power, making him the most active and consequential former attorney general anyone can remember. Serving as a top scholar at the Heritage Foundation, on the board of visitors for The Federalist Society, on the boards of various organizations and a major law school (George Mason), and also as chairman of the Conservative Action Project (in which both of your authors are also involved), General Meese fills the role of a godfather to the modern conservative movement, in law, politics, and policy.

Late in 2009, General Meese shared his thoughts and concerns with us regarding Obama's czars.

As someone who served both as a top presidential advisor in the White House, and then as a top official with operational responsibility as a Cabinet officer and department head, General Meese emphasized that these two functions—advisement and operation—must be kept separate. It's an important safeguard within each administration that those responsible for implementing the president's agenda not be part of the president's White House staff. The advisory role must be kept at arm's length from the operational role.

According to General Meese, aside from all the constitutional issues, there are three problems that cannot be avoided when it comes to the czars.

First, czarism disarms all the safeguards that are in place to stop bad policy. There are various laws, such as the Administrative Procedure Act, and vetting processes that government policies are supposed to pass through before they go into effect. Whenever policy is being formulated and major actions are being considered, these proposals go through these safeguard procedures, much of which is conducted by nonpartisan experts, and parts of which provide transparency to the public to prevent shenanigans from taking place. These processes are able to expose many of the flaws of such proposals, including constitutional problems or legal gray areas, in order to weed out the bad ones.

But the White House is exempt from almost all of these safeguards. And the White House is also an inherently political operation. So the nonpartisan experts are not involved in top-level internal White House deliberations, the vetting doesn't take place, and there is no public transparency. Bad things are bound to happen as a result.

Second, so much power radiates from the president, Meese explains, that when White House staffers are involved in designing policy, they put a thumb on the scales, outweighing the input and actions of operational experts in the relevant government agencies. Whatever the White House actor wants often ends up carrying the day, drowning out important dissenting voices—including the kind of nonpartisan experts mentioned above—that otherwise would provide crucial insight which could be used to shape and improve the policy.

And third, it's critical that the president have completely objective—and at times blunt and even harsh—evaluations of various policies and operations. Every president needs to have trusted White House advisors that will tell him plainly when a policy is not working and must be discarded, or when a high-ranking official is performing badly or has made a terrible mistake and must be replaced. When that key White House advisor is also the one with operational responsibility over a particular policy area, that person is tempted to spin things in the best possible way. Such an advisor will certainly be the last one to tell the president that the president needs to fire that operational manager.

That's because with these czars, the president's advisor and the operational manager are the same person.

Case in Point: Terrorism Czar John Brennan

Only weeks after General Meese shared his insights with your authors, the whole country saw a perfect example.

John Brennan is Barack Obama's terrorism czar. His official title is Deputy National Security Advisor for Homeland Security and Counterterrorism. The reality is that, as a true czar, he's not merely an advisor. Instead, he's an operational manager who should be Senate-confirmed and should be serving in an executive-branch agency such as the CIA or the Pentagon, not the White House.

One of the biggest news stories at the end of 2009 was the so-called "underwear bomber." On Christmas Day, 2009, a Nigerian terrorist named Umar Farouk Abdulmutallab tried to detonate explosives sewn into his underpants to blow up an airliner as it was landing in Detroit after a transatlantic flight.[36] The most-remembered administration response to this failed attack that almost became a disaster was our blissfully clueless Homeland Security Secretary Janet Napolitano, who assured all of us that we should stay calm because "the system worked."[37]

Like heck it did, Madame Secretary.

But just as alarming was the fact that Czar Brennan claimed responsibility.[38] And it appears that Brennan did have at least partial operational control, admitting that he told the director of the National Counterterrorism Center (NCTC) that the director could continue a skiing vacation with his son instead of returning to his post.[39]

The problem is that the director of the NCTC should not be answering to a White House advisor. That director should instead be answering to the DNI (director of national intelligence), who is a Senate-confirmed presidential Cabinet officer, or to the CIA chief, or some other top-ranking official, who in turn answers to the president.

Brennan has had a very distinguished career as an intelligence official. He has a great deal of experience in national security and intelligence analysis. He certainly has a lot to offer as either an operational commander, or as someone advising the president on homeland security.

But in keeping with General Meese's sage observations, Brennan cannot be both at the same time.

This has become patently clear, as Brennan has now become a political actor, saying that top Republicans are playing politics with national security by daring to question the White House response. Brennan made the crazy claim that any criticisms of the Obama administration's utterly pathetic response to this attempted bombing help al-Qaeda, and called top senators and congressmen liars on national television for disagreeing with his account of things.[40] He said there was no problem with the recently revealed discovery that at least 20 percent of the terrorist combatants we capture and then release go back to the battlefield to kill our servicemen.[41] More than that, public officials expressed outrage upon learning that Abdulmutallab was told he had the right to remain silent and have a lawyer after only fifty minutes—that's less than one hour—of being interrogated by U.S. agents. In response, Brennan claimed with a straight face that during those fifty minutes we had extracted every useful piece of information from this terrorist, so it was okay to tell him that he didn't have to answer any more questions and give him a lawyer to advise him of every possible way to make it harder for us to convict him.[42]

In doing so, this longtime national security expert has been reduced to a partisan hack. Czar Brennan has lost credibility with Congress, and these serious mistakes and ill-advised statements have rendered him useless to President Obama and to congressional overseers.

This is yet another example that proves the wisdom of our Founding Fathers. President Obama's czars are dangerous, and they need to go away.

Solution: We'll See You in Court!

The constitutionality of President Obama's czars has never been challenged. In politics, things often must reach a critical mass before people organize to act against them. The simple fact is that before the Obama administration, czars were minor players, either because the scope of their duties was narrow or their tenure was brief. Either way, few people (if any) had a beef with them, so no one's feathers were ruffled enough to bring a lawsuit.

Normally it would be hard for someone to bring a lawsuit against presidential decisions. To have standing to bring suit in federal court, a plaintiff must allege a concrete, personal injury that is fairly traceable to the defendant and can be effectively redressed by the court. The Supreme Court held long ago that if a taxpayer doesn't like the way the government is spending his tax money, that's not a particularized, personal injury sufficient to confer standing to sue.

But plenty of people have standing to bring suit against many of these czars. No one could sue over Richard Holbrooke's actions in the Middle East or the actions of some of these other foreign-policy czars. But any person or company directly impacted by one of these other czars would have standing to sue. Any executive whose pay is cut by the pay czar, any car company on the receiving end of an order from the car czar, or anyone particularly burdened by a direct order of one of these czars, among others, would have standing to sue.

And they should, as soon as possible. The federal courts could make quick work of these unconstitutional officials.

However, this is only a limited solution. Many of these czars, such as John Brennan, cannot be sued because no private citizen would have standing to bring such a suit. The only way to get rid of all of these czars is to get rid of the president those czars serve, which we'll have an opportunity to do in 2012.

All the Emperor's Men

We started with one movie; let's end with another. When Dustin Hoffman and Robert Redford played the legendary journalist team of Woodward and Bernstein in *All the President's Men,* they were telling the sad and sordid story of a president whose power got the better of him. Let's call these two movie stars and tell them we've got a bigger story for them this time.

President Obama specifically and repeatedly condemned George W. Bush for concentrating too much power in the White House outside of congressional oversight, and promised to reverse it. Instead, he has taken this approach of centralizing power in his own hands to an inconceivable level. The hypocrisy here is stunning. President Obama promised transparency during his campaign, condemning what he called the secrecy and unaccountability of the Bush administration. But there's no transparency here at all. These czars are not subject to congressional oversight, do not need to abide by the Administrative Procedure Act, for the most part don't have budgets that Congress can cut to rein them in, and answer only to the president. The shadow government created by President Obama's czars is illegal and dangerous. These czars concentrate more power in the White House than any president has ever possessed in American history, and they cannot be held accountable for their actions, which are exercised mostly in secret.

This government-by-czar strategy is nothing short of an early stage in creating an imperial presidency, unanswerable to the people and repugnant to the Constitution. It is a major component of the Obama blueprint, and the longer we wait to challenge it, the more inroads a single-minded White House will make in our everyday lives.

The Constitution forbids any president to have such power.

Chapter 2

PACKING THE COURTS

The Supreme Court [has] never ventured into the issues of redistribution of wealth and served more basic issues of political and economic justice in this society. . . . It didn't break free from the essential constraints that were placed by the Founding Fathers in the Constitution. . . . I think one of the tragedies of the civil rights movement was because the civil rights movement became so court-focused . . . there was a tendency to lose track of . . . the actual coalitions of power through which you bring about redistributive change. . . . [W]e still suffer from that.

—BARACK OBAMA, JANUARY 18, 2001

Most Americans don't realize exactly what's at stake when it comes to our federal courts, and especially the Supreme Court. We are at a fork in the road. Which direction we take will determine the destiny of this nation. America's chief executive(s) during the next two presidential terms will forever change this country through his appointments to the federal courts. President Obama knows this, and he's made packing the courts part of his blueprint.

What's at Stake

We have a moderate Court today. To be more precise, the current Supreme Court is one step to the right of dead-center; it's a conservative-leaning, moderate Court. If Republicans retake both the Senate and the White House, we could have the first conservative Supreme Court since 1936. If Obama wins a second term, we will not only have a liberal Supreme Court, but it will be the most liberal in history. And we will have this liberal Court for at least a quarter century.

The Court's current makeup, beginning with the chief justice and then in order of seniority, is as follows:

Name	Age	Judicial Philosophy	Appointment
John Roberts (Chief)	55	Center-leaning conservative	Bush 43 (2005)
John Paul Stevens*	90	Very liberal	Ford (1975)
Antonin Scalia	74	Very conservative	Reagan (1986)
Anthony Kennedy	73	Moderate	Reagan (1987)
Clarence Thomas	61	Most conservative	Bush 41 (1991)
Ruth Bader Ginsburg	77	Most liberal	Clinton (1993)
Stephen Breyer	71	Liberal	Clinton (1994)
Samuel Alito	60	Conservative	Bush 43 (2006)
Sonia Sotomayor	55	Liberal	Obama (2009)

Already Obama has appointed one Supreme Court justice. He may well get two more in this first term, as Justice Stevens and Justice Ginsburg are both expected to retire before 2013. If so, then Obama will be the first president since Ronald Reagan to fill three seats on the High Court in a single presidential term.[1] Only five presidents in our history have appointed more justices in one term.[2]

Imminent Vacancies Expected on the Supreme Court

It is widely expected that Justice Ginsburg will step down from the bench in 2011. Although she originally let it be known that she intended to serve at least until 2013, sadly she is battling pancreatic cancer, so if her health forces her from the Court she could very well step down in June of 2011.

However, this expectation could be wrong. Like most Supreme Court justices, Ginsburg has always been a fighter, and may be determined to fight on against her cancer or to live to the end of her days on the bench. That was the choice made by the late Chief Justice William Rehnquist, who lost his own battle with cancer on

---

*   As explained later in this chapter, Justice Stevens most likely will announce his retirement in June 2010, so if you are reading this after that date there is probably a new member on the Supreme Court.

September 3, 2005, while still presiding over the Court. Justice Ginsburg has already hired a full complement of four law clerks for the annual term that begins in October 2010,[3] strongly suggesting that she intends to be serving on the bench into 2011 at least.

Justice Stevens is almost certain to announce his decision to retire in 2010 upon the confirmation of his successor, with an announcement expected in late June 2010. (Depending on when you are reading this, Stevens's retirement may have already taken place.) This apparent decision to retire is a bit surprising, because if Stevens had instead chosen to serve until February of 2011, he would have become the oldest-serving justice in history, beating the current record of ninety years and ten months held by Oliver Wendell Holmes.[4] Many Court watchers expected that Stevens, who is still in good health (it's reported that he still plays tennis, for goodness' sake), would like to beat Holmes's record and then retire during the Court's annual recess in summer of 2011.

But Justice Stevens hired only one law clerk for the annual term starting October 2010, a strong sign of imminent retirement. Supreme Court justices get four law clerks each year. These clerkships are the most sought-after tours of duty for young lawyers, and only the very best of the best get them. They're selected from the most promising clerks serving the judges on the federal courts of appeals. Since these positions are extremely important to a justice's ability to do his work, and because those applying for these clerkships are extremely talented individuals with great job prospects, justices usually hire all four of their clerks well in advance of the next year's cycle, which starts each August as the Court prepares for the official beginning of the annual term in October.

John Paul Stevens usually hires his clerks each autumn for the following year's August. However, this year he only hired one clerk. This single hiring is an important indicator. A retired justice can still choose to hear cases on the federal appellate courts, and many do so. To help them, a retired justice can still have one law clerk per year.

Stevens's hiring of only one clerk for the year starting late summer 2010 is a clear sign of his intent to retire.

Since Obama already appointed Sonia Sotomayor to replace David Hackett Souter in 2009, Stevens's departure would give the president a second Supreme Court appointment. And with Ginsburg's unfortunate health condition, it's more likely than not that Obama will have a third.

In addition to its governing laws and the rules it officially adopts, the Supreme Court operates under a lot of unwritten traditions. One of those traditions is that retiring justices try to stagger their retirements so that two or more vacancies won't occur at the same time. Confirming a new justice takes a lot of effort and captures the focus of the nation, and justices see it as leaving with grace and style to retire one at a time.

Another tradition is that justices try not to retire during a presidential election year. Supreme Court confirmations have always been a big deal, and all the more so since the 1987 confirmation fight over Judge Robert Bork (explained in more detail below). Justices see it as complicating the political landscape and saddling the president with an unnecessary task to deal with a Supreme Court vacancy during an election year. If the incumbent president is running for reelection, then it thrusts his nomination decision to the center stage of the nation, distracting from other issues. And if there is an outgoing two-term president, then he's a lame duck, and the retirement would take the country's attention away from the two presidential nominees vying to lead our country.

A third tradition is to leave during the Court's annual recess. The Supreme Court maintains a very busy schedule from when the term begins on the first Monday of October, until late June when the Court rises at the end of its active term and the annual recess begins. The tradition is to announce your retirement from the bench on the Court's last daily session for the year's term, although some justices let their intentions be known a few weeks ahead of time, or announce in the days after the Court rises. But because there are only nine justices and having a vacancy midterm is very disruptive (among other things, resulting in some 4–4 tie votes on cases that then require a second argument once the new justice is sworn in), most justices do everything possible to only step down during the summer recess.

For all these reasons, since we're looking at one probable vacancy in 2010, if a third seat opens up, it will likely happen in the summer of 2011. There shouldn't be two vacancies at any point in 2010, or any vacancy in 2012, unless health concerns require it. But when a person is battling cancer in her late seventies, anything can happen, so no one should dismiss the possibility.

Of course, it's also possible that no one retires despite the signals that are being sent as of this writing, and thus Obama might not have another vacancy through the remainder of his term. It's also possible that one of the other justices, all of whom seem healthy now, could suddenly develop an unanticipated health problem that forces him or her from the Court. Surprises of both sorts have happened throughout the Court's history.

But as of today, the smart money looks like one—and only one—vacancy right now in 2010, going into the midterm elections, with the possibility of another vacancy in the summer of 2011.

Filling Judicial Vacancies

Article II of the Constitution vests the authority to nominate federal judges in the president.[5] The power is his alone. He doesn't share it with senators, with his legal officers, or with the public. It's one of the most serious and consequential duties that any president has under the Constitution. As explained in more detail later in this chapter, although the Senate has a role in judicial appointments through their confirmation process, those confirmations are designed to stop judicial nominees only in narrow circumstances; the Senate is not a co-appointer of judges (despite what some senators say).

This power of judicial appointments gives a president the opportunity to have an impact on the nation that will long outlast his term in office. Federal judges hold lifetime appointments.[6] Since the Constitution adds that a judge holds lifetime office only during "good behavior," the only way to remove a judge before that judge chooses to retire is for the U.S. House to impeach that judge by a majority vote, and then the U.S. Senate to remove the judge by a two-thirds supermajority vote.[7] In all of American history, only fourteen federal judges have been impeached by the House, and only half of those (seven) have gone on to be removed from office by the Senate.[8] Of these judges, only one Supreme Court jurist has been impeached, Justice Samuel Chase, who remained in office because he was acquitted by the Senate.[9] So aside from those rare cases, any president's judicial picks will continue shaping the law for many years.

Most people don't pay much attention to judicial nominations unless it's a nominee to the Supreme Court. That's a shame, because those lower courts are the highest authority in most cases. The Supreme Court is offered about 8,000 cases a year, and only takes around 80—which is 1 percent.[10] So 99 percent of the time, the decisions of lower courts are the final word. For this reason, those concerned with the rule of law, and especially judicial activism, need to be concerned with the federal appeals courts.

Yet a big part of each president's impact on the Constitution and the rule of law comes from his appointments to the circuit courts of appeals. There are around two hundred federal appeals judges (including "senior judges," who are semiretired and hear cases part-time but no longer fill a regular-service judgeship), whereas there are only nine Supreme Court justices. During one four-year term, a president gets around forty vacancies to fill on the circuit courts, out of 179 seats. A two-term president, then, usually gets to replace almost half of the federal appeals bench.[11]

But President Obama has an opportunity to fill vacancies that he should not have. Once the Democrats took the Senate in 2006, they began slowing down the already-too-slow confirmation process for George W. Bush's judicial nominees. As a result, there were over twenty circuit court seats already vacant when Obama took office. He'll get to fill all of those vacancies, as well as up to forty more that could come before the 2012 election, giving him up to sixty circuit court appointments in his first term alone.

This strategy—part of Obama's blueprint gifted to him by a Democrat-majority Senate—is particularly appalling because it targets our nation's most important appeals courts. Of the thirteen federal appeals courts, the most prestigious and important one is the U.S. Court of Appeals for the District of Columbia Circuit. Why? Because it has exclusive jurisdiction to hear all appeals from federal government agency decisions that are challenged under the Administrative Procedure Act, and also because most lawsuits brought against a Cabinet department, actions of Congress, or the White House are filed in the federal district court in D.C. for trial. All of these vitally important cases end up before the D.C. Circuit when they're appealed.

Next to the D.C. Circuit, the Fourth Circuit is generally considered the most important court.[12] The Fourth Circuit—made up of Maryland, Virginia, West Virginia, North Carolina, and South Carolina—has jurisdiction over the Pentagon, the CIA, and the NSA (National Security Agency), as well as all sorts of military and government agencies and facilities. As a result, many of the War on Terror cases go to the Fourth Circuit, as well as many lawsuits over government policies that don't end up before the D.C. Circuit.

The Democrats deliberately blocked Bush nominees to the Fourth Circuit, hoping for a Democrat to win in 2008 and then to push the Fourth Circuit far to the left. They succeeded. Of the fifteen judgeships on the circuit, four were kept vacant during the last two years of the Bush administration. With one retirement since Obama took over, there are five seats—one-third of the total—that Obama is filling early in his presidency. His first nominee has been confirmed already, and three more have been nominated as of the time of this writing. Of the fourteen appellate nominations Obama has made as of this writing, with vacancies on all thirteen circuits, four of those fourteen are nominations to the Fourth Circuit. Obama has already tilted the balance of one of our most important courts.

It's especially true that Obama, of all people, should not have this opportunity because he was one of the people who created the problem. When Democrats were filibustering Bush's nominees (explained below), Obama was among those seeking to deny Bush's nominees an up-or-down vote. Although he supported a filibuster by voting against cloture to end debate on many qualified nominees,[13] Obama expects to receive the opposite treatment now that he is president.

Do as I say, not as I do. That's leadership for you.

Expanding the Courts

The names and faces of nine people with jurisdiction over the entire nation—our Supreme Court justices—are relatively easy to remember. Most of us ignore a serious peril to our personal liberties that exists among the names and faces of the lower courts.

We've already explained that very few cases get to the Supreme Court. So for most cases, the decisions of the circuit courts of appeals and state supreme courts are the law of the land. But the reality is that those courts are on the verge of a big change, and we need to stop that change from happening.

Barack Obama wants to initiate a plan to increase the size of the federal appellate courts.

Truth be told, the judiciary needs to be expanded. The Judicial Conference of the United States consists of the chief judges of all the circuits across the country and one district judge from one of the districts within each circuit, and is chaired by the chief justice of the United States.[14] The Judicial Conference issued a report in 2008 (as in previous years) in which it said that the federal courts had too many cases and that more judges were needed in order for the courts to do their jobs properly. So the Judicial Conference requested that Congress create twelve new appellate judgeships and fifty new trial judgeships.

(It's critically important to note, however, that in his 2009 year-end report, Chief Justice Roberts said that the courts understand the country is in a tough spot right now, so the judiciary is not asking for more money or any other form of aid from Congress at the moment. Any attempts to force through an expansion of the courts this year, with Democrats dominating the appointment process of these life-tenured judges, should be rebutted with the fact that the judiciary is holding off on requesting any help.)

We've increased the judiciary's size a number of times before, as needed. For example, in 1985 a bill was passed to split the U.S. Court of Appeals for the Fifth Circuit, reassigning several of the states in that circuit—Florida, Georgia, Alabama, and the U.S. territory of Puerto Rico, to form the new Eleventh Circuit. (The states remaining in the Fifth Circuit are Texas, Louisiana, and Mississippi.) More often, legislation simply creates a few more judicial seats, such as was later done in 1990.[15]

Because of ongoing requests after 1990, legislation was introduced to expand the courts more. Specifically, bipartisan legislation was introduced in early 2008 by the Democratic chairman of the Senate Judiciary Committee, Patrick Leahy of Vermont, and the Republican former chairman of that committee, Orrin Hatch of Utah.[16] Critically, though, these judgeships would not have come into existence until January 21, 2009,[17] the day after the next U.S. president would be inaugurated. That means that the then-current president, George W. Bush, would no longer be in office. It was impossible to tell whether the new president would be a Democrat or Republican, and so the legislation wasn't giving either party an advantage.

But now that Democrats control both the White House and the Senate, that old bill is off the table and a completely new piece of legislation is being pushed. Now that the president currently in the White House is clearly focused on appointing as many staunchly liberal judges as he can, Democrat Leahy is changing the rules. He's still pushing for new judgeships in this new bill, but the bill now provides that those judicial seats would be created *immediately*, not after the next presidential election; this way, President Obama and the Democrats' huge Senate majority can ensure that they stack the courts with their kind of jurists.

We don't need to guess how this would play out, because history gives us a perfect example from the Ninth Circuit.

The U.S. Court of Appeals for the Ninth Circuit is the court perhaps best known by non-lawyers for holding that the Pledge of Allegiance is unconstitutional because it mentions "one nation under God." While it's not fair to say that one case sums up an entire federal appellate court, and 99 percent of the time the Ninth Circuit's decisions are the same as those of other courts, it's nonetheless true that the Ninth Circuit is the most liberal federal appeals court in the country.

What is instructive is how it got that way. In 1978, Democrats passed a bill expanding the Ninth Circuit from eighteen judges (already the largest circuit—most circuits have around twelve judges) to twenty-eight judges, creating ten new judicial seats. President Jimmy Carter proceeded to nominate—and the Democratic Senate was quick to confirm—a whole host of solidly liberal judges.

Overnight, the Ninth Circuit became the most liberal court in America. Judges usually try to retire when the White House is controlled by the same kind of president (liberal/conservative, Democrat/Republican) as the president that nominated them. The same is true here, as many of these Ninth Circuit judges retired, or took senior status during the Clinton years, helping to ensure that the Ninth Circuit remained liberal through Clinton's new appointments.

That is what President Obama hopes to do to all thirteen federal appeals courts: pack them with staunchly left judges who will retire in time for a future leftist president to do the same. We need to make sure he doesn't get that chance. Any judgeship bill to make it through Congress needs to provide that the new judicial seats created by that bill will not come into existence until January 21, 2013.

The Need for an Independent Judiciary
The courts must remain free from partisan influences in order to protect our rights. If you're trying to escape the constraints of a writ-

ten constitution, a key element of subverting a democratic republic like ours is to diminish its courts of law and justice.

An independent judiciary is essential to a free country. The courts are a countermajoritarian institution. That means they're designed to stand against popular sentiment and political pressure. They're designed to be able to protect the minority against oppression from the majority.

The Constitution sets up our federal courts to insulate them from politics. Article III says that judges hold lifetime appointments[18] so that no one can remove them from office, and thus judges cannot be pressured to cave in to political pressure to keep their jobs. Article III also provides that no judge's salary can ever be reduced while that judge continues in office.[19] Thus, politicians cannot say, "Well, fine, we can't kick you out of office—but if you don't go along with us on this issue, then your pay will be cut from $180,000 a year to $3,000 a year. Have fun providing for your family on that."

When the same political party controls both the White House and both branches of Congress, the courts are all that stand between the freedoms of average Americans and the partisan designs of an extremist agenda. The basic concept is that if a solid majority of people want something, then they can probably create the political will for Congress to pass legislation and get the president to sign it.

So the courts are needed most when something is unpopular. The courts are empowered to go against the tide to vindicate the Constitution, regardless of how an issue is being portrayed by a less-than-objective media, and a less-than-forthcoming administration.

Many of the seminal Supreme Court decisions that have shaped this nation have been rooted in the Court's independence. The Court struck down several massive expansions of federal power in the New Deal of the 1930s because they exceeded Congress's power to regulate interstate commerce.[20] The Court struck down Harry Truman's seizure of American steel mills as a "wartime necessity," because the president has no such power to co-opt private businesses.[21] The Court abolished the idea that the Constitution allows for racially discriminatory laws under the "separate but equal" rule,[22] holding that "separate but equal" is an unconstitutional violation of the Fourteenth Amendment.[23]

To be sure, the Court has used its independence at times to arrive at wrong conclusions. These cases have done terrible harm to this country, such as creating a constitutional right to abortion,[24] remaking economic policy by buying into man-made global warming,[25] or extending habeas corpus rights to terrorists captured on foreign battlefields and held overseas by our military.[26]

But the solution to those outrages is not to remove judicial independence. The solution is to appoint the right people to our federal courts, and especially the Supreme Court.

Demonizing the Supreme Court

The Supreme Court relies more on public legitimacy than the other branches of our government. Congress has the power of the purse, whereby only Congress can appropriate funds for any federal program or purpose. The president is the commander in chief, with absolute control over the most formidable military in the history of the world. The president also has the extraordinary platform of the bully pulpit to reach out to everyone in the country, and the 535 members of Congress likewise have smaller media platforms through which to persuade and win over the public to support their decisions (a tactic that is often effective even when those decisions are amazingly wrongheaded).

But the Court has none of those. They have no independent funding, and no armed force beyond a few dozen court marshals. Moreover, the justices do their work without public speeches and only speak through their written opinions in the cases presented to them.

So the Supreme Court, as well as the inferior federal courts under the Supreme Court, relies on public legitimacy. The justices rely on our being taught and understanding that the Court is the final arbiter of our Constitution, the guardians of the Supreme Law

STRIKING DOWN
UNCONSTITUTIONAL LAWS

When the Constitution was adopted in 1789 and Americans understood that the United States now had a written charter of government that would be the Supreme Law of the Land, everyone wanted to be clear on one thing: What would happen if Congress passed an unconstitutional law, or the president did something that violated the Constitution? There was always the widespread understanding that somehow the courts would be involved. In 1803, when the Constitution was just fourteen years old, it became official.

President John Adams had appointed William Marbury as a justice of the peace in D.C. shortly before Adams left office. The Democratic-Republicans, led by Thomas Jefferson, had defeated Adams's Federalist Party, not only for the presidency, but also winning a majority in Congress. But Adams's secretary of state had failed to physically deliver the written commission of office to Marbury, without which Marbury could not sit on the bench. President Jefferson ordered James Madison, who was now Jefferson's secretary of state, not to deliver it. The Judiciary Act of 1789 in force at the time allowed for Marbury to file suit in the Supreme Court, and that's exactly what he did, seeking a court order that Secretary Madison had to hand over the judicial commission.

Then the Supreme Court threw both sides for a loop. In the resulting case of *Marbury v. Madison*, the

Court didn't decide the case one way or the other. Instead, they noted that aside from limited matters, such as one states suing another state, Article III of the Constitution only gave the Supreme Court *appellate jurisdiction*—meaning, jurisdiction to hear appeals. In other words, the Supreme Court could not hear trials, and could not act upon lawsuits filed directly at the Court, without first going through a lower court and then coming up on appeal. Although the Court acknowledged that William Marbury was entitled to the commission, the Court held that it lacked the power to issue the order Marbury sought.

The Supreme Court held that this provision from the Judiciary Act was unconstitutional. In doing so, the Court declared the power of judicial review: Courts have the power under the Constitution of interpreting the Constitution, and striking down any inferior laws, whether statutes, regulations, or other government actions, that violate the Constitution.

People didn't realize at the time how significant a power this was. But decades later, when major pieces of legislation wound up being struck down by the Court, America came to realize that this power put the Supreme Court on par with Congress and the president as a fully coequal branch of government.

of the Land, and that when the Supreme Court speaks on a constitutional issue, then that issue has been decided.

Again, that's not to say that the Court doesn't make mistakes. In years past the *Dred Scott* decision held that African Americans were not citizens, and in more recent years, cases like *Roe v. Wade* and *Lawrence v. Texas* have seen the Court wrongly weigh in on social issues where the Constitution is silent.

But those decisions are the exception, not the rule, and the Court can correct those errors over time—or the people can correct them through constitutional amendments if necessary. Far more often than not, the Court does a great job of performing its extremely difficult job for all of us.

Which means that the most toxic thing that can happen with the Court, as damaging as the Court's weighing in on controversial policy issues that don't involve the Constitution, is what happens when our elected leaders assail the Court. Such attacks undermine the Court's legitimacy, and in so doing erode the confidence of the American people in our constitutional system of government. It's the Constitution that empowers the Supreme Court to decide what the Constitution means in different cases, an idea that has not been challenged since *Marbury v. Madison* in 1803.

But the Court was attacked just this past year, in the most damaging way possible. The attack came in the aftermath of the Court's decision in *Citizens United v. FEC*, which was a challenge to the Bipartisan Campaign Reform Act of 2002 (BCRA), better known as McCain-Feingold. Citizens United, a public-interest group led by political veteran David Bossie, made two documentaries during the 2008 primaries, one critical of Barack Obama and the other critical of Hillary Clinton (who at that time was still considered the most likely Democratic nominee). But the FEC blocked the documentary from being distributed on Video On Demand.

The FEC blocked this documentary because the time frame for its sale and promotion fell within BCRA's "blackout" period, during which an electioneering communication (i.e., a message designed to influence how a person will vote in an election) from any group cannot be shared over radio or TV within thirty days of any primary election, or within sixty days of a general election, if that communication mentions the name of any candidate for any federal office. Violating this ban is a federal felony, punishable by five years in federal prison. So if you are a billionaire and choose to spend a million dollars to broadcast campaign ads, that's okay, but if a thousand ordinary people get together to form a corporate organization, and give a thousand dollars each to amass a million dollars to make those same ads, they're federal felons and going to prison.

In *Citizens United*, by a narrow 5–4 vote, the U.S. Supreme Court struck down this censorship law for violating the First Amendment. In an opinion written by Justice Anthony Kennedy, the Court explained that election season is when people most need to hear about the candidates. Looking at what makes America a unique beacon of freedom in the world, Kennedy went on to say that, "Governments are often hostile to speech, but under our law and our tradition it seems stranger than fiction for our Government to make this political speech a crime. Yet this is the statute's purpose and design."

Democrats assailed this Supreme Court decision. Senator Charles Schumer called it "un-American." Barack Obama condemned it as well, and even had the gall and disrespect for the Court and the constitutional duty of addressing a joint session of Congress—where the Court was present as a courtesy to him—to condemn the decision on national television during his 2010 State of the Union, with the justices seated just a few feet in front of him.[27] This deplorable and shameful act by the president of the United States marks a new low in disrespect for our nation's courts.

Reshaping the Supreme Court

So, we've been saying that it's easy to remember the Supreme Court justices when compared to all the other federal judges. Well, the truth is that many of us can't name even one Supreme Court justice. That's totally understandable. Hey, even some lawyers whose work doesn't involve constitutional law or federal issues have trouble naming all nine of them.

But the reality behind those nine Supreme Court seats is that on average in the modern era, each one is occupied by the same person for more than twenty years. So the opportunity to name a Supreme Court justice is the opportunity to shape the Court for years to come. And if one president gets to fill two or more vacancies during his presidency, those appointments can fundamentally alter the course of the nation.

As mentioned above, Justice Stevens is almost certainly retiring, and Justice Ginsburg may also be leaving the Court. Some will say that it's no big deal because Obama will just replace one liberal with another.

That argument is dangerously flawed. You're not replacing two liberal justices with two different liberal justices. Instead, you're replacing two elderly liberal justices who were on their way out with two young liberal justices who will probably still be deciding cases when the ball drops in Times Square on New Year's Eve in 2030.

Just think about that—whoever our next two presidents are, they will both be out of office by then. We could even have gone through a third president by 2030. Do you have school-age children? They'll be grown professionals by then, and maybe have kids of their own.

So these Supreme Court seats are a big deal. When Justice Stevens was appointed, Gerald Ford was president and the country had just gone through Watergate. It was an entirely different world. And it will be an entirely different world again, when Stevens's replacement is herself replaced.[28]

Even so, the bigger impact comes from Obama potentially having the ability to replace a moderate or conservative justice. Look back to the chart of ages at the beginning of this chapter, and you'll see that one moderate justice and one conservative justice are already in their seventies. Only God knows what tomorrow has in store for any of us, regardless of our age. But as you get older, the odds start climbing that something could happen from out of the blue, resulting in death or permanent disability.

There are four liberal votes on the Supreme Court right now. Four votes that none of us have any Second Amendment rights to own any guns whatsoever. Four votes that it's okay for government to discriminate on the basis of race when promoting people in the workforce, as long as it's called affirmative action. Four votes that restrictions on even partial-birth abortion are unconstitutional. Four votes that the government can throw you in federal prison for five years for pooling your money with other citizens to speak out on a political candidate during election season.

One more vote, and they have five. One more vote, and they can do anything they want. One more vote, and President Obama has a Court that may give a green light to his blueprint.

Recent Outrages

Warning! Despite what the media tries to tell you, don't for a minute believe that there is a conservative majority on the Court right now. There are only four conservatives, and one moderate. Although many issues don't break down as conservative-versus-liberal in the Court, when there is an issue that splits along philosophical lines, the current lineup on the Court means we win only when Justice Anthony Kennedy sides with us. In other words, we usually don't have conservative wins; they're often moderate wins instead, and it just so happens that it's an issue where moderates side with us on the Right.

But there have been a number of serious losses in recent years. None of us should think in terms of defending the status quo. The status quo is unacceptable, and will continue to be so until we have a new president and a new Senate to see a fifth conservative justice seated on the Supreme Court.

Consider just a few examples. As we alluded to earlier, in 2007 the Court bought into the global-warming craze, and held that the state of Massachusetts had standing to bring a lawsuit to force the EPA to set up a national regulatory scheme for carbon emissions. In 2008 the Court held that foreign terrorists captured by our military on foreign battlefields and held in overseas facilities have the same rights as American citizens on our own soil to challenge that detention and potentially have a judge order the terrorist released. Also in 2008, the Court took a bite out of the states' ability to govern themselves when it held that it violates the Eighth Amendment's ban on cruel and unusual punishment for a jury in a *state* trial to sentence a child rapist to death, even if *state* law expressly allows that penalty for such a heinous crime. The list goes on, with a dozen or so very unfortunate cases since the Court's current ideological makeup became reality in January 2006.[29]

The Limited Role of Courts in a Free Society
What these recent High Court outrages have in common is that they ignore the limited role of courts in our free society. America is a constitutional democratic republic. It is a republic because it is a representative government, where people do not directly rule but instead choose who it is they want to represent them, speak for them, and make decisions for them. It is democratic because those representatives are chosen by the people, as opposed to being hereditary or appointed. And it is constitutional because the structure, form, and powers of that government are set forth in a charter called a constitution, which is the supreme law of the country.

We've looked at various aspects of the Constitution designed to protect our liberties as individuals, such as the separation of powers and the system of checks and balances. But beyond that, there are certain additional safeguards to limit the power of each branch of government.

To limit the power of the courts, nothing is more important than the case-or-controversy requirement. Article III of the Constitution says that the judicial power extends to "cases" and "controversies."[30] What that means is that the courts, including the Supreme Court, can only exert their power—the judicial power—as part of a case or controversy.[31] The Court has made clear over time that this clause means the courts do not give advisory opinions.[32] They can only act when there is a lawsuit properly brought before them.

Without such a case, the courts have no jurisdiction to act. Without getting into the legal weeds, suffice it to say that such jurisdiction must be authorized both by the Constitution and by a federal statute.[33] Beyond that, the person bringing the lawsuit must have standing, which means that they must have suffered a personal injury that is traceable to the defendant and that the court can remedy by granting the requested relief.

By providing that a court cannot act without standing and these other jurisdictional hooks, the Constitution shields the country from judicial power where it's not appropriate in a democratic republic. The Court explains that the judiciary can only act in a way "consistent with a system of separated powers."[34] The Founding Fathers understood the immense damage that life-appointed, unelected, and unaccountable judges could do unless their power was strictly confined in this fashion. The other exertions of government power, such as deciding what laws to pass or what executive actions to take, would only be carried out by officials who were accountable to the voters through the ballot box.

This limited role for the judiciary is in sharp contrast with Barack Obama's philosophy, as seen by the comments of President Obama's first High Court nominee, Sonia Sotomayor. One of the most controversial statements that Justice Sotomayor said as a judge, which was raised repeatedly in her confirmation hearings to the Supreme Court, was that the federal appeals courts are where "policy is made." That's exactly the attitude of judicial activism, which sees judges as making up some sort of super-legislature, with the power to declare that the Constitution demands whatever that judge thinks to be good, right, or worthwhile.

The Purpose of a Written Constitution

In some countries, like Great Britain, they have what they call a "constitution" and it's enforced as the law, but it's not written. Instead it's a philosophy and method of government discerned through Acts of Parliament, court decisions, and royal action. The problem? One tends to focus only on the actions, traditions, and precedents from the past four hundred years that help one's cause, and ignore the ones that don't help you as much. Although well-meaning judges do their best to set aside biases and agendas, such a subjective process is bound to lead to subjective outcomes.

To avoid such subjectivism, America has a written constitution. The Founding Fathers were driven to start the American Revolution and sign the Declaration of Independence because their rights as Englishmen—that is to say, the rights they claimed under the unwritten English constitution—were being violated by King George III and the British Parliament.

Many of the provisions in the U.S. Constitution were reactions to English abuses. Britain had a national church headed by the king, and at times punished those who preached without a license, so we adopted the Establishment Clause. The British punished and imprisoned colonists who spoke and wrote against the Crown, so we adopted the Free Speech Clause and the Free Press Clause. They tried to disarm the colonists, so we adopted the Second Amendment. The list goes on.

But the greatest anti-British reaction of all was the simple act of writing down a constitution. All of the colonists' grievances could be traced to Parliament violating the colonists' rights under the *unwritten* English constitution, so we reacted by writing down the U.S. Constitution. Their abuses are why we adopted a written document that all could read, so that everyone could tell what powers government has and what rights the people have.

It's passing strange that the Far Left in this country tries to take us back to the British system, declaring rights that are not found in the Constitution (such as abortion, health care, and same-sex marriage) while denying rights that are plainly there in black and white (such as the Second Amendment right to own a gun).

Although the Far Left talks about a "living constitution" that changes over time, it doesn't take more than a third-grade education to understand that the whole point of having a written document is so that we're all reading the same thing. Words written on paper don't change on that paper over time. Words like "abortion" don't suddenly appear on a document, and phrases like "to keep and bear arms" don't mysteriously walk off the page.

That's not to say that the Constitution can't change. It can, and in fact it has—twenty-seven times. A change in the Constitution is called a *constitutional amendment.* Our Founding Fathers were under no delusions. They knew they couldn't get everything right, and they also knew that some things would change over time. So in Article V of the Constitution they provided that the Constitution could be amended, if the amendment was proposed by two-thirds of the House and two-thirds of the Senate, and then ratified by a regular majority vote of the legislatures of three-fourths of the states.

It's a steep hill to climb, but again, that's the whole point. We the People who adopted the Constitution as a sovereign act can also change it by another sovereign act of We the People. But it must be the people, doing so by huge supermajorities—not by five out of nine justices on the Supreme Court.

And not by a president who refuses to abide by the Constitution.

Judicial Activism Remaking Society and Destroying Federalism

Using the power of the courts to do things that are not sanctioned by the Constitution is what is called *judicial activism.* Courts are to interpret and apply the law—whether statutes, regulations, or the Constitution—in accordance with that law's original meaning.

But to cite the Constitution as commanding a result that the Constitution does not in fact require is to usurp the lawmaking process entrusted to the political branches of government—Congress and the president.

It's imperative that the courts only strike down a federal law when that law clearly exceeds the Constitution's limits.[35] Ever since *Marbury v. Madison* was decided in 1803, judicial review is the most potent tool wielded by judges. The power to declare that a statute, passed by the people's elected lawmakers in Congress and signed by their president, violates the Constitution, and therefore to hold that the law is null and void, is a power that courts must resort to only when absolutely necessary. Judicial restraint is critical to maintaining the separation of powers our Founding Fathers gave us.

Judicial restraint is also absolutely needed to save our federal form of government. Going back to what we said in the introduction, the Constitution creates a federal system of government. Certain narrow policy areas, like national security and creating a stable system for interstate commerce, were committed to the federal government.

All other issues were left to the states as sovereign governments. The people of Rhode Island can run Rhode Island—and with it, their own lives—as they see fit. The same goes for Indiana. The same goes for Ohio. The states are what Justice Louis Brandeis called the "laboratories of democracy," trying different things that reflect their own values and priorities. If people don't like it, they can move to a different state. And if something works really well, then other states can decide whether they want to copy that system in their own state. That's federalism.

When courts declare rights not found in the Constitution, they take away the states' ability to decide how to deal with those decisions about personal liberty. When the courts refuse to strike down federal laws that go beyond what the Constitution gives to the federal government, it allows the national government to tread on the freedoms of the people in those states, robbing them of the chance to make those policies for themselves.

In sum, judicial activism takes away our freedom.

Obama Supports Judicial Activism

A statement by Barack Obama from a few years ago shows us what he thinks of judicial activism and the Supreme Court. The Warren Court is considered the most liberal Supreme Court in history, from the mid-1950s until the summer of 1969.[36] Talking about the Warren Court during a 2001 radio interview when he was an Illinois state senator, Obama said:

If you look at the victories and the failures of the civil rights movement and its litigation strategy . . . the Supreme Court never ventured into the issues of redistribution of wealth and served more basic issues of political and economic justice in this society and, to the extent that, as radical as I think people try to characterize the Warren Court, it wasn't that radical. It didn't break free from the essential constraints that were placed by the Founding Fathers in the Constitution, at least as it's been interpreted, and the Warren Court [interpreted it], that, generally, the Constitution . . . says what the states can't do to you, but it doesn't say what the federal government or the state government must do on your behalf. . . . I think one of the tragedies of the civil rights movement was because the civil rights movement became so court-focused . . . there was a tendency to lose track of . . . the actual coalitions of power through which you bring about redistributive change. And in some ways we still suffer from that.[37]

Later in the interview he expanded on that thought in answer to a caller, who asked if ". . . it was too late for that kind of reparative work economically." In response, then-Senator Obama lamented, "I'm not optimistic about bringing about major redistributive change through the courts."[38]

In other words, he regrets that the most liberal Supreme Court in our history was not even more liberal. Barack Obama laments that the Court "never ventured into . . . redistribution of wealth and . . . economic justice." Those are leftist phrases for court-ordered socialism.

That was then, when he could freely speak his mind without being concerned that the national media would spread it to the national voting public. But that was also then, when he had no power to do anything about it. Now he's busy creating a Supreme Court that he thinks will give him what he wants.

Obama Having His Cake and Eating It Too

By remaking the courts—and especially the Supreme Court—in his image, President Obama gets to have his cake and eat it too.

First, President Obama creates courts of judicial activists.

This isn't as hard as it might seem. Although most regular people never hear the names of someone nominated to the Supreme Court before the day that person is first announced by the president, those names are well known in legal circles for years beforehand. For appellate courts, and especially for the Supreme Court, President Obama is only nominating people that his team has vetted. Every person who gets nominated to the Supreme Court has a network of supporters. Aside from that person's being interviewed by the Justice Department and the White House Counsel's Office, reviewing all their writings and works, each of these people has longtime friends. This network includes senators and other top-ranking individuals, some of whom will have long-standing relationships with the president, the attorney general, and senior aides in the White House.

The modern vetting process takes place over years, long before there's a vacancy on the Court. Although you can't read minds or truly know what's in a person's heart, there are key people in each political party who know the legal views and constitutional philosophy of the people on the selective list of those considered to be Supreme Court–caliber. In other words, if you're on the short list to be considered for the Supreme Court, it means that there are people close to the president who know you, know what you believe, know what you stand for, and have a very good idea of how you would decide cases if you were appointed to the bench.

Working from such lists and talking with the people who have known them for years, a president of either party is able to help build a Supreme Court that will reflect the president's philosophy of government and of the Constitution.

For example, it's well known in D.C. that the following people are on Barack Obama's short list for the next Supreme Court vacancy: Judge Diane Wood of the Seventh Circuit, Solicitor General Elena Kagan, Homeland Security Secretary Janet Napolitano, Judge Merrick Garland of the D.C. Circuit, and Michigan Governor Jennifer Granholm.

Beyond that, there are others that are looked at as possible Supreme Court nominees down the road. It's likely that Deputy OMB Director Cass Sunstein, State Department Legal Advisor Harold Koh, and Obama's nominee for assistant attorney general for the Office of Legal Counsel, Dawn Johnsen, are all being groomed to be nominated to the U.S. Court of Appeals for the D.C. Circuit. From there, any of those three could also be nominated to the Supreme Court.

This allows Barack Obama to have it both ways. On the one hand, he can denounce decisions such as the Supreme Court's striking down of a Louisiana law that allows the death penalty for people who rape young children. But on the other hand, it allows for him to create a Supreme Court that will consistently produce such liberal outcomes.

Then he can cry crocodile tears whenever the Court hands down a liberal decision that outrages the rest of the nation, even though it's a predictable result, given the people he appointed to the bench.

For that matter, they're probably the very same decisions he would make if he were a justice on the Supreme Court himself.

FDR's Failed Court-Packing Scheme

Let's change the whole makeup of the federal judiciary. Let's redirect the course of the nation by changing how the Supreme Court basically thinks of the Constitution. Yeah, that's been tried before. It was FDR's court-packing scheme.

As discussed later in chapter 4, President Franklin Delano Roosevelt fundamentally changed the nature of the federal government in the New Deal of the 1930s—but it wasn't easy. A whole series of New Deal programs were struck down by the Supreme Court for exceeding various limits that the Constitution places on certain types of government actions.[39]

In response, FDR decided to try to remake the Supreme Court. The Supreme Court is created by the Constitution, but the exact number of justices on the Court is set by Congress through passing a statute.[40]

FDR wanted Congress to expand the Court by six, for a new total of fifteen justices. He arrived at that number by saying that some of the members of the Court were too old to keep up with the busy workload, so Congress should create a new seat for every justice over the age of seventy.

Everyone knew what was going on, however. It was no secret that FDR had decided that if the Court was going to strike down some of the things he wanted to do, then he would simply pack the Court with a bunch of pro–New Deal justices until he had the votes he needed.

The idea was hugely unpopular with the American people. They understood the court-packing scheme for what it was—a frontal assault on our whole system of separation of powers. FDR's court-packing plan was a blueprint for completely co-opting the third branch of government to become a rubber stamp on the president's agenda.

Public opposition was strong enough to doom the bill that would have expanded the Supreme Court. Unfortunately, that same year, 1937, the Supreme Court also took a big step to the left and started upholding legislation that the justices would have rejected only a year earlier. While part of this was due to FDR filling enough Supreme Court vacancies to make the Court more liberal, it also looked like the Court may have become worried that the court-packing bill might pass, so they sought to head it off by becoming more accommodating to FDR's agenda.[41]

President Obama's court-packing scheme is more subtle. He's only trying to expand the lower federal courts, not the Supreme Court. Instead of adding justices, his plan for the Supreme Court is to win a second term, betting that at least one of the conservative justices can't last until that second term ends in 2017.

But the American people are getting wise to his plan all the same. And if this issue is put before the voters in the right way, President Obama can be on the receiving end of the same backlash that FDR felt in the 1936 and 1938 elections.

Confirmation Standards: The Framers v. Obama

But the issue of how to deal with President Obama's judicial nominees also creates a dilemma for the Republican Party, and conservatives in particular.

For 200 years, the Senate kept to the view of the Founding Fathers that the Senate's role in judicial confirmations was a narrow one. The Senate only evaluated three things when it came to judicial nominees:

- Does the nominee have the intellect and legal education to be able to navigate through the complex problems that make it to the High Court?
- Does the nominee have the experience to show he can handle the stress and strain of that position with grace and poise, and to resist political or popular pressure to faithfully interpret the law?
- Does the nominee have the character needed in a Supreme Court justice, being a person of integrity, honor, and honesty?

This kind of approach is found in *The Federalist* No. 76, written by Alexander Hamilton. Explaining the Senate's confirmation power in the proposed Constitution, Hamilton said that the president has sole discretion in whom he nominates. The Senate's role was to provide a limited check, just to make sure that the president didn't nominate for personal reasons someone who was unqualified, such as a close friend, a family member, or someone to whom the president personally owed a lot of money.

The test that can be distilled out of *The Federalist* No. 76 is that the Senate's role is simply to ensure that the president doesn't nominate someone solely because of that nominee's personal ties to the president. As long as that person could have been nominated by a president who had never met the nominee, someone who's qualified based on their merits, then the Senate should confirm.

So, how can we respond to the judiciary-based part of President Obama's blueprint?

Democrats' Turn for the Worse in 1987

The Democrats changed the rules in 1987. Politics always played a role in Supreme Court confirmations, because it's a major action of the president and the Senate. Even so, a nominee like Antonin Scalia, who was well known as a staunch conservative, was confirmed 98–0 by the Senate in 1986.

How could that happen? Senator Leahy, liberal Democrat from Vermont, summed it up by explaining why he supported Scalia: "Judge Scalia's philosophy is not my philosophy. It is President Reagan's philosophy. In fact, Reagan has earned the right to appoint judges of his political philosophy."[42]

In other words, elections have consequences; this had been the national consensus for two centuries. But then came the 1987 Bork nomination.

Judge Robert H. Bork was Ronald Reagan's nominee in 1987.[43] Bork had a perfect résumé: He taught at Yale Law School, served as U.S. solicitor general, and also served as a judge on the U.S. Court of Appeals for the D.C. Circuit. Yet his nomination went down in defeat because of his "judicial philosophy." Bork was rejected because he was a conservative.

Democrats took the Senate in 1986. After Bork was nominated, Senator Ted Kennedy gave his "Robert Bork's America" speech, in which he said that Bork would create an America where women would die in back-alley abortions and restaurants would be racially segregated.

Why did this happen in 1987?

The 1960s and '70s saw the Supreme Court get involved in making social-value judgments and policy preferences where the Constitution was silent. This tragedy reached a low point with *Roe v. Wade* in 1973. Once the Court was acting as a super-legislature, enacting laws that the Left couldn't get passed, the Left decided to derail nominees that they suspected wouldn't continue this judicial activism.

So the Left savaged Bork, and the White House was caught flat-footed. When Bork went down, Reagan nominated Judge Douglas Ginsburg. When that nomination also went down, Reagan nominated Judge Anthony Kennedy, who at that time was thought to be a solid conservative.

The Far Left continued their campaign-style tactics in the Bush 41 years, trying to derail David Hackett Souter, presuming he was conservative (everyone got that one wrong). Then the Left almost succeeded in stopping Clarence Thomas, who was confirmed by a 52–48 vote.

Republicans tried to restore the process when Democrat Bill Clinton became president. Clinton nominated Ruth Bader Ginsburg to replace Justice Byron White, a moderate. Ginsburg had a long liberal record; she was a former counsel to the American Civil Liberties Union and had written law review articles stridently defending judicial activism.

Nonetheless, Ginsburg was the first woman professor to receive tenure at Columbia Law School, had been a law review editor and top graduate from Columbia, and had served with distinction on the D.C. Circuit. So Republicans overwhelmingly voted to confirm her, with a Senate vote of 96–3.

This went on through the Clinton presidency with judicial nominees, including the 1994 Supreme Court confirmation of Stephen Breyer by an 89–9 vote.

Democrats during the Bush Years

But when Republicans once again took the White House in 2000 and had a majority in the Senate after 2002, Democrats repaid Republican statesmanship by resorting to their old tactics, and then taking them to a whole new level.

The fact that Sonia Sotomayor is the first Hispanic Supreme Court justice is itself proof of Democratic obstructionism. The first Hispanic justice could have been Miguel Estrada, Bush's nominee for the D.C. Circuit. He matches Sotomayor's educational credentials, with degrees from Columbia and Harvard Law, where he was a law review editor. Estrada also clerked for Justice Kennedy on the Supreme Court, and later served as an assistant solicitor general under both Republican and Democrat presidents, and is a partner at one of America's top law firms.

Yet Miguel Estrada was never nominated to the Supreme Court because he was never confirmed to the D.C. Circuit. The Democrats feared that Estrada would eventually sit on the Supreme Court, so they conspired to kill him in the cradle by keeping him off the bench altogether.

Senate Republican staffer Manny Miranda got a hold of an internal strategy memo in which the Democrats on the Senate Judiciary Committee—which would include Charles Schumer and Ted Kennedy—decided to start filibustering judicial nominees to the circuit courts for the first time in history, starting with Estrada.

This leaked memo showed Democrat senators conspiring to stop his confirmation simply because he's Hispanic—a clear instance of racism that never got the attention it deserved. The memo, addressed to Senator Dick Durbin of Illinois, says that a group working with Senate Democrat staff and liberal activists, "identified Miguel Estrada (D.C. Circuit) as especially dangerous, because he has a minimal paper trail, *he is Latino*, and the White House seems to be grooming him for a Supreme Court appointment."[44] His nomination was filibustered for years until he had to withdraw to resume his law practice.

Nor was Miguel Estrada an isolated incident.

For example, aside from Estrada, the most contested fight was over Janice Rogers Brown's nomination to the D.C. Circuit. Brown was a justice on the California Supreme Court, with an extraordinary career. She's also an African American woman, the daughter of a sharecropper, and a single mother. She had an only-in-America success story of going from nothing to everything, and was well known as a solid conservative and a brilliant legal mind. On top of that, she is known as a woman of faith. All in all, Janice Rogers Brown looks like an ideal Supreme Court nominee. So once again, Senate Democrats tried to defeat her. They succeeded for years, until the voters had enough and gave the Republicans fifty-five seats in the 2004 election. Brown was confirmed to the D.C. Circuit several months later.

Supreme Court Confirmation Fights

Bush 43 nonetheless gave us two outstanding jurists. Justice Samuel Alito isn't as conservative as Justices Scalia or Thomas, but he's a fantastic pick, with an extraordinary intellect, vast experience, and even a pleasant personality. And Chief Justice John Roberts, while not as conservative as Justice Alito, is nonetheless a solid and principled jurist with a good judicial philosophy, and is considered one of the most brilliant minds on the Supreme Court. And to boot, he's a man of wit and charm, as the country saw during his confirmation.

Democrats did everything they could to derail Roberts and Alito, as well.

When Roberts was first nominated to replace Sandra Day O'Connor, the Left ginned up within a couple days with a heavy opposition campaign about how Roberts was some wide-eyed extremist.

While that nomination was still pending, Chief Justice William Rehnquist died in office from cancer. President Bush quickly re-nominated Roberts to succeed Rehnquist as chief justice of the United States.

Realizing that they now had two Supreme Court vacancies and Republicans held the Senate, the Left decided to focus their firepower on whoever would come next.

Smart move. Roberts dazzled the country and came across as funny and likable. He had only been a D.C. Circuit judge for two years, so there wasn't much of a paper trail from his decisions. It was impossible to prove what his real views were.[45]

The Democrats couldn't land a glove on him, and some—like Joe Biden—who tried too hard to do so just ended up looking like buffoons. Democrats saw the polls strongly in favor of Roberts, and so the final confirmation vote was 78–22.

Samuel Alito's confirmation was a tougher situation. Unlike Roberts, Alito had a long record as a Third Circuit judge. He was clearly a conservative,[46] and the Democrats hit him with everything they had.

Despite Alito's brilliance and excellent qualifications, the Far Left was so apoplectic over stopping Alito that it looked possible—if unlikely—that the Democrats might even manage to filibuster his nomination. But although he didn't have Roberts's flair for charming repartee, Alito's answers were so eloquent, and he avoided the traps set before him so adeptly, that the Democrats never managed to trip him up.

The pivotal moment came when the Democrats tried to paint Alito as a racist. Sam Alito's wife began to cry. Since she was seated behind him and just slightly to the side, the camera shot caught her in the background, sobbing at the slandering of her husband, as he sat there stoically, taking the abuse without complaint.

The Democrats' boorish tactics backfired. The opposition to Alito faltered. Although almost every Democrat voted against him, the threat of a filibuster collapsed, and he was confirmed by a vote of 58–42.

And, it should be noted, then-Senator Obama voted against Justice Alito. In fact, he voted to filibuster the Alito nomination. More than that, though, he also voted against Roberts, even though he admitted that Roberts was fully qualified to be chief justice.[47]

Maybe Barack Obama had his blueprint in mind even back then.

This Issue Is a Winner for the GOP—If Conservative Judges Are Nominated

The judges issue is a big winner for Republicans and a serious liability for the Democrats, if—and only if—the issue is handled correctly.

The American people do not want activist judges, and do not mind conservative judges when the people understand that a conservative judge means one who will faithfully interpret the Constitution and law as written, and not force a conservative agenda through the courts.

If presented properly to the voters, the courts are an ideal issue. First, it energizes the Republican base, which is essential to any political victory. Second, moderate voters generally favor conservative judges (although it's not a big issue with them), giving them one more reason to vote Republican. And third, moderate voters that do not consider conservative judges a plus nonetheless do not consider them a negative, either; you don't lose any moderate voters by appointing conservative judges.

The only people you lose on conservative judges are liberals—and you don't need their votes to win an election. An issue that energizes your base and is a small to moderate plus with middle voters is a winning issue.

Unfortunately, George W. Bush allowed this issue to fall by the wayside after his second Supreme Court pick—Sam Alito—was confirmed in early 2006. Republicans as a party lost interest in the judicial issue, either thinking they had won or thinking that they had gotten enough out of it, and that the diminishing returns were no longer worth it.

And regrettably, the GOP nominee, Senator John McCain, did not make the courts a campaign issue. He gave only one speech on judges. Conservatives were disappointed by this, but not surprised, as the courts were never a major focus for McCain. John McCain's role in the "Gang of Fourteen"—to avoid abolishing the filibuster for judicial nominees—was greeted with hostility from many on the Right (though some have changed their tune in light of the current political situation). McCain's answers about judges to Pastor Rick Warren during the Saddleback Church debate with Obama were spot-on perfect, and had he spoken like that throughout the campaign, it would have energized conservatives on the topic of judges.

With McCain not forcing the judicial issue and Obama doing everything he could to duck the issue, it never rose to the level of prominence that it otherwise would have in the campaign, to the GOP's detriment on Election Day.[48] The courts were never really a topic of concern in the 2008 campaign, and the race might have been closer had Obama been forced to discuss in detail what sort of judges he'd appoint.

Republicans need to keep one thing in mind when it comes to the courts, and it bears repeating: You cannot win or lose moderates over conservative judges, and to the extent that they care at all, moderates prefer conservative judges because those are the ones that practice judicial restraint. This taps into moderate voters' agreement with the principle that in a democracy, policy matters should be decided by *elected* leaders rather than appointed judges.

All you can do when it comes to the courts is energize your base, or alienate your base. Regardless of their views on specific issues, a majority of the American people want judges who confine themselves to the Constitution and law as written.

Solution: Forcing Lawsuits Now, and Putting Senators on Notice

There are several solutions for combating Obama's blueprint involving the courts.

First, bring all the lawsuits now where we can win Justice Anthony Kennedy over. Let's get some good victories under our belt, in the same vein as the *Citizens United v. FEC* decision for free speech, or the 2008 *D.C. v. Heller* decision holding that the Second Amendment secures an individual right for private citizens to bear arms. And in so doing, let the country see what liberal justices have to say as they oppose these outcomes, and that President Obama's Supreme Court appointments are on the wrong side of these issues.

No precedent is better than bad precedent. When you lose a case, that decision is nonetheless a binding decision that will be upheld by a future Supreme Court unless there is a compelling reason to overrule it. So we shouldn't be reckless in pushing cases. But in situations where we do lose cases despite our best efforts, those losses will only continue to heighten the importance of this issue to the American people.

The other solution is making judicial confirmations a very public and politically costly endeavor. We need to shine the spotlight on controversial nominees. Voting for those nominees will be dangerous for vulnerable Democrat senators, and will help to elect Republican senators who can slam the brakes on the rest of Obama's agenda.

The issue of judges will also remind the American people that President Obama is out of step with the country on this issue, and show them that he has far different priorities than they do about what we look for in a judge.

And although we should all want to return to a confirmation situation where it's accepted that a liberal president can put liberals on the courts, just like a conservative president can appoint conservatives to the courts, at this point the process must be made costly for the Obama White House. Republicans cannot unilaterally disarm. Republicans need to put enough of a squeeze on the process now, so that Democrats are willing to publicly agree to return to the Founders' confirmation standards after the next presidential election. Democrats will only do that if they're made to cry uncle now.

These are limited solutions. The reality is that President Obama is stacking the courts with liberals as you read this. He will likely have two or three Supreme Court appointments, more than fifty circuit court appointments, and over two hundred district court appointments. But elections have consequences; the president has the power to nominate judges, and there will be many judicial vacancies during President Obama's term. As we fight to uphold and restore the

Constitution, we cannot violate the Constitution ourselves. The country will continue to need new judges as vacancies occur.

This is especially true given the unprecedented role that the courts are taking in national security after the Supreme Court's 2008 *Boumediene v. Bush* decision, which we've referenced in this chapter. Article III of the Constitution allows courts only a minimal role in national security. The president has tremendous power when it comes to national security, and that power becomes truly immense once Congress authorizes war, as happened after 9/11.

So it's an utter outrage that President Obama has allowed Attorney General Holder and the Justice Department to take a leading role in the War on Terror. The underwear bomber we discussed in chapter 1 is being tried in civilian court. Gitmo detainees are probably being moved to a civilian prison in Illinois. There might even be civilian trials for terrorists such as 9/11 mastermind Khalid Sheikh Mohammed.

In each of these cases, all the constitutional protections that American citizens enjoy would apply to these foreign terrorists. These protections include the presumption of innocence, the right to a jury trial, to challenge witnesses, to challenge evidence, and to exclude any evidence obtained before Miranda rights were given or confessions made before a lawyer was consulted, and countless other rights.

The Constitution sets up a system whereby it's better for one hundred guilty citizens to go free than for a single innocent citizen to be condemned. It draws a bright line between war and law enforcement, though. There is a bright line between foreign policy and domestic policy, and between the rights of citizens versus foreign wartime enemies. Thrusting these issues into our civilian federal courts destroys these distinctions, empowers judges to act where the Constitution gives no such power, and cheapens all of the precious rights on which every American relies.

We need the courts to be a top issue in 2012, and for the next president—a Republican president—to be firmly committed to doing what it takes to get the right kind of judges on our nation's courts. Let's replace President Obama's judiciary blueprint with our own.

CHAPTER 3

THE UNCHECKED PRESIDENT

The president is not a king—free to take any action he chooses, without limitation by law.
—SENATOR CHARLES SCHUMER (D-NY),
JANUARY 9, 2006

Barack Obama's blueprint establishes an imperial president. Although this doesn't mean that such a president can do anything he wants, it does mean that he wields such enormous power that it amounts to a critical mass, where it's hard to think of anything that can stop him once he's gained momentum.

One of the themes we looked at in the introduction is our Founding Fathers' focus on checks and balances. They regarded all government as dangerous, but they also knew that it would be less dangerous if the various power centers had checks over the others. With a "fight fire with fire" approach, the Founders wanted to use one type of government power to check another.

The elaborate system of checks and balances, along with the separation of powers, was the form of government they devised as a result. The federal government possessed certain powers, and the states held the remainder. Within the federal government, all power is divided into three types: legislative, executive, and judicial. And each of these three types of federal power were set in tension with the other two, so that none of them could break free and oppress the American people.

The Constitution says that "The executive power shall be vested in a president of the United States of America."[1] In doing so, the Constitution gives all the executive power of the government, which includes military, law enforcement, and administration, to one person alone.

But the Constitution also denies to him whatever power is not executive in nature. The Constitution vests all of the federal government's legislative power to Congress, not the president.[2] The legislative power is the power to make laws. The Constitution likewise vests all of the judicial power in the Supreme Court, and under the Court to whatever lower courts Congress would later create to assist the Supreme Court.[3] The judicial power is the power to say "what the law is."[4] In other words, it's the power to interpret the Constitution and inferior federal laws whenever such issues arise.

You've heard the cynical version of the Golden Rule? "He who has the gold, makes the rules." Well that's not always true. When the head of the military has no limits on his power, "he who has the guns can shoot he who has the gold. Therefore, he who has the guns makes the rules."

No one is more dangerous to ordinary people than a man with complete power over the military, national security, antiterrorism, and law enforcement. Denying the president lawmaking power, and also any power to say "what the law is," is part of the check that the Constitution imposes on the presidency to protect you and me from our head of state.

Barack Obama's blueprint calls for casting off the limits that the Constitution puts on him. President Obama's blueprint for using executive orders, administrative regulations, and international law will give him a way to exercise lawmaking power in violation of Article I of the Constitution, and to avoid judicial review of his actions in violation of Article III. And to help carry out his plans, he's building his own private civilian army of dedicated followers, in violation of Article II.

WHEN LAWMAKING BECOMES LAWBREAKING

To get around the Constitution's commitment of the power to make laws to Congress (and Congress alone), Barack Obama is going to make laws by executive fiat, but then call them something other than laws. He's going to call them "executive orders" and "regulations."

Getting the Words Right

To be completely accurate, we need to say what we mean by "laws." The Constitution typically uses the term "law" in reference to statutes. A statute is an Act of Congress, passed as an exercise of the legislative power, and either signed by the president or enacted over the president's veto with a two-thirds congressional vote. When we speak about "laws" in this chapter, we're referring to pieces of legislation passed by Congress.

But in the broadest sense, a "law" is any legal determination or government edict with the power to bind others through imposing legal obligations or declaring legal rights. Of those, there are two types of law: enacted law and case law.

Enacted laws are laws adopted by government. At the federal level, the highest law we recognize is the U.S. Constitution, which is the Supreme Law of the Land.[5] Under the Constitution are statutes enacted by Congress. Under those statutes come regulations, which we're about to examine because of how President Obama can abuse them. Under regulations come executive orders by the president, and various types of determinations by boards or commissions, or other actions by government agencies that don't meet the legal requirements to be considered regulations.

Case law is made of court decisions.[6] The authority of the decision depends on which court issues it, and what the legal issue is. Each court only has power where it has jurisdiction, whether that's only part of a state, or a federal appeals court with jurisdiction over several states.[7] So long as it has jurisdiction, whatever a court decides becomes the binding interpretation of that law.[8] Unless that court is reversed by a higher court, or overrules its own precedent in some future case, the case law created by that initial decision continues to be binding.[9]

But when the Constitution confers "lawmaking" power to Congress, that refers to the legislative power. And it's a power that Barack Obama is not allowed to have.

Taking Care to "Take Care"

Law is a tricky issue, one that President Obama is using to his advantage.

Only Congress has legislative power, but laws usually aren't self-executing. Most of the time they need all sorts of rules and regulations to fill in the fine print of how they're implemented. This is done through the rulemaking process.

Rules and regulations are where the rubber meets the road when it comes to the law. Congress passes a statute, with all sorts of requirements and mandates. How exactly those provisions are going to be administered by agents of the executive branch is usually a big question mark.

You can argue that there's a constitutional basis for the executive branch making some rules and regulations. The Constitution requires the president, as chief executive, to, "take care that the laws be faithfully executed."[10] This appropriately labeled Take Care Clause grants each president the power to create regulations, in such a manner as provided by Congress, to carry out the various Acts of Congress.

The key here, though, is the mandate from that clause. The president is to make sure the laws are *faithfully executed*; he's not allowed to make law himself.

Herein lies the tricky balancing act, one that is easily subject to abuse even under good circumstances. When you have a president intent on causing trouble, we can see a train wreck in a hurry.

It's also possible that the Take Care Clause doesn't authorize regulations, but if that's true, then most regulations on the books these days are unconstitutional. Since no court is ever going to go there, we'll stick regulations under the Take Care Clause and move on.

Obama Wasn't the First to Use Regulations

To be completely fair, using regulations to advance his agenda isn't something President Obama is inventing out of whole cloth. Executive orders and regulations have been abused for decades, and in one sense, all Obama is doing is taking the abuse to the next level.

Back in the day of our first president, George Washington, the executive branch was small. There were in essence only three major departments: State, Treasury, and War (the predecessor of the Defense Department). There was an attorney general, but no Justice Department. (The A.G. was essentially just the president's full-time lawyer, something of a hybrid of today's White House counsel and the solicitor general, who argues for the government in the Supreme Court; he didn't even make the same salary as the secretaries of State, Treasury, and War.) The president's Cabinet was small enough that the postmaster general was a member. (Although this may have been influenced by the fact that America's first postmaster general was no less than Benjamin Franklin.) The first administrative official came when Congress authorized our first president to appoint someone to estimate duties on imports.[11]

True to the institution's nature—and our Founding Fathers' fear—our government grew over time. New departments were added,[12] and with new departments came their natural bureaucratic desire to protect and expand their own turf. In addition, career civil servants were created to provide consistency in government operations when a new administration began,[13] although also creating a faceless, nameless bureaucracy of people who can almost never be fired, no matter how ineffective, and a large voting bloc of people who usually vote for whichever presidential or congressional candidate promises more government spending.

But with FDR's New Deal in the 1930s, the federal government mushroomed in size and scope. All of a sudden there were agencies regulating trucks, electricity, unions, and the stock market. This created the modern administrative state, of countless alphabet-soup government commissions, boards, and other administrative bodies.

The rise of the administrative state even led one famous Supreme Court jurist, Justice Robert Jackson, to write in one case that "The rise of administrative bodies probably has been the most significant legal trend of the last century. . . . They have become a veritable fourth branch of the Government, which has deranged our three-branch legal theories."[14]

What had Justice Jackson so concerned was that it looked more and more as though these administrative agencies were doing more than just making procedures to implement and execute laws passed by Congress. An elaborate process was created by Congress for agencies to make legally binding rules and regulations, under the Administrative Procedure Act (APA) that we briefly discussed with the czars in chapter 1.[15] These agencies were actually making substantive policy through their regulations.

But isn't policymaking in fact lawmaking? *If it looks like a law, and it smells like a law* . . . Yes, it is. In fact, one way you could define lawmaking is the process by which public policy is established. So how can administrative agencies do this?

Predictably, there was even a lawsuit over whether agencies could make policy. Eventually a group sued over rules being imposed under the Trade Commission Act by the Federal Trade Commission. And in this landmark case, the U.S. Court of Appeals for the D.C. Circuit upheld the concept that Congress can empower administrative agencies to promulgate regulations that look an awful lot like laws passed by Congress.[16]

This really cleared the air on one issue: The executive branch could use regulations to make public policy in a way that looks as though it's congressional lawmaking. There was already a long line of controversial regulations under which people and organizations chafed, and after this decision, that line continued unabated.

So what's the problem here? Well, there are two: First, if something is unconstitutional (like the executive branch making laws), the American people don't like it regardless of its having been done previously. And second, here, in 2010, is the fact that Barack Obama is taking these things to a whole new level.

Obama's Illegal Plans for Regulations

It's always been accepted that there are certain limits on how much policy can be made through rulemaking and regulations. The idea was that "small" policy decisions could be made by agencies to keep members of Congress from worrying their little heads over (relatively) nitpicky issues that would require them to seriously delve into complex policy areas.

(The reality is that if as a country we forced Congress to take these things seriously and do their homework, then they'd have less time on their hands to try pushing monster-sized pork bills—aka, "stimulus"—or taking over parts of our private sector, such as automakers, banks, or medicine. Idle hands are the devil's playground, especially in the cesspool by the Potomac. We need to occupy those hands with some honest work. Maybe we should give 'em back the nitpicky policy issues, or [gasp!] at least expect that they read the bills that they make into law.)

Like other areas of government, then, there's something of a statesmanlike gentlemen's agreement concerning regulations. The president wouldn't use regulations to do anything too big, and in return Congress wouldn't insist that regulations be only procedural, and instead allow for agencies to make some substantive policy decisions rather than have to rely on Congress.

But this agreement rests on one thing. As we'll see elsewhere in this book, self-government only works when each of the branches of government restrains itself. Each branch of government needs to have a sense of what its proper role is and then limit itself to act within that function. For regulations that's always meant the executive branch making regulations only on smaller things so as to respect Congress's lawmaking power.

The problem here is that President Obama has signaled he's willing to take regulations to a whole new level. He's willing to do things through regulations that are so big, they have always been considered something that only Congress could do by passing a statute.

The perfect example is cap and trade, which is the proposal to regulate carbon emissions. We'll closely examine what's in play when it comes to cap and trade and the economy, discussed in chapter 5. In that chapter, we'll be looking at what that scheme would mean if enacted by legislation.

But now that the carbon emissions legislation is on the ropes, President Obama is threatening to do cap and trade through executive action.[17]

The cap-and-trade legislation kept stalling in the Senate, until finally it looked like it was on life support. *Oh no you don't,* said the president. Obama wanted cap and trade passed before he went on yet another junket to Copenhagen, this time for a big-government, capitalism-bashing environmental summit. Gotta look good to the Europeans, right?

Trying to give Congress a nice swift kick in the pants (more of that warm and fuzzy hope 'n' change to reform the way Washington works, we guess) to do what they're told, President Obama's EPA chief made a completely unprompted and unsolicited public announcement. EPA Administrator Lisa Jackson announced that if Congress did not enact a cap-and-trade system to regulate carbon emissions in America, then the EPA would do it for them.

More than that, the White House warned that if Jackson did this herself, it would be a much harsher system that American businesses would hate. Therefore, the White House explained, Congress should do it, so that cap and trade would be a nicer, more pleasant, less suffocating system than what Jackson and the EPA would create.

Such charming people.

This may have been a bluff, but it's one that backfired on the president big-time. Shocked at this blatant Chicago-style threat, Congress froze. Nothing passed the Senate, and the ever-charismatic Harry Reid made it clear that he didn't know when anything would ever pass in the Senate on that front. Obama went to Copenhagen without any emissions-control legislation, resulting in yet another embarrassing failure of our president, giving big grins and striking impressive poses for photos, but not actually delivering any results for this country.

Not that we're complaining this time. Cap and trade would be horrible for America, and so failing to make any international deal is wonderful news that in a way is also good for President Obama, because it's one less disaster that can come back to haunt him in 2012.

But it may not have been a bluff.

As we'll see in chapter 5, the cost of cap and trade to the U.S. economy could be more than two *trillion* dollars, and would redesign our economy through central-government planning to an even greater extent than a government takeover of health care (as difficult to believe as that may seem).

Yet in December 2009 the Environmental Protection Agency issued an endangerment finding that carbon emissions (which come from anything with an engine, such as your car, your fireplace, or your local power plant) create global warming and endanger the health of the American people,[18] which is the first step in starting to develop a massive book of federal regulations to control carbon emissions.

In other words, President Obama's EPA has started the process for a $2 trillion takeover of part of the American economy, and it isn't even going through Congress. Just think about that. Even with big Democrat majorities and far-left leadership in both houses, cap and trade is bad enough that even Congress won't pass it. There are Democrats who are scared of it. So Obama is positioning to cram it through.

The Constitution does not allow the president to do this, and it amounts to an illegal power grab. But President Obama's blueprint calls for him to have this power, and he's just daring someone to stop him.

Executive Orders

For some things, however, President Obama isn't even using regulations. He's just making law directly through executive orders. Even though administrative regulations are made by executive agencies, and the head and various officials in those agencies are appointed by the president,[19] even then the president doesn't have complete control over them.

That's because regulations are made through the Administrative Procedure Act (APA), which we've referenced a couple times before. (Please don't worry, and don't put down the book. We're not going to launch into a lecture on the APA; it's just one paragraph. We know that the very sound of its name, the phrase "administrative procedure," sounds like a bureaucratic nightmare reminiscent of a root canal.)

The APA requires agencies to give public notice that they're going to be considering making new regulations, and to publish that notice in the *Federal Register* where the media picks up on it. Then, when the proposed regs are drafted, the agency has to publish them in the *Federal Register*, hold public hearings, and then open up a period for public comment. During this time, anyone can speak up, and public-interest groups can alert their members and they—along with university professors, think tanks, and experts—can submit all their analyses and studies and comments on these proposed regs. All that goes into the record. If the agency wants to revise the proposed regs because of what the agency learns during this time, it needs to publish the revised regs and allow more comment. After all this is over, then—and only then—can the agency issue regulations that carry the force of law.

Regulations are something that presidents largely control, and it's hard to get the public interested in anything called "notice of proposed rulemaking." But because adopting regs is a public process, there can be a big outcry if the government tries crafting regulations that have a serious impact on people's lives.

Because of that, when President Obama can't get something done through legislation and can't think of a way to make his desires fit into existing regulations, he's willing to just fulfill them through executive orders. Executive orders are official and numbered orders issued by the president to direct the actions of people serving in the executive branch, and that carry the force of law with those government personnel.

One such example occurred in February 2010. That month President Obama created a "debt commission." A bill had been cosponsored in the Senate by Democrat Kent Conrad and (retiring) Republican Judd Gregg. This bill would have created a bipartisan commission similar to the BRAC Commission, used for military base closings. In order to reduce the federal budget deficit, this proposed commission would have put a package of major financial measures on the table, and then Congress would have had to vote that package up or down without amendments.

But conservative think tanks and advocacy groups smelled a rat. This legislation would have enabled the commission to recommend both spending cuts and tax increases to reduce the budget deficit. These groups understood that the government's problem isn't that it doesn't bring in enough money; the problem is that regardless of how much money government brings in, it spends even more. Tax increases should be off the table; and there should be a commission, but it should only be empowered to lay out a package of spending cuts. When this understanding took hold, the legislation went down in defeat.

So Barack Obama has created that same commission by executive order. Congress didn't give him what he wanted in a statute, so he just ordered it into existence.

Such a commission is legal so long as it has no power, and its findings are advisory only. (It's still bad policy, as we'll see in chapter 5, but at least it would be legal.) But the Constitution requires that any measures for federal spending must come from Congress.[20] The Constitution more specifically also requires that any measures for raising revenue must start in the U.S. House, and cannot start in the Senate.[21]

It's not clear at this time what Obama's plans are for this commission, or even if this may be a useless commission that never does much of anything (which would put it on par with many other boards and commissions in D.C., the members of which somehow nonetheless make ridiculous salaries). But if he tries to use it to cut a single dollar of federal spending or raise a single dollar of taxes, then this commission, created by executive order, would be unconstitutional.

The Solution that Might Not Be: The Congressional Review Act

Do we have any defense against wrongheaded regulations? Some might argue that we do, and they might point to the Congressional Review Act (CRA).[22]

The Congressional Review Act provides that if a set of regulations would have enough of an impact on our country that it should be regarded as a set of "major rules," then once adopted, any such rules must be submitted to Congress, and the new set of regs wouldn't go into effect for sixty days. During that time, if Congress passes a joint resolution rejecting the regs, they're thrown out. Moreover, even if they do go into effect but then Congress disapproves of them through a CRA resolution, then the disapproval is retroactive, meaning it's as if the regs were never passed, and never went into effect.

Great! We've got a nice congressional check on the executive branch here, right? The problem is that this joint resolution has to be signed by the president, just like any ordinary legislation. Since Obama will continue as president until January 20, 2013, we're not going to get his signature on any of those things even if we take back both houses of Congress in 2010.

Just like any other legislation, a president's veto can be overridden by a two-thirds vote in both houses of Congress. But since few if any Democrats are going to turn against Obama, it's hard to see how Republicans could gather two-thirds in both chambers, no matter how well we do in the 2010 elections.

So the bottom line is that it's hard to see how CRA could be of any use to the GOP before the next presidential election. If Republicans take both Congress and the White House, then the next administration could use CRA resolutions to undo a lot of the craziness that the Obama administration is doing. But that's an eternity away in politics, so it doesn't offer much help at the moment.

Solution: The Nondelegation Doctrine and the APA

Instead, one thing we can use to go after these regulations is the nondelegation doctrine.

When FDR went nuts with the New Deal and the Supreme Court was pushing back, the Court declared the principle of nondelegation. As we've seen, the Constitution vests all the legislative power possessed by the federal government in Congress.[23] It had already been long established in American law that Congress could not delegate its legislative power,[24] a doctrine traceable all the way to the early days of the republic.[25]

But what does it mean to "delegate" legislative power? The Court explained in 1928 that this means Congress can allow the executive branch to fill in the gaps so long as Congress declares an "intelligible principle" about what the policy is, and that the executive branch can act so long as the regulations it makes follow and implement that principle given in the legislation.[26]

As you might guess, the courts try to give the two elected branches of the government the benefit of the doubt when it comes to this issue. But in 1935 the Supreme Court struck down two major pieces of the New Deal for violating the nondelegation doctrine. The first the Court struck down, holding that "Congress has declared no policy, has established no standard, has laid down no rule."[27] In the second, when the Court struck down the law involved, it did so holding that "Congress cannot delegate legislative power to the President to exercise an unfettered discretion to make whatever laws he thinks may be needed or advisable. . . ."[28]

The Supreme Court hasn't used the nondelegation doctrine to strike down any laws since the 1930s, but that doctrine is still on the books, and the words just cited—as well as many others like them—could be used against several parts of Barack Obama's agenda.

The other option is the APA, yet again. The details here would bore you fast (unless you just love to sit up at night reading through books on federal regulations), but in brief, agencies are limited in how they can interpret statutes in that they only have room to interpret them if the statute is somehow ambiguous, and courts will only defer to the agency's interpretation when there is a genuinely cloudy issue.[29] Beyond that, other types of agency action can be overturned by a court if the action was "arbitrary and capricious" or an abuse of discretion.[30] Still others can be overturned if the action is unsupported by the evidence.[31]

That may all sound annoying, but the good news is that it would be annoying for Barack Obama if his subordinates were dragged into court to defend really obnoxious regulations under these legal standards. The courts are there to protect us.

As we'll see through the rest of this book, the Constitution is alive and well. So long as we have courts willing to uphold it, Barack Obama's blueprint for an imperial presidency is in trouble.

INTERNATIONAL LAW

Another element of Obama's power-grab blueprint is foreign law. For years the Far Left has pushed for more global government at the expense of American values and American sovereignty. In many ways, from increasing deference to the United Nations to building transnational institutions to citing the laws of foreign countries, liberals seek to make Americans "citizens of the world."

Now they have a president who can't move fast enough to omit the "American" in every American citizen. *"We are the world . . ."*

Shining City on a Hill

Ever since America was first settled, the people living here have known this land to be an extraordinary place. The Pilgrims were among our first colonists, settling in what we now call New England.

Believing that this was a land of extraordinary opportunity, blessed with abundant resources and shielded from much of Europe's corrupting influences, one pastor was inspired to deliver a sermon that would echo through the ages. Puritan clergyman John Winthrop preached a homily entitled "A Model of Christian Charity" shortly before his ship of settlers reached the American shore.

Drawing on language from the Sermon on the Mount in the Gospel of Matthew, Reverend Winthrop announced that "We shall be as a city upon a hill."[32] This language later found its way into a speech by President John F. Kennedy. And then it became the basis of Ronald Reagan's declaration that America was a "shining city upon a hill," in the Great Communicator's farewell speech to the nation.[33]

This sentiment is the foundation of *American exceptionalism*— that America enjoys a unique place in the world as a source of hope and a beacon of light.

It's an idea often traced to Alexis de Tocqueville, who wrote to the world about this inspiring nation when we were still young in *Democracy in America*. De Tocqueville's amazement in the 1830s about this free country has endured through the years. It was still fresh in Abraham Lincoln's Gettysburg Address and Second Inaugural. It rings in the speeches of Kennedy and Reagan. And free people across the globe still hear its call and believe in American exceptionalism.

Obama on American Exceptionalism

However, it seems there's nothing exceptional about American exceptionalism to our current president. When asked overseas in 2009 if he believed in American exceptionalism, Barack Obama replied, "I believe in American exceptionalism, just as I suspect that the Brits believe in British exceptionalism and the Greeks believe in Greek exceptionalism."[34]

Of course, that's no different than the self-esteem-building platitude, "Everyone's a winner!" This is the same ridiculous philosophy that says everyone should get a trophy for participating, because everyone's a champion just for trying.

If there is nothing exceptional about America's exceptionalism, then our nation's not an exception at all. An exception is something different from the norm. We're not taking a giant leap here—that's the *definition* of an exception. If everyone is "exceptional," then it means no country is exceptional, including the United States.

This was President Obama's impossible straddling of the issue, essentially saying, "America is the greatest nation on earth. And Britain is the greatest nation on earth. And Greece is the greatest nation on earth. And . . . etc." In other words, Barack Obama says that citizens of every nation consider their own nation special, but he isn't willing to assert that America truly is the greatest nation on earth.

You make us proud, Mr. President.

Our Freedom Makes Us Exceptional

In almost all foreign lands, people don't have the broad array of rights to protect them against their government that we do here in America, and in no country do they have all the rights that we enjoy under our Constitution. Most Americans take for granted their right to post criticisms of the president or Congress on the Internet, or to write a letter to the editor to vent on some public issue. We readily expect that we can go to political rallies, attend the church of our choosing, share our faith, and gather with our friends.

The police can't enter our house on a whim or search our property, and we can't be forced to incriminate ourselves. If accused of a crime, we have the right to legal assistance and a speedy jury trial. We can't be tortured or burdened with excessive fines or bails.

We have the right to vote. We can't be deprived of life, liberty, or property without due process of law. We have rights as individuals and as families.

And to secure all these rights against a government that might choose to ignore the Constitution, we even have the Second Amendment right to bear arms as a perpetual insurance policy that We the People will always ultimately be in charge of our own country. (Try to find another government that welcomes *that* right, of their own people holding the government in check by force of arms.)

But such things cannot be said for much of the world. No country fully shares our values, and many are fiercely hostile to what we believe.

Much of the world is militantly secular, and many countries that are not secular are held in the vise grip of militant Islam. In some countries you cannot say anything the government opposes, and even in many where you can, you still can't criticize the government.

America is a truly exceptional place to live.

Presidential Power in Foreign Affairs

So, we have a man who doesn't believe in American exceptionalism, and the Constitution puts him, as president, in charge of U.S. foreign policy. He's not just "in charge," either. With very few exceptions, the president's power in foreign affairs is absolute.

As the Supreme Court has said, quoting from as early as 1800, the early years of the republic, "The President is the sole organ of the nation in its external relations, and its sole representative with foreign nations. . . . The President is the constitutional representative of the United States with regard to foreign nations."[35] In all these years, the Supreme Court has never tried to scale back this principle.

Although it may seem like some form of consolation that the president can't enter into treaties without two-thirds of the Senate ratifying the agreement, you shouldn't take any comfort from that. There is also something called an executive agreement, where the

Supreme Court has upheld the president's power to bind the country by a document that looks just like a treaty (and walks like a treaty, and talks like a treaty, and smells like a treaty, but somehow isn't a treaty). But these executive agreements are approved by a regular majority vote of both houses of Congress, instead of a supermajority in the Senate.[36]

It's even more serious than that. What about agreements where the president can't get Congress to go along at all? The Court has also upheld the president's power to bind us to agreements simply with his signature, without any action of either house of Congress.[37]

President Obama has that same power today.

Crippling Our Economy

He represents us but doesn't think we're exceptional. He can bind us to international agreements with a stroke of his pen. What's more, President Obama is trying to use international law to subvert the U.S. economy in favor of international expectations and values. Most countries don't agree with America's free-market, capitalist system. We use it because tough competition with minimal regulation fosters innovation, increases productivity, and creates more wealth for more people, benefiting everyone. Many countries reject that approach because of a paternalistic softness; they're afraid of letting anyone fall through the cracks. But the reality remains that you cannot have a vibrant, competitive economy unless companies (or people that can't make the cut) are allowed to fail. (More on this in chapter 5.)

But in light of that, it infuriates those who believe in the American system that President Obama is pushing for an international regulatory scheme for economic institutions. Such regulations would come from the policies of the International Monetary Fund (IMF), and would serve as a regime for global economic regulation.[38]

Such a system would make regulations based on the failed economic theories of a bunch of other countries. These systems look to "fairness" and "economic justice" and spreading the wealth. This reflects President Obama's own beliefs, as we'll see in chapters 4 and 5, and that's why he's trying to tie our economy to this international system. He'll try to do it, and he'll look to his blueprint for the method. (Hint: See the previous section, "Presidential Power in Foreign Affairs.")

NTBT: Endangering our National Security

Barack Obama, as our sole representative in foreign affairs, can also endanger our national security by committing us to the Nuclear Test Ban Treaty (NTBT).

Ronald Reagan's foreign policy was predicated on strength. Reagan believed in foreign diplomacy where the other country understood that the United States had the most powerful military in the world, a vast apparatus of intelligence gathering and processing using the most advanced technologies, and a nuclear arsenal that could annihilate any country that forced us to use those terrifying weapons.

Even our mortal foe, the Soviet Union, was kept at bay for years through détente before Reagan came along. This détente was facilitated through MAD: Mutual Assured Destruction. Even the Soviets decided that they would not act with their nukes against U.S. assets because the United States would use nuclear weapons in return, and we would all die.

For an atheistic people who believed that there is nothing after death, there isn't much incentive to all die as a nation in a forest of mushroom clouds.

Yet President Obama is trying to commit us to a treaty, NTBT, that would comprehensively outlaw nuclear testing. Our national security experts have made it clear that we need to be able to do nuclear testing (which is essentially done underground to prevent harm from radioactive fallout) to maintain our nuclear arsenal. This arsenal is the sum and substance of our nuclear deterrent.

Without such a deterrent, we become increasingly reliant on the United Nations for our security. Also without that deterrent, we are increasingly subject to being coerced into going along with other nations and not standing up for U.S. interests.

A president who commits us to something like the NTBT pushes us more in the direction of global government, undermining our sovereignty and our security. Although there's nothing unconstitutional about using such presidential power, it undermines our constitutional government by making us beholden to countries whose laws are much different than ours.

When in Rome ... Get Tried by a Foreign Court

Another thing to look out for—something lurking in the corner of our president's plan—is Barack Obama's putting us back on track to be subject to the International Criminal Court (ICC).

The ICC was established by a treaty called the Rome Statute of 1998.[39] President Bill Clinton signed the treaty on behalf of the United States on December 31, 2000, when he was leaving office.[40] (As in just twenty days before leaving office, as a parting gift to the incoming Republican president.) When George W. Bush was president, he ordered that the U.S. signature to the Rome Statute be physically removed.[41]

No treaty can be binding on this country unless it is both signed by the president and ratified by a two-thirds vote of the Senate. With the U.S. signature removed, the Senate cannot act.

But Barack Obama could re-sign the treaty on behalf of the United States. With his massive majority in the Senate, he would have a better chance than Bill Clinton ever had at getting it ratified. And even if it were not ratified, he could test the Supreme Court to take a first-ever step of invalidating a presidential foreign agreement by calling it an "executive agreement," and ordering our government to treat the ICC's decision as binding.

The ICC could then try American citizens abroad in accordance with international law. U.S. soldiers and agents acting abroad could be subjected to foreign law and foreign penalties.

It would be a huge step forward for global government, making America more like the rest of the world and subject to the laws of foreign nations. Foreign nations, where governments have much more power over their people, unconstrained by a Constitution and a robust Bill of Rights.

The kinds of countries where a chief of state like President Obama could do anything he wanted.

Solution: Supreme Court to the Rescue

Statutes and treaties are of equal authority.[42] Because of that, Congress cannot do anything by treaty that it could not do by statute. So just as the Supreme Court can strike down a federal statute that runs afoul of the Constitution, it can also strike down a treaty that is unconstitutional.

Because they are of equal authority in Article VI of the Constitution, under the last-in-time rule, when a federal statute and a treaty are in conflict, the more recent of the two to be enacted is considered to have repealed the inconsistent part of the earlier one.[43]

Although executive agreements have always been upheld by the Supreme Court, they must have less legal weight than treaties. Statutes must be passed by the House and Senate and signed by the president. Treaties must be signed by the president and ratified by two-thirds of the Senate. Executive agreements, in contrast, can just be signed by the president alone.

We therefore have two ways to fight whatever Barack Obama does through agreements with foreign countries. If Republicans can retake Congress, they can deny any approval to executive agreements that undermine American sovereignty or values. If Obama signs an executive agreement and declares it binding without any congressional action, then retaking the White House and Congress would allow the new president to disavow the agreement, or the new president could sign into law a new statute passed by Congress that would nullify the agreement (or even a treaty) under the last-in-time rule.

Without waiting for 2013 to make that happen, however, the Supreme Court could strike down an unconstitutional executive agreement right now.

So if the Supreme Court can strike down a statute or treaty that violates the Constitution, then the Court can all the more easily strike down an unconstitutional executive agreement, especially one that was unilaterally imposed by President Obama without any congressional vote. Although the Court has never struck down such an agreement before, because it gives great deference to the president on foreign policy issues, the rule that no legal action can trump the Constitution puts the Court in the position to hold anything unconstitutional.

The Supreme Court showed as recently as 2008 its willingness to reject even the president's assertion of foreign policy primacy when it held against the president regarding the execution of Mexican nationals in *Medellin v. Texas*.[44] The Court did not strike down the treaty being cited in that case; instead, it held that the treaty was not self-executing, and so couldn't be enforced without Congress passing a statute to implement its provisions.

But it still gives us all a lot of hope, because it shows that the current Supreme Court is unwilling to give any president a blank check when it comes to foreign policy. Even the president's vast foreign-policy power is not absolute.

The Supreme Court has indicated its willingness to uphold the U.S. Constitution against assertions of power by the president. We need to be ready to bring suit, asking the Court to do exactly that if Barack Obama oversteps his bounds, citing international law.

Oh, and by the way—any U.S. president has the constitutional authority to immediately withdraw us from any treaty that we've joined,[45] or to issue a new interpretation of what that treaty means. So a new president could instantly get us out of any treaty mess that Barack Obama puts us in. Remember that in 2012.

DOMESTIC ARMY

Strap on your combat boots. Barack Obama, in order to forcefully make the presidency an unchecked office, wants to use every American as manpower to carry out his agenda. Obama has indicated that he wanted such a force, and that he planned to get one.

During the campaign, Barack Obama said:

> *We cannot continue to rely only on our military in order to achieve the national security objectives that we've set. We've got to have a civilian national security force that's just as powerful, just as strong, just as well funded.*

Maybe Obama's statement sounds a bit murky all by itself. What does he mean? Fortunately, his never-quiet White House chief of staff elaborated on it for us:

> *Citizenship is not an entitlement program. It comes with responsibilities. Everybody somewhere between the ages of 18 and 25 will serve three months of basic training and understanding in a kind of civil defense. That universal sense of service, somewhere between ages 18 and 25, will give Americans once again a sense of what they are to be American and their contribution to a country and a common experience. And you look at World War II, now that was a draft—this is not a draft, it is universal service—it is not an accident that we started our big march towards civil rights in expanding post–World War II, because of the country coming through an experience together.*[46]

Look at that language (and since we want to give credit where it's due, we note that he got through that entire statement without using any profanity at all, so there's a first for everything). Basic training. Universal service. He's talking about the government owning civilians the way they own people in the military. (By the way, that could make it unconstitutional as a violation of the Thirteenth Amendment.[47])

Not to be left out of the fun, First Lady Michelle Obama said, "Barack Obama will require you to work. Barack will never allow you to go back to your lives as usual, uninvolved, uninformed."[48] She went on to say that he will *force* you to be engaged.[49] (Again, a Thirteenth Amendment violation.)

What is going on here?

Only Two Possibilities, Both Terrible: Behind Door #1

One possibility is that it's not as ominous as it sounds. It may simply be mobilizing and funding ultra-left forces to push their radical agenda. (It's unfortunate that a plan we can describe only by words such as "ultra-left" and "radical" is the *least* alarming possibility.)

We might have a clue as to what this security army is supposed to do. Before the election, on December 1, 2007, Barack Obama attended a meeting with community organizers that was videotaped, clips of which you've no doubt seen if you watch political news. Obama was asked if he would agree to meet with a delegation from the Association of Community Organizations for Reform Now (ACORN) and other left-wing "community organizations" in his first one hundred days as president. At this meeting he answered the audience by saying, "Yes," but that, "Before I even get inaugurated, during the transition we're going to be calling all of you in to help us shape the agenda . . . [s]o that you have input into the agenda of the next presidency of the United States of America."[50]

The problem is that the agenda of these organizations is a radical one. It goes beyond their support for abortion on demand, ending the death penalty, amnesty for illegal aliens, and racial preferences. They also favor free government-run health care, free government-provided "decent" (translate as "expensive to the taxpayer") housing, free college education, and other entitlements that they regard as free, but which means the American taxpayer would be on the hook for hundreds of billions of dollars per year in providing.

Given the extremist nature of some of these organizations and their policies—organizations like ACORN, with whom Obama openly shares his blueprint—it's both tragic and stunning that video clips like Obama's quotation given above did not virally spread around the Internet and sink his candidacy for the White House.

It's especially stunning since these are the same people who sparked our economic crash during the campaign. Obama regained the lead in the election when the market took a nosedive, but the cause of the market's plummet should also have caused Obama's poll numbers to plunge. And that's exactly what would have happened if the truth had been quickly and effectively communicated to the electorate.

Remember, the market crash was brought about by the bursting of the housing bubble. The housing market sharply declined with delinquencies and foreclosures. Banks that had issued the mortgages on those delinquent and foreclosed houses were then taking massive losses. Financial institutions had wrapped those mortgages into investments that they had sold into the markets, and as the value of those mortgages collapsed, those investments turned sour. That's what caused the demise of Lehman Brothers and the would-be demise of AIG and Bear Stearns. As those firms collapsed or teetered on the brink, investors panicked, and the market crashed.

But why were there so many bad mortgages out there? There are three reasons. First, to be fair, much of this was driven by irresponsible people buying twice as much house as they could afford, and equally irresponsible banks that decided to go to the racetrack in terms of their lending policies, approving these ridiculous mortgages.

Second, Fannie Mae and Freddie Mac screwed up the entire housing market. These government-chartered entities were bastardized hybrids of government agency and public corporation. These quasi-governmental monstrosities pushed all sorts of utterly reckless and unconscionable lending practices, funneling people who had no economic foundation to support a home into home ownership. The support of these two half-government operations also gave banks and investment houses a false sense of security on the soundness of these assets.

There's a third part of the problem, though. The final part came from these far-left groups like ACORN. Under the Community Reinvestment Act (CRA)[51]—the result of liberal politicians wrecking the private market—banks had to "reinvest" to a certain extent into their local communities by providing mortgages that normally would not have been approved. These organizations essentially shook down the banks, threatening that unless the banks gave in to their demands, these groups would act on the provisions of the CRA that gave these local community organizers (the same work that Barack Obama used to do for a living) the power to object to these banks opening new branches or expanding their business. So, these banks wrote countless mortgages that they shouldn't have, pushing more toxic assets into the investment markets.

These community organizers and their destructive actions could be part of what Obama refers to as his domestic army. If so, he doesn't mean an "army" in the sense of armed units with weapons, using deadly force. Instead, he's referring to an "army" of activists, politically mobilizing people and advancing the president's blueprint for the far-left power grab discussed in this book.

These are the people that Barack Obama invites to be part of his government. Just imagine the chaos of the housing crash infecting other areas of national policy, as these reckless extremists allow their wrongheaded thinking, extortionist tactics, and self-aggrandizing goals to steer the federal government.

They would be involved in voter registration, opening community centers and implementing public programs. They would work to essentially create a massive, permanent political campaign to try to directly sell President Obama's agenda to the American people. And they would also work to defeat Obama's political opposition in elections to create a Congress, statehouses, and governorships that are more amenable to President Obama's plans for America.

That's where the staggering sum of $534 billion comes in. (Remember, that's the annual budget for the military, and, as quoted at the beginning of this chapter, Obama says his domestic army will be as well funded as the U.S. military.) These people would have access to this inconceivable sum to buy influence and win elections. In terms of elections, they would have an unlimited budget for a campaign to "educate" voters on what the issues are and who is supporting the "best" ideas. They could pay for carpet coverage on TV, radio, mail, the Internet, and even door-to-door "helpers." This money would overwhelm whatever funds the conservative candidates could raise, tilting the playing field in favor of the Left.

Aside from those elements of a political "reeducation" plan (because even the most extravagant of such "educational" campaigns couldn't cost more than maybe $20 billion), they could directly buy or finance whatever they want. They could give massive grants to non-Left organizations that meet these groups' other requirements. These grants would just be bribes—irresistible financial temptations to organizations minding their own business to change their positions on what they support and who they hire. They could give untold sums to create newspapers that only carry far-left viewpoints and endow professorships at every university for academic research showing the "proof" of the benefits of socialism and collectivism, or writing lengthy books on the dangerousness of gun ownership or conservative Christianity. They could hire public-school teachers that could teach new classes in "civics" and "public values" to indoctrinate children, fund after-school programs where children are treated to great food and entertainment in exchange for listening to, or participating in, all sorts of activities that instill a radical-left, secular mind-set.

With that much money, the possibilities are endless. Yet Obama promises this "army" will be as large and well funded as our military, so if it's not something like this, then the president ought to explain what he meant.

Only Two Possibilities, Both Terrible: Behind Door #2

Unfortunately, the other option is worse.

We're reluctant to even discuss this because it's so inherently extreme, but the words driving our concern that Door #2 is a possibility came from the president's own mouth (along with the words of his wife and his chief of staff), so it can't be ignored.

Essentially, every oppressive, far-left regime in the world has some version of a "ministry of internal security." These are the secret police who constantly monitor private citizens, pay informants in every neighborhood, and keep files on potential troublemakers, all in the name of "security."

The worst regimes in the world have had such organizations, from the Gestapo to the Soviets' KGB. In some countries, such as the Soviet Union, these were uniformed services with military discipline. In other countries, such as the Basij Resistance Force in Iran, they are relatively disorganized, militia-like units where their officers are undercover.

Either way, they are constantly on the lookout for those who are disloyal to the government and its exalted leaders. They are the eyes and ears of a massively powerful central government, stopping free speech and quelling public unrest.

Again, it's difficult to even write about these things because it very quickly becomes black-helicopter conspiracy fare. But again, it is Barack Obama who said he wanted to create a domestic security force with over two million people and over a half-trillion-dollar budget. What in the world was he talking about? He owes us all an explanation.

Apollo Alliance

We should assume that he meant the first option: an "army" of activists and community organizers. Let's proceed on that assumption to figure out where it would begin.

Could it be that Obama has already begun assembling this domestic army? Two million people are a lot of people. To mobilize hordes of this size, it would make sense that you would seek to draw upon preexisting groups that were supportive of your agenda as the "special forces" troops of such an army, and to form part of the "officer corps" to provide leadership.

Considering those things, it's worth noting that many of the far-left supporters in Obama's camp have now formed an umbrella organization to pool their resources and give their enormous numbers a centralized command structure. It's called the Apollo Alliance.[52]

The Apollo Alliance brings together a number of activists from all sorts of left-wing organizations. It acts as an umbrella group to keep many far-left actors on the same page.

The question becomes: How can such an organization be assembled under the direction of the White House, if it's all composed of private-sector people? After all, there are handlers and gatekeepers in the White House. The Secret Service keeps security logs of every person who visits the White House. Courts can—and have—ordered those records to be produced when someone seeks them for a proper purpose in a court case.

So President Obama would also need someone close to him to help organize and build this army. It would have to be someone working directly for the president so that no paper trail of records would be created when that person speaks with Obama and Rahm Emanuel. It would also have to be someone who is not subject to congressional oversight, because that would mean the person would run the risk of being asked about such activities under oath, forcing him to give answers that would cause a public outcry.

One of the founding members of the Apollo Alliance is none other than Van Jones, the avowed communist who until recently was serving as one of President Obama's czars (chapter 1). So there was someone in the White House itself, with Cabinet-level authority—even though he never went through Senate confirmation, and thus cannot be compelled to testify before Congress regarding his activities—who was directly advising the president, and is now one of the leaders of this alliance.

We noted in chapter 1 that the public got wise to Van Jones, and he had to resign in disgrace. We also noted, however, that Jones is back on the public scene, albeit not back on the White House payroll.

Given that there was one, there's no reason to believe that there are not more people who are part of this plan—a plan announced by the president himself—who are not working in the White House.

That's especially true since Obama's closest advisor and one of the architects of his blueprint, Valerie Jarrett, is the one who recruited communist Van Jones, as we showed in chapter 1. Who else is Valerie Jarrett talking to these days? Who else did she recruit? No one has the president's ear more than Jarrett. Who is she working with as a go-between and messenger to and from the Oval Office?

No Solution, Because We Don't Know the Problem

At this point, there's no way to know what to do about this problem. Who can possibly even understand the problem yet? We haven't seen this army. We don't know what President Obama meant by it. In some ways, that makes this issue especially frightening. It's the fear of the unknown.

Right now, what we need is information. The president and his chief of staff should be made to explain what they meant with the material quoted above. Michelle Obama should be asked the same thing in interviews.

The Military Protects Us; These People Don't

What's perhaps most chilling about this whole domestic army that President Obama and his people talk about is how these people are different from our real military.

The U.S. military is full of people who want to serve. Some of them just want a job, and are willing to risk their safety and undergo hardship to have one. Some want to develop a skill set or earn money for college, and are willing to work hard and sacrifice to get that. Still others are career military, who love this country and take pride in the idea that they can help protect their country and those they love who live here.

None of these people are political extremists. They're not wide-eyed ideologues. They're just patriotic Americans, who in the ranks of enlisted personnel take an oath to uphold the Constitution and obey the chain of command.

Atop this military pyramid of enlisted servicemen (including non-commissioned officers) is the officer corps. Every commissioned military officer is a college graduate, an educated person who undergoes a background and character check. And every single officer takes the following oath of office as a prerequisite of receiving his commission:

I . . . do solemnly swear that I will support and defend the Constitution of the United States against all enemies, foreign and domestic; that I will bear true faith and allegiance to the same; that I take this obligation freely, without any mental reservation or purpose of evasion; and that I will well and faithfully discharge the duties of the office on which I am about to enter. So help me God.[53]

Every officer in our military takes an oath to support the Constitution. More than that, they swear to protect it against all enemies—not only foreign, but even domestic. Our military may serve under the president, but they are serving under whoever currently holds the office; they do not serve the president himself. The U.S. Armed Forces instead serves the American people, and it does this by defending the Constitution.

President Obama's domestic army couldn't be more different in this regard. We don't know all the facts until Obama and his inner circle explain their bizarre statements regarding what this domestic army is, but we do know that they won't be people who go through a military academy. They likely won't be people screened for felony convictions or crimes involving violence, deceit, or fraud. And they will be focused on serving President Obama, not the United States.

Crossing the Rubicon: A Lesson from History

In the English language, we use the phrase "crossing the Rubicon" as a metaphor for passing the point of no return. The phrase comes from the days of the Roman Republic, which was the form of government Rome enjoyed before it became the Roman Empire. Because the Senate of Rome—representing the people of Rome— feared a military leader taking power by force, it was Roman law that no army could march on the lands of Italy carrying weapons. Armies could only march in battle-ready formation through the lands of the Republic beyond the borders of Italy, where they would be safely removed from the capital city of Rome itself.

The ruling body of the Roman Republic was the Senate, which was led by two consuls who held their office for limited terms. One consul, Julius Caesar, had soared in popularity with the Roman people because of his amazing military victories and how he had expanded the reach of Rome. The Roman Senate feared Caesar's popularity, as did Pompey, the other consul. While Caesar was living in Gaul (modern France), governing that region of the Republic, Pompey and the Senate issued an order that Caesar must disband his army and relinquish his command.

Deciding to fight, and intent on taking over the Republic for himself—and transforming it into an empire—Caesar mobilized his army and marched to Italy. When he reached the Rubicon River at the border of Italy, he knew this was his last chance. If he led his legions across the Rubicon, he would have broken this ancient law and committed a crime from which there would be no going back.

He then crossed the Rubicon, and led his army in a military march on Rome. The rest is history.

One lesson from that time echoes through the ages to Americans today. We do not permit the U.S. military to operate domestically. The Posse Comitatus Act specifically forbids the military from operating on U.S. soil unless Congress—not the president, only Congress—issues a declaration temporarily suspending this prohibition to deal with an emergency.[54]

We Need Answers

This may in fact not be as big of a problem as it seems. But when the president of the United States starts talking about walking a domestic army full of people who answer to him instead of the American people and the Constitution, funded with hundreds of billions of dollars, we should all be worried.

We must all demand answers as to what this army would be, and what President Obama wants to do with it. As in the days of ancient Rome, such a domestic army doesn't belong in the United States of America, answering to a president who is amassing such vast power to himself. Such a domestic army seems like it would be a critical part of Barack Obama's blueprint, and not understanding exactly what it is or what he wants to do with it is something that should make us all lose sleep at night.

The scariest parts of President Obama's blueprint are the parts we don't know about yet.

CHAPTER 4

HEALTH CARE

The time has come for universal health care in America. . . . I am absolutely determined that by the end of the first term . . . we should have universal health care in this country.
—BARACK OBAMA, JANUARY 25, 2007

Under the theories that the Government presents. . . it is difficult to perceive any limitation on federal power, even in areas. . . where States historically have been sovereign. Thus, if we were to accept the Government's arguments, we are hard pressed to posit any activity by an individual that Congress is without power to regulate.
—UNITED STATES V. LOPEZ, 514 U.S. 549, 564 (1995)

For more than a year, a chorus of voices has argued that President Barack Obama's health-care plan is bad policy. There are plenty of books about Obamacare out there now, and even more articles and columns (including ours, both separately and jointly).

But the point we emphasize, and the one that not enough people are discussing, is that key parts of Obamacare are also unconstitutional. Beginning in 2009, we have written some of the first columns detailing how and why parts of Obamacare are unconstitutional.

Although one of your authors (Blackwell) has done a lot of national television on the topic, and your other author (Klukowski) lectures at law schools around the country on this issue, we've noticed that no one else has really laid out in depth exactly how and why essential provisions of Obamacare violate the Supreme Law of the Land.

People need this information in more depth than is possible in a sound bite or a column. Regardless of what has passed Congress already, or what we've managed to stop, from the time we're writing this to the time that you're reading it, this issue is not going to go away. It goes to the very heart of President Obama's blueprint for an imperial presidency. So we'll go in-depth here.

Obamacare Is Unconstitutional

As we explained in the introduction, the federal government is one of enumerated powers. Unless there is a specific provision of the Constitution authorizing a particular federal law, then that law is unconstitutional.

Parts of Obamacare are unconstitutional. Not the whole thing—the bill was more than two thousand pages long, and much of it was outrageously stupid, but that doesn't make those parts unconstitutional. There is no provision in the Constitution that forbids Congress from doing idiotic things on a galactic scale. (If there were, the courts would be overloaded with striking down congressional actions.)

But some aspects of Obamacare are worse than simply crazy—they violate the Constitution. And these unconstitutional provisions are actually essential parts of the statute; if they go down, then the whole house of cards collapses.

Obamacare Individual Mandate Is Unconstitutional

The central provision in Obamacare is the "individual mandate"—the requirement that American citizens must purchase health insurance or be subject to a financial penalty. If a person refuses to pay that penalty, then they're committing a federal crime.

It's utterly unprecedented for the federal government to try to compel American citizens—as private individuals—to make a particular purchase or become a federal criminal with the possibility of prison time for their noncompliance.[1] It's the archetype of an oppressive, overbearing government, and the exact opposite of a free society with a limited government.

We've written on this for months. We jointly coauthored a column with Senator Orrin Hatch of Utah on the mandate's unconstitutionality,[2] and both of us signed a public memorandum of the Conservative Action Project and its chairman, former U.S. Attorney General Ed Meese. Beyond that, one of your authors (Klukowski) has written on this issue since October of 2009, for *Politico*, Fox News, and the *Washington Examiner*.[3] We have joined other legal analysts who have written on this as well, so by now, it's no secret that the mandate is unconstitutional.

This Isn't Car Insurance, Mr. President

The most aggravating comparison that Barack Obama and his apologists make for Obamacare's individual mandate is that it's just like car insurance. President Obama himself made that analogy in an ABC interview.[4] You have to get car insurance, they argue, so you have to get health insurance, too. No difference, and no big deal.

Good grief, this is absurd. What makes this argument so aggravating is that it is so completely and ridiculously wrong. Having car insurance is not like making people get health-care insurance. Not at all.[5]

There are two enormous differences between states requiring car insurance and the feds requiring health insurance. Either one is enough to blow the individual mandate out of the water. Taken together, it's hard to see how anyone who knows constitutional law can even make Obama's analogy with a straight face. We wonder how the faculty of Harvard Law School feels about their school's most-recognized graduate.

First, the state car insurance mandate versus the federal health insurance mandate gets back to the fundamental difference between state and federal governments as explained by the Supreme Court, which we discussed in the introduction. The states are governments of general jurisdiction with police power. This police power includes the authority to make laws for public health and safety. Requiring people to get car insurance before driving falls squarely within this police power, as this serves to ensure proper coverage for injuries or property damage that come as a result of car crashes.

The federal government, by contrast, has no police power. It has only the specific powers delegated to it by the U.S. Constitution. There is nothing in the Constitution about car insurance; thus, the federal government could not require anyone to have it.[6]

Second, Obama is not telling the truth when he says that states require people to get car insurance. No one is *required* to get car insurance. As an American citizen, you have a constitutional right to travel.[7] However, using a car—which is a massive, powerful, and sometimes-deadly machine—as your chosen means to travel on public roads is not a right; it is a conditional privilege granted by state government.[8] If you choose to ride the bus or subway instead of driving, you don't need car insurance. If you choose to walk or ride your bicycle to your destination, you don't need car insurance. Or if you just drive your car around your own private roads and never venture onto the public roads, you don't need car insurance.

So President Obama is not telling the truth. You only need car insurance if you voluntarily choose to operate a motor vehicle on public roads. If you use public transportation, or travel without a car, or stay on private land, you can go all your life without car insurance without ever breaking the law, or ever being subject to any government penalty.

It would be ridiculous to have to lecture a graduate of Harvard Law School like Barack Obama on this issue, but the reality is that there's no need to lecture. It's a real stretch to suggest that President Obama never considered these things. He has to know that no one is required to get car insurance, and that state governments are fundamentally different from the federal government.

Which means he has to know that what he's telling America is untrue. Is that the kind of "change" he had in mind—telling us with a straight face something he knows not to be true?

The fact that he's resorting to such completely absurd arguments reveals two things: First, he must be aware of how flimsy the legal grounds are for what he's doing, and so he's trying to concoct an explanation that flies in the face of constitutional law. And second, it reveals the ultimate goal of his plan: to make the federal government a government of general jurisdiction—a government with police power—to minimize and eventually eliminate state sovereignty. He seeks a national government with complete authority over people's lives. Arguments like these are how he gets there.

Commerce Clause

Most of Obamacare's supporters say that the individual mandate is authorized by Congress's authority to regulate interstate commerce, found in the Constitution's Commerce Clause.[9] Although you can make a liberal case for that argument, it's just dead wrong.

There was a vast expansion of federal power in the 1930s. When all of those sweeping new laws were being passed, the courts were required to reinterpret the Constitution as giving the federal government vastly expanded powers. Otherwise, whole fields of federal legislation would have been mowed down by the courts.

That's exactly what happened in the early years of the New Deal. Dozens of major Supreme Court cases came out of that period, defining—and then redefining—the size and scope of the federal government's power over the states and in the lives of private citizens. The Court made some judgments that kept the growth of government at bay. As an example, the Supreme Court struck down several of the major components of FDR's New Deal on Commerce Clause grounds, the last one of these cases being the Court's 1936 holding in *Carter v. Carter Coal Co.* that coal mining is not "commerce."[10]

Change came in a big way in 1942 when the Supreme Court decided *Wickard v. Filburn.*[11] In *Wickard*, a certain wheat farmer who was only allowed to grow eleven acres under the Agricultural Adjustment Act decided to grow twenty-three acres instead, using the extra acres to feed his family and livestock.[12] He fought the penalty that was assessed against him all the way to the Supreme Court. In a watershed case, the Court (which by that time had become fairly liberal) upheld Congress's power to regulate crop production and authorize penalties, because the Court held that although the extra crops were never sold or even moved off his property, the farmer's use of the wheat could have "a substantial economic effect on interstate commerce."[13]

Wickard was the high-water mark in federal power under the Commerce Clause. This extremely broad interpretation of congressional power was reinforced by the liberal Warren Court of the 1960s. In 1964 the Court held that Congress could regulate a hotel whose guests were mostly out-of-state.[14] The Court also held in a separate case that the Commerce Clause authorized regulating a local eatery because it served food that had traveled across state lines.[15]

Many legal experts believed that the Court had turned the Commerce Clause into nothing more than a rubber-stamp green light for federal laws. Justice Clarence Thomas wrote in the 2000 case *United States v. Morrison* that:

> . . . the very notion of a "substantial effects" test under the Commerce Clause is inconsistent with the original understanding of Congress' power and with this Court's early Commerce Clause cases. By continuing to apply this rootless and malleable standard, however circumscribed, the Court has encouraged the Federal Government to persist in its view that the Commerce Clause has virtually no limits. Until this Court replaces its existing Commerce Clause jurisprudence with a standard more consistent with the original understanding, we will continue to see Congress appropriating police powers under the guise of regulating commerce.[16]

The Commerce Clause was considered a dead letter after these early cases. (A "dead letter" means a law or constitutional provision that for whatever reason cannot be used any longer in a meaningful way in court.) After these decisions, it was thought that any federal law could be upheld under such a liberal standard of "interstate commerce." Everything seemed to fall within "interstate commerce."

But then in 1995, the Supreme Court struck down the Gun-Free School Zones Act in *United States v. Lopez*.[17] This is not to say that firearms should be in or near schools. Instead, as also explained in this book's introduction, *Lopez* held that public-safety laws are part of the police power, which is a power possessed and applied by state governments, not the federal government.[18]

This bombshell—the first time in sixty-nine years that the Court had struck down a federal law for violating the Commerce Clause—was then followed up just five years later. In *United States v. Morrison*, the Court struck down the Violence Against Women Act.[19] Violence against any innocent person is appalling, and any decent man rightfully clenches his fists in anger at the thought of any woman—who is someone's daughter, and often someone's mother as well—being brutalized by any man. This is an especially emotional issue since much of the violence covered by that law is actually rape. Such violence must be punished to the full extent of the law, and is a felony in all fifty states.

Nonetheless, as disgusting and heinous as rape is, it's not a commercial action. And so the Court struck down the federal law for violating the Commerce Clause, and interfering with a matter that the Constitution leaves to the states.[20]

We can never lose sight of the fact that the federal government is designed to be a limited government. Many things that are good and important are outside the reach of federal power. And that limitation is for our own protection.

Going back to one sentence from *Lopez* sums up the problem with the Obamacare individual mandate: "Thus, if we were to accept the Government's arguments, we are hard pressed to posit any activity by an individual that Congress is without power to regulate."[21] Team Obama is resting the individual mandate on exactly the same argument that the Court rejected in *Lopez* and *Morrison*—a theory of boundless federal power, where Congress and the president can do whatever they want.

The Constitution gives them no such power.

Taxing and Spending Clause

The next option for Obama, Reid, and Pelosi to square Obamacare with the Constitution is to try to cram it into the Taxing and Spending Clause.[22] This clause covers the power of the federal government to take money from persons and companies by way of taxes, and also the power to spend money from the U.S. Treasury.

The taxing and spending power is broad enough that there once was a time when it was hard for the federal courts to imagine taxes that would run afoul of constitutional limits.[23] But that was in a day when the federal government was a tiny fraction of what it is today, with little visible influence over people on a daily basis. Besides, there's a huge difference between "broad" and "unfettered." It looks like some of the taxes in Obamacare may finally cross the line.

The one provision of Obamacare that most clearly violates the Taxing and Spending Clause is the fees/penalties for the individual mandate. Still, if the Democrats can't cram the individual mandate into the Commerce Clause, then they will do their darnedest to convince the courts that the monetary penalty for an individual not having insurance is a "tax" under the Taxing and Spending Clause.

That clause of the Constitution allows several types of taxation. The clause reads, "The Congress shall have power to lay and collect taxes, duties, imposts and excises . . . but all duties, imposts and excises shall be uniform through the United States."[24]

These are all legal terms. Duties and imposts are taxes imposed on purchases. Excises can be taxes on certain purchases, such as alcohol or tobacco ("sin taxes"); license fees for special professions, such as being a lawyer; or corporate fees, such as an annual renewal fee for a company's business license. The Uniformity Clause that you just read requires that all these tax rates be the same throughout the country.

The Constitution later adds, "No capitation, or other direct, tax shall be laid, unless in proportion to the census. . . ."[25] A capitation tax (or "per-head" tax) is a tax that everyone pays (or at least everyone with a head—we can all think of people who might be exempt, most of them in Washington, D.C.). The census comment there gives us the apportionment rule: If Congress imposes a direct tax on people, everyone in each state must pay exactly the same amount.

The only other type of constitutional taxation is an income tax, authorized by the Sixteenth Amendment. That amendment allows Congress to impose a direct tax on incomes that doesn't need to be apportioned; instead, each person pays based on how much they make.[26]

The first point to make here is that there's a difference between the Obamacare mandate and the penalty. The mandate is the government command to buy insurance, and the penalty is what you get socked with if you don't make that buy. The mandate itself can't be a tax, because a tax is money that you pay to the government. The mandate isn't a legal requirement to give money to the government. Instead, it's a legal requirement to give money to a private health insurance company. So the mandate is not a tax.

This is such a critical point to make: The mandate itself is separate from the penalty. If the mandate is unconstitutional, then we don't even have to look at the penalty. If the mandate is unconstitutional, then the penalty falls with it.

For the sake of argument, let's assume that the mandate is constitutional; even then, the penalty for failing to comply with the Obamacare mandate falls within none of these four constitutional taxation options.

Some might say that the penalty is just some generic "tax." That argument was long ago decided. When the federal government first imposed an income tax, it was struck down by the Supreme Court in *Pollock v. Farmer's Loan & Trust* in 1895.[27] Why? Because the Court insisted that there is no generic catchall "tax," and that the only kinds of federal tax allowed by the Constitution were the specific types mentioned above.

The Court held that there are only two kinds of taxes: direct and indirect. Indirect taxes are taxes that can be passed on to others through purchasing goods, such as duties on imports.[28] Direct taxes are taxes directly on individuals, where you can't pass it on to others.[29] The Court had made clear back in 1866 that all direct taxes are subject to the apportionment rule, where every person in each state pays the same amount, and all indirect taxes must be uniform throughout the country.[30]

So in *Pollock* the Court struck down an income tax, saying it was none of these. The Court held it was a direct tax, but it was not apportioned the same throughout all the people of each state; instead, it varied based on your income.[31]

That's why the Sixteenth Amendment to the Constitution had to be adopted in order for the feds to ever create an income tax. (We're sure some of them wish they could take it back.) If there was just a generic power to tax, then the Court could have declared the income tax to come under that power. The fact that they had to pass a constitutional amendment, which was ratified in 1913, shows how serious the constitutional taxation limits are.

The penalties imposed under the Obamacare mandate don't fit into any constitutionally recognized tax categories, so it can't be authorized by the Taxing and Spending Clause.

General Welfare Clause

Obamacare supporters who have come to terms with the fact that neither the Commerce Clause nor the Taxing and Spending Clause authorize the Obamacare mandate are throwing a Hail Mary: the General Welfare Clause.[32]

That's when you know you're desperate.

When you're studying for the bar exam after law school, one thing they tell you during the lectures on constitutional law is never to rely on the General Welfare Clause as the answer to a question. It's a perennial trick choice on the bar exam. If you're stuck on a question and the General Welfare Clause is choice "C," the only thing you need to know about choosing C is that it's the wrong answer.

And yet, when House Majority Leader Steny Hoyer was confronted with the fact that there were growing concerns that the Obamacare mandate was unconstitutional, he responded that it was authorized by—you guessed it—the General Welfare Clause.[33] (Did Hoyer pass the bar? It's hard to tell from that comment.)

The General Welfare Clause of the Constitution confers no power to the government whatsoever. It's simply a phrase in the Taxing and Spending Clause that says Congress can tax and spend money, "to pay the debts and provide for the common defence and general welfare of the United States. . . ."[34] Taxing and spending must be for the general (i.e., national) welfare, as opposed to the welfare of a particular state.

The General Welfare Clause *limits* the federal government's powers—it doesn't *expand* them. What it means is that every budget item that Congress spends money on must be for the general welfare of the nation, and that every tax it imposes likewise must be imposed for the nation's benefit.

And why is this clause a *limiting* clause? Why can't Congress have a power to do things for the "general welfare"? Because, the Supreme Court says—quoting one of the most famous Supreme Court justices and constitutional scholars of all time, Justice Joseph Story—that if such a theory were adopted, "it is obvious that, [because] of the generality of the words, to 'provide for the . . . general welfare,' the government of the United States [would be], in reality, a government of . . . unlimited powers. . . ."[35]

Thus, the Supreme Court explains that to read words about providing for "the general welfare" to be a source of power would give the federal government absolutely unlimited power. All the government would have to do was proclaim that whatever it was doing was for the *general welfare*, using these words like a magical incantation, giving it the power to do anything it wants.

Instead, the Court makes clear that the General Welfare Clause can only *limit* federal power by striking down taxes or spending that do not serve the general welfare. The Supreme Court has never used the General Welfare Clause to authorize any federal action whatsoever, or to empower the government to do anything that's not independently sanctioned by another provision in the Constitution. That provision can't authorize anything, including Barack Obama's individual mandate.

There is one thing, however, that the General Welfare Clause can do. And irony of ironies, it's foursquare relevant to the Obamacare debacle.

Bribing Senators Can Violate the General Welfare Clause—And Did This Time

As just noted in the previous section, the General Welfare Clause has the power to limit congressional taxes and spending. As explained in chapter 5, that doesn't make earmarks or other directed spending unconstitutional, because those things are supposedly for the benefit of the entire nation (despite the fact that you couldn't say that with a straight face when it comes to most of the things on which Congress spends money).

But congressional spending specifically directed to the benefit of one state violates the General Welfare Clause, and that's exactly what happened when Harry Reid bought off two U.S. senators to get the votes he needed to pass Obamacare.

First came "the Louisiana Purchase." Senator Mary Landrieu, Democrat from Louisiana (who could be vulnerable in a 2012 reelection fight), sold her vote for Obamacare for $300 million. Landrieu held out in the beginning, expressing concerns about the plan's horrifying cost. Then she met with Harry Reid, and came out supporting the bill. Initial press reports said that Landrieu had secured $100 million in federal money for Louisiana.[36] Evidently insulted by the suggestion that she could be bought off for $100 million, Landrieu promptly took to the airwaves to clarify that she wasn't for sale for anything less than $300 million, and that she wouldn't settle for one dollar less to vote against the best interests of this country.[37]

That's statesmanship. We expect a chapter about Landrieu in the next edition of *Profiles in Courage*. When you're offered thirty pieces of silver, make it absolutely clear that you won't sell your soul for anything less than ninety.

Whether a court would hold this provision to violate the General Welfare Clause is unclear. The language of this buyoff was that it would go to any state that had been designated a federal major disaster area in the past seven years.[38] That sounds like a very odd qualification, doesn't it? Gee, it just so happens that the only state in the country that meets that criterion is Louisiana (because of Hurricane Katrina).

The issue is whether the courts would accept the wording of a spending measure at face value, or instead look past the mere words to its obvious meaning. If a judge were to go with the plain wording, then it's possible that other states could have qualified for the money, and therefore it could be national in scope. But if a court is willing to look beyond the words on their face, taking into account the circumstances and the obvious intention of this provision, then it should not survive a General Welfare Clause challenge.

But then came "Cash for Cloture," where we don't have to deal with this problem of second-guessing the language in the bill.

It originally looked as though Senator Ben Nelson, Democrat from Nebraska, was going to take a principled stand against Obamacare, specifically because of its taxpayer funding for abortions.[39] But then Nelson emerged from a meeting with the perpetually scowling Harry Reid, where Nelson announced that the new "compromise" language now offered on abortion was good enough for him.[40] (This, despite the fact that pro-life groups railed against the language because it doesn't stop the funding the way Nelson said it would.)

Within hours, however, the truth became public knowledge: Ben Nelson sold his vote in exchange for a new provision in the health-care bill: Although states would have to pay for the expansion of Medicaid in the legislation, Nebraska—and Nebraska alone—would forever be exempt from any additional Medicaid expenditures.[41] Congress would cover Nebraska's expense. In other words, the other forty-nine states in America would permanently be subsidizing Nebraska's increased Medicaid bills.

It is exceedingly hard to violate the General Welfare Clause. As explained above, all the Clause requires is for Congress to say that whatever it's spending money on is in the national interest.

Ben Nelson's thirty pieces of silver violates the General Welfare Clause. Congratulations, Senator—some scholars didn't think such a thing was possible. The Supreme Court has made clear in *United States v. Butler* that the word "general" means that congressional spending must be for "general" (that is, "national") interest, as opposed to the interest of only one state.[42] Even though an awful lot of congressional spending is in fact intended to benefit some local concern at the taxpayers' expense, the language used is general, and therefore can pass constitutional muster.

Not so with Senator Nelson's "Cash for Cloture." The Obamacare legislation singles out Nebraska *by name* as being exempt from all additional Medicaid payments, meaning that those expenses will be covered by federal money extracted from the other forty-nine states. This is something that the General Welfare Clause will not allow. This provision becomes a federal expenditure for the benefit of one state, and to the detriment of the American taxpayer.

As this book was being edited, the White House released a new version of President Obama's health-care bill. Predictably, the Cornhusker Kickback was such a bald-faced bribe (aside from being unconstitutional) that it was abandoned in the president's version of the legislation. That being the case, depending on which version passes, we may not have a chance to challenge Ben Nelson's bribe in court, but we may still have a shot at Landrieu's.

There were sweetheart deals for other senators as well, for Florida (Bill Nelson), Vermont (Bernie Sanders), Connecticut (Chris Dodd), and others. But while those were appalling, it's likely that no court would hold that they violate the General Welfare Clause. It was just national leaders putting their own political support base ahead of the country's well-being.

Shameful, but not illegal. It's just politics as usual these days, where officials who are tasked with representing their states in the national interest instead promote their states' interest at the expense of the nation.

Employer Mandate is a Different Story

Unfortunately, the legal case against the employer mandate—requiring employers to offer health insurance plans and penalizing those that don't—is a much closer case. Although a constitutional challenge to the employer mandate should still tip in favor of striking down this part of Obamacare as a matter of first principles, the reality is that Justice Anthony Kennedy's previous Commerce Clause cases—specifically, his concurring opinion in *Lopez*,[43] as well as the opinion by Justice John Paul Stevens that Kennedy joined in *Gonzales v. Raich*[44]—make it unlikely that a constitutional challenge would succeed on this question for as long as Kennedy is the swing vote on the Court.

In addition to the Commerce Clause, it's likely that the employer mandate also passes constitutional muster under the Taxing and Spending Clause. The Supreme Court has held that excise taxes upon employers are reasonable in exchange for allowing the business to employ other people.[45] That's the theory the Court used to uphold employers' payroll tax obligations for their employees.[46] Although the employer mandate might be a bridge too far for the Supreme Court and could be struck down as a consequence, the smart money would be on the Court's upholding that particular provision under either the Commerce Clause or the Taxing and Spending Clause.

But whether it's legal or not, it's terrible policy. It will kill jobs and bloat the government. We'd have a lot more to say if we had the space of a whole book to devote to health care. As shown throughout the rest of the chapter, the parts of Obamacare that don't violate the Constitution do violate our capitalist, free-market system that has made our economy—and our health-care system—the envy of the world.

But just because it's terrible policy doesn't make it unconstitutional. As much as we'd like to see the employer mandate be struck down in court, the employer mandate isn't likely to suffer the same fate that the individual mandate should suffer.

Abolishing State Sovereignty

We started this chapter by taking President Obama to task for comparing the individual mandate to states requiring car insurance. It should be clear to any Harvard Law School grad that such an argument is so ridiculous, it's laughable. There's a reason that he's making this comparison: President Barack Obama is trying to end the system of federalism in this country. In plain English, he's working to abolish state sovereignty.

In the American system, each of the fifty states is a sovereign entity. The states formed a federation in which they ceded to all of us certain parts of their sovereignty in order to form a national government. The federal government has control over those areas that the states gave up. In every other area, the states are still sovereign, and do not have to bow to the wishes of Washington, D.C.

State sovereignty is part of what makes America such a great place to live. You get to live in any state you choose, selecting the one that best reflects your values, your culture, and your personal priorities. For us, although our duties have taken us to different places for a time, our home states of Ohio (Blackwell) and Indiana (Klukowski), side by side in America's heartland, are the best places on earth to live and raise a family.

The key to state sovereignty is that the federal government has only limited jurisdiction, with only the powers delegated to it by the Constitution. If you abolish that limit and give the federal government the kind of police power held by the states, then state governments themselves will be effectively abolished, because Washington, D.C., will control everything.

If he could abolish state sovereignty, then Barack Obama would become the chief authority figure in every aspect of life in America. It's the ultimate power grab. That's what President Obama's blueprint is all about.

Wow, Something that Actually Violates the Tenth Amendment

There's a huge difference between what many people think the Tenth Amendment means and what it actually means. The Tenth Amendment reads, "The powers not delegated to the United States by the Constitution, nor prohibited by it to the states, are reserved to the states respectively, or to the people."[47]

The Tenth Amendment. It is what folks on our side of the aisle try to cite every time the feds overstep what every normal person understands to be the boundaries of anything you can call a limited government. You see the Tenth Amendment invoked regularly, especially under the current Obama-Pelosi-Reid government.

In reality, the courts have construed the Tenth Amendment in such a way that not much violates it. Whether that's right or not, that's what the Supreme Court has done, and it's in charge of interpreting the Constitution. It would take a significant rightward shift on the Court to broaden the reach of the Tenth Amendment.

For a while, when the Supreme Court pulled back from its leftmost days during the Warren Court, and some conservative and moderate justices appointed by Richard Nixon and Ronald Reagan had joined the Court, there was reason to hope that the Tenth Amendment could be a resurgent force in American law.

Hope swelled after the Court invoked the Tenth Amendment to strike down a minimum-wage measure in *League of Cities v. Usery*.[48] The Court declared, consistent with an earlier case, that, "This Court has never doubted that there are limits upon the power of Congress to override state sovereignty, even when exercising its otherwise plenary powers to tax or to regulate interstate commerce. . . ."[49]

However, only a few years later, this excellent opinion written by William Rehnquist was overruled, when Justice Harry Blackmun—the author of *Roe v. Wade,* who continued to drift to the left the longer he was on the Court—switched his vote from *League of Cities,* and wrote the Court's opinion in *Garcia v. San Antonio Transit Authority.*[50] *Garcia* completely gutted the good work that had started in *League of Cities,* and left everyone thinking that the Tenth Amendment was a dead letter. After *Garcia,* it was hard to violate the Tenth Amendment.

But like the gift that keeps on giving, Obamacare gives us one final constitutional violation: It actually violates the Tenth Amendment. Specifically, it violates what's called the "anti-commandeering principle."

As mentioned above, the Tenth Amendment went for so many decades without being used to strike down a federal law (aside from *League of Cities*) that it—like the Commerce Clause was for a time—came to be regarded as not having any real teeth.

But in 1992 the Supreme Court brought the Tenth Amendment back to life when it considered a case challenging a federal law that required each state to pass legislation that would enact a particular federal program. In *New York v. United States,* the Supreme Court held that this violated the Tenth Amendment, declaring that "the Constitution has never been understood to confer upon Congress the ability to require the states to govern according to Congress' instructions."[51]

The Court then extended that principle in *Printz v. United States.* This case was brought by Sheriff Jay Printz from Ravalli County, Montana, who, like one of your authors (Blackwell), serves on the board of directors of the National Rifle Association. In *Printz,* the Court struck down a provision of the Brady Act gun-control law that required local law enforcement to run federal background checks on purchasers.[52]

These cases made clear that the Tenth Amendment does not allow the federal government to commandeer—or take authority over—any branch or part of state or local government.

That creates a problem for Obamacare, which requires states to pass statutes and enact regulations—with staff to administer those regulations—to create statewide nonprofit insurance exchanges in each state.[53]

In Supreme Court cases, lawyers and scholars argue how that case is like one particular previous case, or unlike another case. This method of comparing and distinguishing cases is how we develop the law, and is part of the basis of how courts decide cases.

What's amazing about this Obamacare case is that there's no guesswork relating to previous cases; this is *New York* and *Printz* all over again. The only difference is that Obamacare is worse. If the laws discussed in *New York* and *Printz* were a little bit unconstitutional, the Obamacare demands for state insurance exchanges are more unconstitutional.

It looks like it's time for another Tenth Amendment case, if President Obama manages to ram his health-care bill through Congress.

Can Obamacare Pass Without a Vote?

We also want to briefly note one development as this book is being edited.

In the second half of March 2010, Democrats are debating ramming the Senate version of Obamacare through the House with a cheap political stunt. To shelter Democratic congressmen from having to vote on this wildly unpopular legislation (there's nothing quite so admirable as a congressman hiding under his desk and trying to slip one past his constituents), Speaker Nancy Pelosi might have a solution.

Every piece of legislation is passed according to certain rules, such as how much debate time will be allocated on the House floor or how many amendments can be offered. Rules Committee Chairwoman Louise Slaughter is trying to craft a rule saying that the Senate bill is "deemed" to be passed, whereby if members of Congress vote for the rule, the Speaker will count it as a vote for the Senate Obamacare bill itself. That way, if a majority votes for the rule, then

Obamacare will pass the House and go to the president for his signature, with those Democratic congressmen being able to say, "I never voted for the bill. I just voted for a procedural rule."

From a policy standpoint, this is deplorable. Worse than simply voting for Obamacare, this vote amounts to voting for Obamacare *and* trying to deceive your voters. It is a cowardly and craven act— the worst form of sleazy politics.

But is it constitutional? Nobody knows.

The Presentment Clause of Article I, Section 7 requires that any bill must pass both the House and Senate before going to the president. Does this coward-vote trick satisfy the constitutional requirement?

This is form versus substance, and you can make an argument both ways. One argument is that whatever the first chamber votes on, the second chamber must vote on exactly that same measure. The opposing argument is that if everyone casting the House vote knows that they're voting to move the Obamacare bill from the Senate, then a majority vote for the Slaughter Rule should be considered a majority vote for Obamacare.

On this question, your author Klukowski thinks that the constitutional standard should be a mirror-image rule: whatever the first chamber votes on, the second chamber must vote on exactly the same measure, in exactly the same form, to send the bill to the president. But the reality is that no such situation has ever been litigated in court, so nobody knows.

If by the time you read this chapter, the House did pass the bill with such an underhanded trick, then you can bet that there's a lawsuit under way right now on exactly this issue. If so, it could be the best shot at striking down the entire Obamacare monstrosity.

Obamacare Is also Bad Policy

It's beyond the scope of this book to look at all the ways that Obamacare is bad; we're only tackling the constitutional issues. But a few key policy points need to be made to round out the picture on this looming monstrosity.

According to the Congressional Budget Office (CBO), Obama's health-care plan would create at minimum—at *minimum*—an annual deficit of $240 billion all by itself. That was CBO's original estimate. As of the time of this writing, CBO says it can't even score the bill right now because the White House isn't coughing up enough of the facts for CBO to tell us how much this would really cost.

This assumes that there's no government insurance program. The Heritage Foundation commissioned a private study which concluded that 83 million Americans would be transferred from their private insurance plans to the government program. So the numbers CBO gives are not even counting the 83 million government handouts.

Aside from the constitutional problems we've looked at, it seems that the whole debate over Obamacare stems from three defective suppositions. The first is a misunderstanding of the nature of government—a failure to understand that by its very nature, government is wasteful, self-serving, and tends toward corruption.

The second is economic. Perhaps the fundamental flaw with liberal economic policy is that it doesn't understand the core economic law of supply and demand. The less something costs, the more people abuse it and waste it. If you give everyone health care that they don't think they're paying for, it can only lead to more headaches and shortfalls than we have now.

Finally, we're all going to have to face the reality of our own lifestyles. Instead of making government responsible for our health, we need to be good stewards of our own health.

For example, a tenth of our nation's health-care expenses stems from the simple fact that we abuse our abundance in this country by eating too much. The truth is that 9.1 percent of all health-care costs are caused by obesity.[54]

Until we confront these sorts of issues, and look to what each of us can do to be good consumers of health care and good stewards of our own personal health, no government-run program will fix our problems—even if Obamacare were something we could afford (which we can't) and even if it were constitutional (which it's not).

But again, all that is another book entirely.

Rationing Care

One final point must be made regarding the inescapable consequence of the governmental principle and economic principle just mentioned.

Once government gets into the business of dictating care, rationing decisions are inevitable. The definition of economics is the allocation of scarce resources. One of the first principles you learn in an introductory economics course is that all resources are scarce; there is no valuable resource for which there is an unlimited supply. And so for every resource or product, there is a price at which a certain quantity is to be had, at the intersection of the supply and demand curves on the economic charts.

But when you make something free, the demand curve shifts hard over the margin because no one gives any thought to cost. As a result, supply is outstripped by demand. In plain English, it means that when something is free, there's never enough to go around.

This means that decisions need to be made about who gets what. Right now those decisions are made by insurance professionals or individuals willing to pay out of pocket, all according to their means and how much they need it. But when government is the only payer, it means government will decide who gets what, when, where, and how.

It means government starts rationing care.

This Is about Control, Not "Reform"

When times are tough, people say, "Well, at least you have your health." We tend to treat it as a cliché. But it's not.

Both authors have had health episodes. Blackwell has had a stroke and prostate cancer. Klukowski is younger and hasn't faced those issues, but came down with appendicitis while traveling in

Egypt, was treated by his doctor wife (the one you read about in the introduction) with medications they could obtain in Cairo, and was later told by his American surgeon that his wife's outstanding medical instincts probably saved his life.

But aside from those potentially deadly events, all of us have dealt with the flu or a stomach illness that left us literally on our backs, completely unable to function. At times like these, we're all reminded that although we tend to take our health for granted, when your health is bad, it can dominate every moment of every day. It causes you constant pain, and can be a burden to those who love you.

Considering the intimate, personal, and significant effects of individual health, it's clear what controlling health care means: It means controlling people's lives.

To give credit where it's due, Rush Limbaugh spelled some of this out in an interview.[55] If you control people's health care, you control their lives. You can tell them what to eat, whether and how much to smoke, and what prevention to take. You can tell them where to live, where to work, what lifestyle to lead. All you need to do is make medical treatments contingent on their abiding by certain "reasonable" conditions that government decrees to be for their own good. If you don't comply, you don't get treated.

This is especially true for parents. If your own health care is on the line, that moves you to a certain extent. But if you have children—especially very young children, or those with special needs—you don't take any chances. Most parents love their children so much that they will sacrifice almost anything to care for them.

Obamacare gives the government control over our children's health. Make no mistake—that's nothing but leverage to control their parents.

Solutions: Elections and Lawsuits

America's health-care system is the best in the world, but it needs serious improvements. Those improvements require major legislation. First off, we need tort reform to save $70 to $120 billion a year, because right now about one-fourth of medical tests and procedures are not medically called for, and come about as part of "defensive medicine"—also called "legal medicine"—where doctors are required to follow wasteful policies that are put in place to protect against lawsuits.

Other needs are also well known:

- We need wellness/prevention programs to reduce chronic health problems and catch many types of major illnesses before they become catastrophic (and catastrophically expensive).
- We need small business associations where smaller employers can pool together like a large corporation or a union to spread the risk and be able to get good coverage rates for all their employees.
- We need private electronic medical records—managed by individuals and private entities, not the government—so that administrative costs can be cut by many billions of dollars; medical response times can be cut to a fraction of what they are today; and to help avoid medical errors.
- We need to be able to buy insurance across state lines, so that everyone can shop around for the best plan that fits their needs, at the best price.
- And we need to provide economic incentives for the consumer, to help encourage people to make decisions that are better for their health and their pocketbook.

But obviously these things can't happen until a conservative Republican—not just a Republican, but a conservative one—wins the presidency, and leads a Republican-majority House and Senate to implement all of this through major legislation.

In the meantime, our only hope is in the courts. We've shown how the individual mandate is unconstitutional. The employer mandate is unconstitutional. The state exchanges are unconstitutional. Even some of the bribes given to secure votes for Obamacare are unconstitutional. Each of these are essential parts of Obamacare, so if the president's health-care bill passes, it will include these unconstitutional provisions.

If the House Democrats use the Slaughter Rule to ram the Obamacare package through with a shameful procedural stunt, then the entire bill may become unconstitutional. The final vote is occurring as this manuscript goes off to print, and it appears that the public outcry has risen to such a level that the Democrats are abandoning the Slaughter rule in favor of a straight-up vote on the Senate bill. Regardless, this latest outrage proves the truth of a statement just made by Democratic Congressman Alcee Hastings of Florida. (Congressman Hastings was formerly Judge Hastings, until he became one of the only federal judges in U.S. history to be impeached and removed from office, in his case due to bribery and perjury—both felonies.) Regarding the way Obamacare has been rammed through Congress, Hastings said, "When the deal goes down, all this talk about rules—we make them up as we go along."

Apparently Obama's congressional Democrats don't mind trampling the rule of law underfoot.

With a constitutional challenge to Obamacare imminent, we note in closing that the Obamacare bill doesn't have a severability provision, which is a standard disclaimer that if part of a law is struck down, the remainder remains in force. Without a severability clause, a court gets to decide if every aspect of a bill is essential, such that Congress didn't want to pass only parts of it. Courts presume that a law is severable, but have the power to find that the law stands or falls as one unit. Should a court come to that conclusion, and find any part of the law unconstitutional, then it could strike down the whole thing. It's rare, but it happens. And now we'll see if it does.

We need to do everything possible to keep Obamacare from becoming law. But if it passes, then we need to go to court, in a systematic and organized fashion, with the right legal team, the right plaintiffs, and the right legal strategy, to have the unconstitutional leviathan of Obamacare struck down by the U.S. Supreme Court.

Chapter 5

"WE'RE ALL SOCIALISTS NOW": THE ECONOMY

In short, attempts to equalize economic results lead to greater—and more dangerous—inequality in political power. This was the central theme of Hayek's The Road to Serfdom, *where the goal of simultaneously combining freedom and equality of outcome in democratic socialism was declared "unachievable" as a result, but dangerous as a process change pointing toward despotism.*
—THOMAS SOWELL, *A CONFLICT OF VISIONS* (1987)

You never want a serious crisis to go to waste. And what I mean by that is an opportunity to do things you think you could not do before.
—WHITE HOUSE CHIEF OF STAFF RAHM EMANUEL, NOVEMBER 19, 2008

The February 16, 2009, cover of *Newsweek* magazine shows two hands shaking in an iconic fashion. In this handshake, one hand is red and one blue, symbolizing that all of America—both red states and blue states—agree on something.

The shape, angles, and colors of the hands reveal something else. If these hands were black and white instead of red and blue, they would form the logo of the Socialist Party.[1]

The hands are shaking, as if in agreement. What do we agree on? In big, bold letters, *Newsweek* puts this title caption with the handshake: WE'RE ALL SOCIALISTS NOW.

The heck we are!

It's likely that some people at *Newsweek* (probably many of them) want that to be true. To be fair, we'll add that *Newsweek* surely isn't pushing for Eastern Bloc–style oppressive socialism. Most of those on the Left are instead pushing for European-style, big-government socialism. It's living the European dream instead of the American dream.

We've rapidly become a culture where earning money does not entitle you to it, but wanting it does.

Living the European Dream

In the aftermath of Barack Obama's election, it looked as though big-government collectivism—of which socialism is a form—was ascendant in the United States.

The inescapable problem is that you cannot have a vibrant and flourishing economy using any form of socialist model. The European countries are living proof of that. Filled with intelligent and educated workers, European economies consistently fail to match the economic growth rate regularly achieved in the United States. The economies in Europe languish in comparison to America.

The European economic model focuses on stability, not advancement. Although European economic policymakers like making profits, they're not very concerned about making profits. Instead, the focus is on avoiding loss. As the president of the European Central Bank said, "The most difficult question is still open: Europe, America, China, are they ready to modify their macroeconomic policies in the future—by following the advice of the IMF and under pressure from their peers, for the common good, and world economic stability?"[2]

But Americans live and thrive by the notion of "no risk, no reward." Robust economic growth can only come through risk. Although risk must be managed and careful calculations need to be made, the reality is that you cannot take risk out of the equation if you want to strive for an upward economic trajectory.

Nevertheless, in the past year and a half, European-style policies have been rushing like a torrent out of Washington, D.C.

The first of these European-style responses to economic woes regrettably started under Republican George W. Bush. Although much of the criticism we could offer on what President Bush started and President Obama has continued is policy-based in terms of what kind of governmental role, tax structure, and regulatory scheme best leads to economic growth, all that is beyond the scope of this book.

Instead, we want to emphasize how many of these policies amount—yet again—to a power grab by President Obama.

Newsweek had it just a little bit right on their February 16, 2009, cover. You and I may not be socialists, but given his policies, it seems legitimate to ask whether our president and his congressional leadership might be.

Déjà Vu All Over Again: Bush/Obama = Hoover/Roosevelt

Before delving into how Team Obama is taking over parts of the economy, it's worth noting that something like this presidential two-step of a moderate Republican enabling a liberal Democrat happened once before in American history.

The 1920s were called the "Roaring Twenties" because of the flourishing economy and overall optimism of that decade. Republican Calvin Coolidge was president during much of that time. Taxes were low, regulations were minimal, federal spending was controlled, and the economy surged.

Then in 1928 Republican Herbert Hoover was elected president. During his first year, the stock market crashed, mostly in September and October of 1929. The crash was largely fueled by irresponsible excess on the part of millions of consumers, as well as speculation on risky investments and borrowing large amounts of money for use as leverage to acquire investments. The crash was also fueled by dropping European demand for American imports as Europe struggled to rebuild its economy after World War I. These, as well as other factors, put the market in a vulnerable position.

But this market decline was also spurred by big-government action. The latter part of the 1929 decline coincided with the private sector's learning that Herbert Hoover would not oppose the proposed Smoot-Hawley Tariff Act, which became law in 1930.[3] The investment community understood this tariff to be one of the most severe protectionist bills ever passed. Such a bill would kill jobs and stifle growth, and some investors reacted accordingly.

Once the market began its steep decline, panicked consumers pulled back on their spending, immediately causing an economic downturn that began to spiral. The United States went into recession.

Economists don't all agree on why exactly the government response to the recession allowed it to get worse and worse, until it turned into the Great Depression. One leading theory was proposed by Nobel Laureate Milton Friedman. He suggested that the Federal Reserve's reaction—tightening the money supply—forced the liquidation of all sorts of assets at fire-sale prices, burning through useful assets and keeping millions from having the money they needed to service their debts and pay their bills. These people were simultaneously walloped with falling incomes, rising unemployment, and an inability to get loans.[4]

(For those who try to ignore Milton Friedman, it's worth noting that current Federal Reserve Chairman Ben Bernanke has endorsed this view.[5] For those on the Left who would like to dismiss Bernanke as Bush's guy, we'd be happy to point out that President Obama has reappointed Bernanke to continue as Fed chairman.)

Regardless of what exactly caused the Great Depression, the big picture remains that Herbert Hoover was a moderate, not a conservative. Despite the incessant talk from Obama and his Democrats that Hoover was all about unregulated markets, nothing could be further from the truth. He was a market interventionist, and the recession his presidency began with turned into a depression.[6] And the act that helped push the economy over the edge was Hoover's big tax hike in 1932,[7] surging the top tax rate to a whopping 63 percent. This is the exact opposite of what a conservative would have done in a falling economy.

Hoover's big-government interventionism opened the door for Franklin Roosevelt. Once a supposedly "pro-business" Republican set the precedent of interfering with the economy, especially a wealthy businessman like Hoover, FDR had all the political cover in the world to do it.

So this is what FDR did, except that he put Hoover's approach on steroids. As we've seen previously in this book, and as we'll see in several instances later, FDR exploded the size and scope of the federal government. He invented one new government agency after another, and had the federal government move into whole new sectors of the economy.

The United States had a fundamentally different economy in late 1941, when we entered World War II, than we did in early 1929, when Calvin Coolidge left office.

George W. Bush may have done the same thing in our own generation as Hoover did during his term in office.

We won't pile on President Bush. His leadership in the aftermath of 9/11 was magnificent. His cutting taxes helped spur economic growth. His judicial appointments were for the most part outstanding. And many of his ideas that did not become law—such as reforming Social Security and Medicare—were exactly the right things to push for; they only failed to pass because several Republicans rejected conservative principles.

But on the issues of government spending and government involvement in the economy, George W. Bush's actions led to a host of problems. His flood of federal spending and record deficits exceeding $400 billion gave Obama cover to run even deeper deficits. And Bush's major intervention in the markets in the closing months of 2008 likewise gives Obama cover for an expansion of big government.

But on both deficit spending and government expansion into the private sector, President Obama has overreached. The deficit spending levels Obama has gone to, reaching toward $2 trillion a year, are leading to a historic backlash. And the outright socialist policies

President Obama has enacted and continues to push, amounting to an outright takeover of whole sectors of our economy, have violently shaken the American people awake.

So while Bush may have acted as Obama's Hoover, giving Obama a lot of political cover, it wasn't nearly enough to excuse Obama for what he's doing today.

CHAIRMAN OBAMA: SOVEREIGN FUND

If you ask an average Joe or Jane in your neighborhood or where you work to tell you three things that the government is doing right now that really tick them off, every list you get will include the following: *People don't like the government taking over private companies.*

Americans just kind of know in their gut that the government isn't supposed to be controlling businesses in this country, especially big corporations that employ thousands upon thousands of people. We live in a free market with a capitalist system, and a limited government is supposed to exist in a completely different sphere of our lives.

To use the technical term for it, when governments own companies, they usually do so through what's called a *sovereign fund.* That's like a holding company, except that it's wholly owned by the state as part of the sovereign government of the nation instead of an investment firm.

Lots of countries across the world use sovereign funds, but they're countries like China and Venezuela—not the United States.

Still, sovereign funds are exactly what the bailouts have created. They've literally given the United States government a seat on the board. More than that, the government has leveraged the position it gained in the bailouts to take a controlling interest in companies, which means the government essentially chairs the board of directors. And since the government is led by one man, it means that the president is the one controlling these companies.

President Obama is the de facto chairman of the board, controlling several of America's most important companies. Chairman Obama has seized control of corporate America.

Preferring Preferred Stock

The United States government has a controlling interest in a number of companies. President Obama has a seat on the board of directors for AIG. President Obama controls General Motors. President Obama also took control of Chrysler.

How did the government take control of these companies? When the bailouts started around the time of the 2008 election, at the insistence of the government, the companies on the verge of going under issued preferred stock, which they sold to the U.S. government.

There's a reason they issued stock instead of bonds. Stock is an ownership stake in the company, whereas bonds are debt instruments. These companies were already on life support. For them to suddenly list billions more in debts would make them look even more pathetic, driving away future investors and putting them in a position to possibly run up even more debt.

So instead they issued preferred stock, which the government purchased with billions of dollars of your taxpayer money to infuse the morbid companies with much-needed cash. Stock certificates can be issued with different features and terms, as listed on the stock certificates. Like most preferred stock, the terms of these shares put the government at the head of the line in terms of recouping the taxpayers' investment.

But then a funny thing happened on the way to Solvency Land. Once Barack Obama was in office, his Treasury Department converted the preferred stock into common stock. Then he took over those companies.

This maneuver was what everyone should have expected from government buying preferred stock. Anyone with a business degree or a law degree (who paid attention in class), or who works in securities or corporate finance can tell you that there are two distinctive features about preferred stock. We've already looked at the first item: Preferred stock is at the front of the line in terms of cash distributions.

But the second one is the kicker here: Preferred stock is convertible into common stock. Common stock is voting stock, which means that if you convert your preferred stock to common stock, you can then vote for board of director positions. If you have enough shares of common stock, you can guarantee yourself a seat on the board. And if you have enough shares to take over the board, then you have a controlling interest in the company. In other words, it means you've taken over the corporation.

The U.S. government had an awful lot of shares . . . so President Obama took control.

How did the government try to pass it off?

First, it allowed observers to come to the natural conclusion that this preferred stock wasn't really any better than any other debt obligation. Observers still saw these debt-ridden companies as toxic. So to free these corporations from the blemishes on their records of being saddled with debt that had to be serviced—debt payments that would be made by way of preferred dividends ahead of dividend distributions to ordinary shareholders—the Treasury Department oh-so-kindly decided to just become an ordinary shareholder. (This is completely disingenuous as an explanation, because everyone involved knew all this up front. There were no surprises.) But again, Treasury held a lot of shares, so all of a sudden—look at that! We own the company! Who would've guessed?

Of course, the Obama administration is quick to add that they don't actually control any of these companies. But the facts prove that statement false. When President Obama decided he didn't like how the CEO of General Motors (or is it Government Motors?) was handling things, President Obama fired him.[8] If you can fire the CEO of a company, then you own that company. Period. No ifs, ands, or buts. President Obama fired the CEO of GM; therefore, Obama owns GM. It's his company.

So, has this plan to rehabilitate these companies worked, at least? Has it been worth it? Are they making money again? Hardly. GM sales were down 22 percent in the first half of 2009.[9] AIG is also in lousy shape.[10] And even the companies that do look like they've stabilized are in trouble for other reasons, such as Goldman Sachs (a major financial supporter of Barack Obama), now being investigated for overseas shenanigans.[11]

But then again, when a government controls a company through a sovereign fund, that government is not focused on making profits. The government just sinks more taxpayer money into those companies whenever it's needed, always saying, "Well, gee, we've already spent so much, we can't let this company fail now." In other words, with a straight face, these politicians try to make it sound like they're doing us a favor by throwing good money after bad.

President Obama doesn't care if his companies lose money. He's never worked for a for-profit venture; he has no experience with businesses needing to turn a profit. And unlike any other CEO in the country, he doesn't plan on having to issue financial statements or answer for his lack of profitability.

Demonizing the Free Market

We talked in the introduction about how part of Barack Obama's modus operandi is to always find someone else to blame for everything. He always has to find a bogeyman to demonize.

When it comes to the economy, it's simple to finger the enemy. The enemy is the free market, and anyone who prominently works in it.

How many times in 2008 did you hear references to Herbert Hoover after the markets tanked in September? Time and time again, you heard that George W. Bush was Herbert C. Hoover. (Which is a bit ironic for us to mention, given that we made that comparison earlier in this chapter; the difference lies in *why* the Democrats were making the comparison.)

According to the Obama-Pelosi-Reid narrative, what led to the 1929 economic crash was the free market. They say that an economy without heavy government control is a time bomb, because people in business are greedy and self-serving (as opposed to the shimmering angels who inhabit government bureaucracies). The moral of the story of the Great Depression, they claim, is that we need more government control. Corrupt fat cats cannot be allowed to run businesses without government having a seat at the table.

Of course, what we saw earlier in this chapter puts the lie to such myths. The Great Depression came about through individual irresponsibility at home and economic weakness in Europe, coupled with the protectionist policies of moderate (*not conservative*) Herbert Hoover, tax increases from Hoover, and the Federal Reserve constricting the money supply.

The reality, then, is that the government's role in the 1920s and 1930s helped create and then worsened the Great Depression. And the same was true with the 2008 market dive that led to the situation we're still grappling with in 2010.

Housing Nightmares, Thanks to Government and Leftists

The perfect example of government causing our current predicament is housing. In 1968—the height of big government—the federal government created Fannie Mae and Freddie Mac to support low-income home ownership. Fannie and Freddie are GSEs (government-supported enterprises), a perverse hybrid of a private corporation and a government agency—with the worst features of both.

Then came the Community Reinvestment Act (CRA), discussed in chapter 3, which was signed by Jimmy Carter.[12] In typical heavy-handed government fashion, CRA requires that banks donate a certain amount of their loan capacity to low-income applicants. CRA also allows for agitator groups like ACORN to have a say in preventing banks from opening new offices or locations if those leftist organizations don't think that the businesses are giving away enough money.

It's a classic shakedown.

So ACORN and these other agitator groups coerce banks to loosen their lending practices, cajoling them into making loans to some people who have no business getting them. Then Fannie and Freddie grease the skids for more people to get into homes they can't afford. Then wide-eyed liberals in Congress, such as Congressman Barney Frank, pushed Fannie and Freddie to lower their standards even more. (For example, Frank is famous for saying that he wanted Fannie and Freddie to "roll the dice" to give out riskier loans so that more low-income people could get a house.[13] Another time, he said that Fannie and Freddie "are not facing any kind of financial crisis."[14]) So government big shots were pushing these GSEs to become ever more reckless.

(To be sure, there's plenty of blame to go around: Many individual homeowners bought twice as much house as they could afford, and many corporate executives went to the racetrack with their money, going for the greedy extra buck by pushing unwise loans on people—but that's another book.)

Then investment houses, seeing that quasi-governmental corporations (Fannie and Freddie) were supporting these subprime mortgages, decided to collateralize them into investment derivatives. They bundled these unstable mortgages into investments, and sold them onto the market. When it became clear that Fannie and Freddie were recklessly out of control and jumping without a parachute, those investments tanked. This in turn crashed the market while starting massive foreclosures and a number of bank failures, which continued to set off a row of dominoes falling, one after the other. That's how we got into the economic mess that we're in today.

That's what happens when government becomes an actor in the private sector.

But at least government involvement in housing works, right? At least it does some good, right? Haven't they gotten their act together? Well, if they had, there wouldn't be recent headlines like FANNIE SEEKS $15.3 BILLION IN U.S. AID AFTER 10TH STRAIGHT LOSS.[15]

Okay, well at least government has learned its lesson about interfering in the housing market then, right? Not when you see 2010 headlines such as OBAMA MAY PROHIBIT HOME-LOAN FORECLOSURES WITHOUT HAMP REVIEW.[16] In other words, we may already be repeating the same folly.

Possibly Illegal, But Not Unconstitutional

Unfortunately, all of this government involvement, owning corporations and acting like a private-sector entity, may be terribly wrongheaded policy, but it's not unconstitutional. (Had the Founders ever imagined that the government would go this far off a cliff, they may well have stuck in a provision in the Constitution to forbid it, but they didn't.)

That's not to say that laws aren't being broken. When the federal government stepped in to violate the contract terms of Chrysler's corporate bonds, the State of Indiana wisely sought to get a court to stop this governmental rewriting of the rules mid-game. It went all the way to the Supreme Court, but the Court noted that a major corporate merger would be scuttled if the deal was not finalized within days, and, not having time for full briefing and arguments on the issue before that deadline, the Court declined to intervene (while making it very clear that the Court was not in any way saying that what the government had done was legal).[17]

So laws are being trampled underfoot in this whole process, sometimes at such a pace that the courts can't even intervene.

One of the reasons that America is so prosperous is that we attract investment capital from all over the world. Domestic investors keep their money here, and foreign investors send their money here, because we have a stable legal regime that enforces contracts and respects property rights, and we have a predictable body of business-friendly laws that inspire confidence the world over.

What happened in 2009 shook that confidence. We cannot rewrite contracts that were entered into between private parties—such as Chrysler and its bondholders—with both parties' consent, and then proceed to jettison contract laws and ignore bankruptcy laws, and expect that everyone will still trust us as a nation with their money.

So while all of these actions may not be unconstitutional, they might be illegal in that they violate statutes and regulations that are important to our economy.

Either way, these misadventures are a lousy way to run an economy. President Obama is acting like an imperial president, leading his government into areas of the private sector where government does not belong.

Solution: Get Out of the Business of Running Business

To the extent that laws may have been broken, remedies and relief can be sought in court by the specific people or organizations that are directly harmed by these actions. But as the lawsuit brought by Indiana shows, the courts are more than a little reluctant to weigh in on these things when deadlines are looming right around the corner, so the odds of winning these disputes in court are not very good.

Instead, there are really only two solutions.

The first is to retake at least one house of Congress with a conservative Republican majority that understands the bitter lesson we're learning as a country on this front, and vows to never pass legislation that takes over businesses or industries. It's not enough that they be Republican; they also need to be led by the stalwarts that we're seeing on TV and radio these days, railing against these big-government takeovers, and pledging to fight them.

Even then, however, there's an awful lot that President Obama can do without additional legislation. So the second solution is that we need to elect a new president in 2012 who understands that government involvement in economic matters, such as taking ownership and control of businesses, is a terrible idea.

We need a president who understands that he's the CEO of a nation, not of an automaker or investment bank.

GREEN AROUND THE GILLS: CAP AND TRADE

As if we haven't already seen enough government involvement in the economy, the reality is that one area of Obama's economic blueprint is even more dangerous to our freedom and our prosperity as a people, and that's cap and trade.

Cap and trade is the proposed system for regulating and controlling emissions of carbon dioxide (CO_2) into the atmosphere. It's based on the increasingly discredited theory of man-made global warming. This theory states—with religious dogmatism—that the earth is warming, that this warming is caused by increasing levels of so-called "greenhouse gases" in the earth's atmosphere (of which CO_2 is the most prominent), and that this increase in greenhouse gas levels is caused by human activity.

Cap and trade is a proposed system under which people and organizations can buy permits to emit carbon. If they don't need their allotment, they can sell it on an open exchange market. That way carbon producers have to pay more and more money to emit carbon, giving them an economic incentive to emit less.

There are plenty of books out there on cap and trade, so we're not going into it here. Instead, we just want to show how cap and trade factors in as a part of Barack Obama's blueprint to build an imperial presidency.

Cap and Trade Doesn't Work

The fallacy about such a system is obvious: If carbon emissions are killing the planet—and all of us with it—then what we would need to do is stop carbon emissions, not make money by reducing emissions. Cap and trade is like saying that smoking kills you, and you smoke two packs a day, so now we're going to charge you more so that you only smoke one pack a day.

The problem is that if smoking kills you and there is no safe level of smoking, then still allowing you to smoke one pack a day is going to kill you; it's just going to take a little longer.

So even if cap and trade regulated 100 percent of carbon emissions, it still wouldn't work because it would not produce the desired outcome.

But that doesn't matter, because cap and trade doesn't work.

This cap-and-trade system is subject to enormous fraud. Republican Congressmen Joe Barton of Texas, the ranking member on the House Energy Committee, and Greg Walden of Oregon, the ranking member on the Government Oversight Committee, managed to get a federal court order for the unsealing of documents from a California cap-and-trade scandal.[18]

The state of California had its own state version of cap and trade, and it's been an unmitigated economic failure. But one noteworthy side issue is that an economist from Cal Tech named Anne Masters Sholtz was also convicted of fraud, selling fake emissions allowance cards for millions of dollars.[19]

There's nothing to stop this at the federal level. On the contrary; with the feds, you're talking about corporations that do business across multiple state lines, and even internationally. A comprehensive cap-and-trade system would require regulating untold millions of carbon-emitting sources. The bureaucratic nightmare growing out of such a monstrosity opens the potential for fraud on a scale of tens of billions of dollars a year, every dollar of which is both a loss to the taxpayer as well as a loss to the private sector, which could otherwise use those dollars to create well-paying jobs.

So even if cap and trade could work—and it doesn't—it would create an entirely new black market that would further erode our economic health, as well as the rule of law.

It's All about Control

So why would whole political parties and entire governments devote massive efforts to enact a system that doesn't work? Sure, there are true believers out there, so they do it because they think their lives are at stake. But what about all the others, who know that the facts don't add up?

Like health care, regulating carbon emissions is all about control. The Industrial Revolution went from the mid-1800s through the early 1900s. After it was completed, the world's developed economies all shared one common characteristic: They all burn fossil fuels. All the time. In everything they do.

The one defining aspect of "organic chemistry" is that it involves carbon. The element of carbon, which is found in the cells of all plants and animals, is released every time we burn a fuel that comes from what used to be living things. Carbon emissions result from the burning of coal, oil, natural gas, gasoline, kerosene, diesel, ethanol—you name it. If it has a combustion engine, then it emits carbon. Therefore, to regulate everything that emits carbon means having the power to control every aspect of our economy.

Foreign "Friends"

President Obama makes certain every time he goes abroad to continue his apology tour, in which he explains how awful the United States is, and how we need to be more like other countries. (You know, Cuba, Iran, North Korea—all of those shining beacons of light out there.) He's always telling our foreign friends how much he wants to cooperate with them and work with them.

Foreign officials from some countries, who are bent on dragging the United States down to the level of the rest of the world, understand that cap and trade can bring the United States down to their level. And they openly admit it. A former European Union minister said, "Kyoto is about the economy, about leveling the playing field for big businesses worldwide."[20]

This goes back to something we saw at the beginning of this chapter. Many countries—especially many in Europe—think of economics in terms of stability and equality. We reject that concept in America. We compete to win. And we believe that if everyone competes to win, then everyone can generate wealth and move forward in progress and prosperity.

Yet some of these "friends" want us to have the same level of economic prosperity that they have, and no more. Many of these countries prize a quality-of-life type of career, where no one is allowed to work more than thirty-five or forty hours a week, with guaranteed generous vacations (such as four weeks a year or so). They see America's fast-paced system as somewhat immoral, forcing people to work "too many" hours, or to work "too hard."

Some of them are like the guy at the factory who doesn't like the go-getter on the assembly line, whose speed, focus, and dedication makes that first guy look bad. So they want us to slow down and be more like them. If cap and trade can force us to their level, then so much the better.

With friends like these . . .

Gateway to World Government

The United States emits roughly 20 percent of these greenhouse gases.[21] That means that even if there were a 100 percent effective cap-and-trade system in place here, and even if it did work (which continues to amuse us, because it's such a joke), then 80 percent of the carbon emissions in the world would be completely outside the jurisdiction of a U.S. cap-and-trade system.

Unfortunately, a *global* warming problem is a problem for, well, the entire globe. So even the best American cap-and-trade system would be useless, unless it were done in concert with the rest of the world.

That's why cap and trade is a huge issue for people who are pushing for developing a world government. We're not just talking about a one-world, new-world-order type of government. No; we're talking about proponents of building and expanding the powers of the United Nations, the IMF, the World Bank, the European Union, and every other international and transnational body you can think of—whatever will help erode national sovereignty and move us toward one global community.

Cap and trade is big with those transnationalists. Here's how they do it:

First, they pronounce the situation as dire. While avoiding hysterics, these alarmists speak in apocalyptic terms of what the world will look like if we don't all do what they say. True to form, our own president is already making these crazy predictions. President Obama says that failing to reverse climate change would be an "irreversible catastrophe" for the entire planet.[22] Okay, that's pretty grim; it doesn't get more serious than that.

Second, you say that the whole plan will collapse and fail unless we get beyond national boundaries and require every nation to act on decisions made by other nations. Again playing his part in this sci-fi drama, President Obama says, "We cannot meet this challenge unless all the largest emitters of greenhouse gas pollution act together."[23]

Al Gore explained, "It is the awareness itself that will drive the change, and one of the ways it will drive the change is through global governance and global agreements." Gore understands that cap and trade (aka, cap and tax) cannot succeed without world government. China and India, who equal our CO_2 emissions now and are rapidly growing past us, have said that they will never agree to cap and tax. Therefore, the only way it can work is if there is a global governing body that has the power to tax every nation on Earth.

Referring to Kyoto, former French President Jacques Chirac touted it as "the first component of an authentic global governance."[24] When coupled with globalist movements on other fronts, such as the IMF chief calling for a world currency[25] (under the watchful eye of the benevolent IMF, of course), such statements show a clear drive toward global government.

The critical issue at the center of international cap and trade is control on a global scale. Every industrialized nation on Earth has a carbon-based economy. To create a global cap-and-trade regime is to create a global economic control system. Everyone needs to make money to buy food, acquire housing, and provide health care and education for their children. To have every source of CO_2 subject to licenses, permits, and inspections by a global authority is to create an agency of world government, one with real teeth that everyone on the planet will need to obey.

As we saw in chapter 3, the authority of any U.S. president is almost absolute when it comes to foreign affairs. To the extent that the United States would be involved in any global cap-and-trade regulatory agency, the president would exercise massive power to make decisions about how the U.S. economy would "fulfill its international obligations" to this world body through ordering how our domestic economy would develop.

So cap and trade is also part of Barack Obama's blueprint to build an imperial presidency. And it's a part that subverts our constitutional framework, in which the people's elected representatives in Congress make policy decisions, with those decisions subject to judicial review in our courts.

Solution: APA Lawsuit and Congressional Review Act

After reading this far, you'll be surprised by our comment here: Cap and trade is constitutional. It's a terrible idea. It's lousy policy. It will kill jobs and wreck the U.S. economy, but nonetheless, it's not unconstitutional.

At least, it's not unconstitutional in this country. The constitutional court of France ruled at the end of 2009 that a tax on carbon emissions does violate France's constitution.[26] It's a sad commentary on the state of American politics when we're enacting policies that the courts of France—a big-government system with many socialist policies—considers so bad that it violates the French charter of government.

But while cap and trade doesn't violate the U.S. Constitution, there is a way to beat it in court. In chapter 3 we discussed the Administrative Procedure Act, and looked at all the various standards that a U.S. court applies when someone sues over regulations promulgated by executive-branch agencies.

So long as cap and trade is done through administrative regulations, we could beat it with the APA. As we saw in chapter 3, EPA Administrator Lisa Jackson is threatening to enact cap and trade through regulatory means. Should Team Obama follow through on its threat, it would have to go through the rulemaking process described in chapter 3.

However, this APA solution doesn't exist if cap and trade is created through legislation. The APA only controls regulations made by executive agencies. Part of the underlying idea of the APA is that administrative agencies shouldn't be doing much by way of making big public-policy decisions. The Administrative Procedure Act is supposed to put real limits on what administrative agencies can do.[27] But Congress is completely free to make wrongheaded policy decisions all day long. (There's a decent chance that Congress may have done so since you started reading this chapter, in fact.) So no matter how much of a job killer it is or how badly it could tank our economy, if Congress decides to enact cap and trade, there's no legal remedy that can be used to stop it.

Strolling Through Oz: Stimulus

One of the biggest outrages from 2009—which is really saying something, because 2009 was a year full of outrages—was the stupendously massive spending binge called *the stimulus*.

Yet again, this wasn't something out of whole cloth. Other presidents had stimulus bills before, the most recent before Obama's being George W. Bush's stimulus in 2008.[28]

But as we've seen with other issues in this book, President Obama took it to a whole new level. His stimulus bill was a shocking—utterly unprecedented and jaw-dropping—$787 billion. The federal government had never dropped that kind of cash before—on anything.

While the stimulus bill wasn't illegal, there are several points about it that need to be made because of how it fits into President Obama's blueprint.

The first is that it didn't stimulate anything. When the stimulus was signed, unemployment stood at 7.6 percent.[29] We were told that it had to be passed to keep unemployment from breaking 8 percent, and that joblessness certainly wouldn't go higher than 8.5 percent if the bill were passed.[30] Instead, it has risen above 10 percent, is hovering just under 10 percent at the time of this writing, and could again climb. Although some say that the majority of stimulus money is yet to be spent, President Obama's top economist—Christina Romer, chairman of the Council of Economic Advisors—says that most of the stimulus impact on jobs was in 2009, not 2010 or anytime thereafter.[31]

On top of all that, it cost a lot more than $787 billion. Due to typical government failures in anticipating tax revenues, the package is actually costing $862 billion so far.[32]

In terms of immediate impact, the stimulus amounted to little more than a liberal wish list for spending. Far-left members of Congress and the administration had a field day, with unlimited money to pour into whatever their pet projects were. For example, there was $800,000 for a backup runway for a little-used airport, the whole existence of which is just a testament to one of the longtime princes of pork, the recently deceased John Murtha.[33] Another example is that Oklahoma received over $1 million to build a guardrail for a certain lake, but it turns out that the lake doesn't even exist.[34]

If the stimulus didn't stimulate, then what was the point of it? Why was it really passed? There were two goals for the stimulus bill, and it remains to be seen whether it achieves them or not.

The first goal is to redistribute wealth. The Obama stimulus is a massive system to take money from companies and wealthy individuals through higher taxes and then give that money to lower-income individuals by way of entitlements and spending on projects involving lower-income labor. The spending is happening now, and President Obama is pushing for all sorts of new taxes, through letting the Bush tax cuts expire, adding fees and taxes to businesses (which will be passed along to consumers), and talk of "surtaxes" (which are just "taxes") on people making over a certain amount of money.

It's taking money from some and giving it to those with less. That's income redistribution.

The second goal of the Obama stimulus is to addict people to bigger government. These spending items are designed to fuel new government programs and new projects. Eventually, the money will run out, because it was a one-time shot in the arm; then, all sorts of stories will come out, bemoaning what will happen to all these people or organizations once the money is gone. Such stories have already started coming out in the media.[35]

The idea is to create programs that will make people dependent on government money. Then people will cry out for that money as the initial stimulus wears off. If more money is allocated in government budgets, this becomes a permanent increase in the size and scope of government.

Increasing government, and fostering voters' reliance on government programs, increases the power of those people who head the government. People like President Obama.

Earmarks

As we've seen already, one of the least-constrained federal powers is the spending power—the power to spend money from the U.S. Treasury. For example, military spending bills cannot cover more than two years.[36] (This prevents wars from continuing in perpetuity because the people's elected representatives have to decide every year or two whether to keep funding them.)

Most federal spending need only satisfy the General Welfare Clause of the Constitution, which merely requires that spending be for the national (that is to say, "general") welfare, as opposed to the welfare of a particular state.[37] This a deferential standard; courts are supposed to defer to Congress's finding that the general welfare is being served, unless it's just plainly evident that it is serving the interest of a single state or narrow region at the national expense.[38]

That's why most earmarks are constitutional. An earmark is a specific allocation of tax money to be given to a specific recipient.

They are constitutional, but they're nonetheless wrong. Not everything that is wasteful, or stupid, or an abuse of the people's trust is a violation of the Constitution. When funds are earmarked, the earmark designates a specific sum of tax money to go to a specific recipient for a specific project. It bypasses a competitive process by which various firms would compete for a contract to help ensure that the best deal is reached to efficiently use public money.

The way the earmark process works is truly pathetic. First, the House passes an appropriations bill. When that bill is in the Appropriations Committee, there are all sorts of pork-barrel items crammed into that bill. Much of this is done as favors from the chairmen of the thirteen subcommittees, who are collectively known as the "cardinals." On top of that, the chairman of the entire committee has enormous opportunity to insert projects himself.

The bill is thus compiled from the various subcommittees back to the whole committee, where it is then sent to the House floor. At that point, many of these wasteful provisions come to light; some principled statesmen will rail against them, but many people look out for themselves and back each other up in order to gain political favor for future projects. (You scratch my back, and I'll scratch yours.) This sort of waste—wasting money on an absolutely incomprehensible scale—is what our federal government has been reduced to.

So why are we discussing earmark spending if it's constitutional? Because earmarks, too, are all about control. It's usually about doing favors for fellow members of Congress or making people back home grateful. But when the president and his team insert specific budget items for some purpose or group, or sign off on the president's congressional supporters doing the same, it's used to enhance control at taxpayers' expense.

In ancient and medieval times, monarchs helped maintain their rule by granting land titles. In many countries only the king would have permanent title to land. They would grant land estates, or take them away, as a favorite method of rewarding friends and punishing enemies.

Earmarks are the land grants of our time, and they give great power to those with the ability to hand them out. Despite swearing to end no-bid contracts, the Obama administration has already been caught granting one to a generous financial donor to Democrat candidates.[39]

Although not illegal, this is exactly the kind of power the Obama blueprint seeks to invest in ever-greater measure in the presidency.

Solution: Throw the Bums Out

The only solution to this problem is to elect officials that truly take their duties seriously and who will stop the utter insanity of spending our nation into bankruptcy. Congress and the Obama administration are burying our children under a mountain of debt, and creating the growing possibility of a catastrophic economic downturn in our own lifetimes.

There are some officials who take their duties seriously and are ready to fight this insanity. Growing numbers of House members are taking a strong stand on this issue, with thirteen earning a 100 percent rating from the Club for Growth (where one of your authors, Blackwell, serves on the board of directors), including one member of the House leadership (Congressman Mike Pence of Indiana).[40] On the Senate side, for example, Senators Jim DeMint and Tom Coburn are perhaps the most dedicated and consistent opponents of this wasteful spending, as seen in the National Taxpayers Union grades (where, again, Blackwell serves on the board).[41]

This shows the benefits of recent trends in Republican elections, and it should be noted that John McCain, the GOP nominee for president in 2008, was also one of the leading opponents of pork-barrel spending in Congress. With a few exceptions, all of the most outspoken leaders on this issue are newer additions to the House and Senate. Many Republicans from before the 1994 Republican Revolution, and especially those from before Ronald Reagan's 1980 election, are among the worst pork-barrel spenders. And because chairmanships are awarded on the basis of seniority in both chambers, those holding the reins of both committees—under both Democrat and Republican majorities—have been big spenders that have driven this country further and further into debt. As these officials are replaced by those elected in the newer political climate, desperately needed change may finally come in this area.

Such change cannot happen with the force that's needed to save this nation, however, unless the party leaders and committee chairmen make it a leadership priority. It's not enough to have House and Senate leaders who are themselves good on this issue when it comes to their own state or district. We need leaders that will stand up to their own membership, and enforce spending discipline in appropriations bills.

But this solution can't truly succeed without one essential element: We finally need a president who is dead serious on this issue. We need a U.S. president who will use the power of the bully pulpit to tell the American people how dire the spending situation is, and use the power of his veto pen to reject every spending bill that includes pork-barrel spending.

All congressional spending should be subject to an open bid except in cases of emergency. Emergency situations should be limited to national security or military matters related to congressionally authorized wars. Such emergencies should be public, well-defined, of a nonrenewable limited duration, and acknowledged as emergencies by both Congress and the White House.

MORE CONTROLS: TAXES

There are many other topics that could be explored in this chapter. The use of the tax code to manipulate behavior, encouraging certain actions and discouraging others, is certainly one example of a type of control that needs to be examined.

One final point that needs to be mentioned, though, is the structure of the tax base. By increasing taxes on higher-income persons and businesses, and subsidizing more and more people to the point where they pay no taxes, President Obama is building a two-class tax structure. As soon as 51 percent or more of Americans pay no income tax at all, then there will be no public will to stop the government from imposing draconian taxes on the upper classes.

This kills jobs and stifles economic growth. Such a tax structure creates an us-versus-them class warfare. In a participatory tax system, enough people need to be paying taxes so that everyone votes to keep them low.

President Obama's strategy to pile all the taxes on a minority of the population is designed to give him the political backing to enact skyrocketing tax increases to "spread the wealth."

But the point is clear from what we've seen here: Government ownership of companies has created a de facto sovereign fund. Cap and trade is a sham, one that is nonetheless still being pushed in order to control the economy. And targeted spending—usually earmarks, but most recently this insane stimulus spending—is used to advance certain priorities, reward the president's supporters, and redistribute wealth.

The more involved the government is in the economy, the less free we are. While the Constitution does not forbid much of this involvement, it nonetheless flies in the face of the idea of limited government.

Such power over of the economy is dangerous. None of us is safe from an imperial presidency.

CHAPTER 6

BARACK THE VOTE: ELECTIONS

To give Congress the power, under the guise of regulating the "Manner" by which the census is taken, to select among various estimation techniques having credible (or even incredible) "expert" support is to give the party controlling Congress the power to distort representation in its own favor.
—DEPARTMENT OF COMMERCE V.
U.S. HOUSE OF REPRESENTATIVES, 525 U.S. 316, 348
(1999) (SCALIA, J., CONCURRING IN PART).

The fact that voter fraud is generally not recognized as a serious problem by press, public and law enforcement, creates a perfect environment for it to flourish.
—LARRY SABATO AND GLENN SIMPSON,
DIRTY LITTLE SECRETS (1996)

Given the profoundly disturbing actions we've seen in the previous chapters, a lot of people ask us one question: How can President Obama and the Democrats think they can survive an election after they try all these things the American people are so against? After all, the most potent defense against subverting constitutional safeguards and building an imperial presidency is that sooner or later, the voters get wise to what you are doing, and then they vote you out of office.

The answer is that Barack Obama's blueprint includes a strategy to shield him and his congressional supporters from a massive voter backlash. Within the master plan exists a specific blueprint to alter how elections play out in this country.

The election blueprint is a five-point plan for reshaping the political and electoral landscape of America, to make sure that Barack Obama can be reelected no matter how unpopular his policies are, and that staunch liberals can keep control of Congress over the long term. The election blueprint calls for:

- Amnesty for illegal aliens
- Card check
- Politicizing the census
- Giving congressional representation to the District of Columbia
- Nationwide same-day voter registration and universal registration

By achieving most or all of these five electioneering items, Team Obama can ensure that they will win elections in an environment where they would otherwise be completely swept out of office. These five items would subvert the current electoral system, making it a key part of the Obama blueprint.

AMNESTY FOR ILLEGAL ALIENS
Of all the things that President Obama and his congressional supporters can do to cement their hold on power through elections, nothing can compare to granting amnesty to millions of illegal aliens.

Illegal Aliens Are Not Undocumented Workers
At the outset, we'd like to make a point about terminology that conservatives and Republicans need to take to heart. We need to refer to these people, without the slightest venom or hostility, as "illegal aliens."

The people we're talking about are not "undocumented workers." They are not "undocumented immigrants." And they are not "illegal workers." Those are all misnomers, and they all hurt those who want an immigration policy that advances our national interests and respects the rule of law.

First, they're not "immigrants." An immigrant is someone from another country who moves to a new country and becomes a citizen there. If someone is an alien, then they are not an immigrant as that term is commonly understood and defined. It's also possible that you can blur the lines a bit and include as immigrants people who have permanently moved to another country to make it their home and become part of that nation's community, but don't go on to become citizens.

We all know what true immigrants look like in this country. Many of the most passionate patriots in America are immigrants. They love this country because they know what life is like where they used to live. They're proud to take their oath to become an American, and many proudly display the American flag, to which they pledge their allegiance. They tend to work hard, save their money, and impress upon their children constantly that they live in a land of opportunity where they can achieve anything if they set their minds to it and do the hard work to pursue their dreams. And they learn English, because it is the commercial language in the United States. A person cannot excel in their career without a working knowledge of the common language.

But neither one of these definitions is true with these aliens that are referred to as immigrants. Millions here make no effort to learn English. Most neither assimilate into American culture, nor do they plan to do so. They expect to return one day to their home country, whether that is Mexico or some other nation. When immigration reform legislation was being debated in 2006, they marched in vast numbers,[1] proudly waving the Mexican flag and chanting *Sí, se puede* ("Yes, we can"). Those are the actions of foreigners, not of immigrants.

Second, many of them are not "workers," either. The unemployment rate in this country is far too high. Even so, the unemployment rate for illegal aliens is even higher, well into double digits.[2] Therefore, many illegal aliens are not workers at all. Moreover, there are more than 250,000 illegal aliens in federal prisons (federal only, excluding state prisons where most criminals are kept).[3] This means that approximately 17 percent of the federal prison population is illegal aliens,[4] a number that is vastly disproportionate to their numbers in this country, since illegal aliens make up only 3 to 4 percent of the U.S. population.

Third, we shouldn't use the term "undocumented." Many countries in the world require people to carry papers with them that they must show to government officers on demand. People can't travel from place to place to live somewhere without proper, government-issued papers. The word "undocumented" carries this connotation of, "Let me see your papers." Some of the scariest words that a person will ever hear in such countries is to be told by a police officer, "Your papers are not in order," because of the ugly consequences that can follow such a pronouncement. It casts in a sympathetic light those without documents as people outside an unnecessary and oppressive big-government system.

Besides that, millions of illegal aliens do have documents—they're just fraudulent documents.[5] Identity theft is part and parcel of how illegal aliens get jobs, presenting fake social security numbers, work visas, and passports. This kind of identity theft on a massive scale causes serious economic damage and countless problems for millions of victims.[6] So using the word "undocumented" ignores this ugly reality. The issue with these people—and it's important to remember that they are people—is not that they don't have the right papers; it's that they're here in violation of our country's laws.

Hispanic Swing Vote

The reality is that most of the illegal aliens in this country are Hispanic. People of Hispanic descent are quintessential swing voters, tending to split in opposite directions on economic issues versus social issues.

You can't paint any ethnic or racial group with a broad brush. One of your authors (Blackwell) is African American, yet votes Republican and is a pro-gun NRA member who opposes tax increases, all the opposite of what polls would suggest. So it's important to remember that for any of the features we describe here, you can find plenty of Hispanics on the other side of the issue. But polling numbers are good indicators of how specific blocs of people are leaning, and that's why we look at them here.

On economic issues, polling shows that Hispanics tend to favor large government entitlements. Part of this is doubtless fueled by the fact that those Hispanics who are not fluent in English find it hard to get good-paying jobs, and so are more inclined to support programs that give more social services, paid for by higher taxes on high-income earners, since lower-income individuals wouldn't be paying those.

In the opposite direction, Hispanics tend to be strongly conservative on social issues. They're pro-life, pro-marriage, and support strong families. This is consistent with the culture and religious heritage of Hispanic countries.

These social views are unlikely to change, nor should they. These views are derived from a strong Roman Catholic culture, with a growing minority of Evangelicals, and a heavy societal emphasis on marriage, children, and households.

The economic views can be changed if the policies are couched in the right terms. There is no cultural heritage driving big-government preferences for Hispanics. Many Hispanics are successful small-business owners. If shown how entrepreneurship, education, and long-term planning allow for hard work to pay off with a good-paying career, Hispanics could be swayed in larger numbers to support pro-business policies and free-market economics. This is especially true given how hardworking many Hispanics are.

It's also important to remember that these numbers are for Hispanics as a demographic bloc. Most Hispanics in this country are law-abiding Americans, and no different from any other ethnic group.

Such Hispanics are not the focus of President Obama's amnesty plan. He doesn't think he would win over additional millions of Hispanic votes by granting amnesty to illegal aliens. Instead, he thinks he would win the lifetime allegiance of the vast majority of those illegal aliens if they were to become voting citizens, and so that's what he wants to do.

Discouraging Numbers

A proper conversation on immigration policy is beyond the scope of this book, but a few aspects have to be understood in the context of President Obama's blueprint. If we're going to get this issue of immigration right as a country, then we need to jettison the euphemisms and understand the underlying facts. This sets the stage as to how Barack Obama is using the illegal alien issue to cement his own grip on power.

Several facts should be noted about illegal aliens in this country. Studies show that perhaps 80 percent of illegal aliens have criminal backgrounds, and 40 percent have been convicted of violent crimes. Between 25 to 50 percent of gang members are illegal aliens, and 90 percent of the members of MS-13, the most violent and infamous Mexican gang operating within the U.S., are criminals.[7]

The statistics from both this section and the previous section create a complex picture. On the one hand, Hispanics as a whole are a rapidly growing swing-vote bloc, which tend to lean Republican on social issues but lean Democrat on economic issues. But on the other hand, a substantial number of Hispanics in this country are also illegal aliens. Most are people just desperately trying to create a better life, not meaning to cause harm to anyone. A minority of those illegal aliens, however, are involved in criminal activity.

Fashioning a policy response to such a situation is a nightmare. Some draconian measures would fall heavily on those illegal aliens who are known by other local Hispanics in their neighborhoods as hard workers desperately seeking a break, making them sympathetic figures. Such measures could chase Hispanics to the Left, into the arms of Democratic politicians promising gentler treatment. But to allow the current situation to continue will only allow the problem to grow, until there are tens of millions of people in this country illegally, millions of whom have children that are now American citizens.

Discussing a sane approach to tackling this enormous problem takes more space than this chapter allows. But what we can discuss is that Barack Obama's plan for this issue is purely political.

Mass-Producing Voters

The reason why Team Obama wants to grant amnesty gets to the heart of this problem. It's the most cynical form of pandering politics.

Most illegal aliens here are low-skilled or unskilled labor. As such, they are mostly suited for very low-wage or minimum-wage work. Many are paid even less than minimum wage (where, it should be noted, the employer is the one breaking the law more than the employee), as these workers are exploited by some businessmen.

Beyond that, they do not have the tools for economic advancement. As noted above, it is almost impossible to thrive in the American economy without a working knowledge of English, because although there is no official language in the United States, English is still the commercial language in this country. It is also difficult to accumulate wealth without an education, which again cannot be had without English and without full access to the educational system.

As a result, a large, permanent population of illegal aliens means creating a permanent economic underclass. These people have heightened odds of engaging in criminal activity and of raising children in poverty.

But more than that, it also means that the vast majority of these people, if newly minted as voters by an Obama amnesty program, will favor economic entitlements. Free health care, free or subsidized housing, generous food subsidies, and educational subsidies would all have much higher public support.

It also means that many of these former illegal aliens will favor higher graduated taxes to pay for more entitlements. A graduated tax is an income tax that increases as you make more money. If all these new entitlements were going to be paid for by higher tax rates starting at, say, $50,000 or $70,000, then many of these new voters would support such tax hikes because they wouldn't expect to ever get hit by the new rates.

Solution: Beat Amnesty Legislation at All Costs

The Constitution gives Congress plenary authority over immigration and naturalization.[8] What that means is that Congress has unlimited power to pass laws defining who can enter the United States and who can become a citizen of the United States, and what the process is by which those aliens become citizens.

That means that if Congress wants to pass a bill declaring that every illegal alien on American soil suddenly becomes a U.S. citizen, and President Obama signs that bill, then it becomes the law of the land. Team Obama and congressional Democrats have the power right now to make millions of illegal aliens into U.S. citizens. And once that citizenship is granted, it is almost certain that it cannot be taken away.[9]

So the only solution is to stop amnesty legislation. Any law that transforms millions of illegal aliens into citizens would give the Democrats an enormous boost in political power that could forever cement their status as the majority party holding power in this country. And if that law also included the right to bring in family members living abroad, citing the important and admittedly laudable purpose of reuniting families and keeping loved ones together, then millions more could be added to the Democratic Party rolls.

Given that there could be no later court fix, no regulatory fix, and that even passing a new law would not reverse whatever effects had already taken place, there is no substitute for stopping this bill. Amnesty will forever plunge conservatives into the political wilderness. Although the Republican Party may reemerge as a competitive party by embracing policies that are to the liking of those millions of new voters, the GOP would no longer be a conservative party, and an important aspect of the blueprint for a permanent big government will be accomplished.

And this is a problem that needs to be fixed. Ronald Reagan offered an amnesty program in 1986 through the Simpson-Mazzoli Act.[10] As many as 2.7 million illegal aliens were made American citizens through that program.[11] But when that law was signed, it was understood that it would be a one-time deal to wipe the slate clean, and that afterwards the federal government would crack down on employers who were breaking the law by hiring illegal aliens, to make sure the problem never recurred. Instead, now it's about five times worse than it was in the 1980s, and only in a period of twenty years.

So amnesty has been tried once before. Far from fixing America's problem with illegal aliens, it just made it terribly worse.

Major legislation is needed for the current problem of illegal aliens; there can be no doubt about that. But such a law must embody a policy that meets the labor needs of American businesses in a way that respects the rule of law. When an American worker cannot be found to fill a job, there should be a system in place to match a willing, foreign-born worker, one without any criminal history or other problems, with a willing employer, who will pay a legal wage.

But such a program should be for temporary workers to enable them to provide for their family abroad while helping American businesses to prosper. It should not involve permanent residence and must not involve citizenship. And it should include biometric and computerized tracking such that those foreign workers are only in this country for as long as they are working at their assigned jobs, and that they are removed from this country as soon as they finish their time of work, or are terminated from the job, or commit a crime—any crime.

One thing that cannot be allowed is for Team Obama to simply create more than 10 million new voters who lack the language or skill set to prosper in this country, creating a permanent underclass that will simply vote for a Democratic Party that promises an ever-larger Nanny State, paid for by someone else. Such an amnesty program would simply take millions of human beings and exploit them for votes to gain enduring political power.

CARD CHECK

Another key way that President Obama plans on getting reelected and keeping his supporters in power is through the union extortionist bill known as "card check."

The legislation is falsely titled the Employee Free Choice Act (EFCA).[12] Under current federal law (the modern version of the Wagner Act),[13] if enough workers call for a workplace to join a union, then the National Labor Relations Board (NLRB) comes to the business to conduct an election using secret ballots. If a majority of workers, each one voting confidentially by secret ballot, vote to organize, then that business becomes a unionized business.

If card check were to pass, then all it would take to unionize a workplace would be a majority of employees *publicly* signing a card. Outside union organizers would know which employees had signed a card and which ones had not, and could directly approach those holdouts to "educate" them on the virtues of union membership. Think about the potential employee intimidation and even violence for workers who refuse to sign such cards, stories of which are plentiful both online and with major news outlets. There are plenty of union elections where a majority of employees *call for* a secret-ballot union vote, but when the vote is held, a majority end up *voting against* unionizing.

Why? Because they were intimidated, and didn't want to publicly admit that they don't want a union. But when given a secret ballot, they vote for what they really want.

Foot Soldiers for Obama

So how would card check be part of Barack Obama's blueprint?

First, a lot of union money goes straight into the coffers of Democratic candidates. For example, in 2008 unions gave $74.5 million to candidates, $68.3 million going to Democrats.[14] But that number is misleading, because money is only a small part of what unions do for Democrats.

Labor unions are the foot soldiers for the modern Democratic Party. They provide tens of thousands of volunteers for campaign events, distributing literature, handling voter registration and "education," putting up signs, and running get-out-the-vote efforts. Such efforts are not officially tracked because they are officially spontaneous "volunteer" activities, as otherwise much of these contributions would be considered in-kind campaign contributions that would have to be reported to the Federal Election Commission (FEC). But it's easy to estimate that the monetary value of these efforts reaches into the hundreds of millions of dollars.

Unions are also a dying breed. According to our own Labor Department, only 12.3 percent of employees are union members.[15] Just thirty years ago, that number stood at almost twice that number, at over 20 percent.[16] In previous decades, the numbers were far higher. And many union members are retirees who joined unions in the 1950s or 1960s, who vote union largely out of good memories from their days at the factory, the plant, the jobsite, or the mill. These older union members are not being replaced by a younger generation in sufficient numbers to keep unions going strong.

So card check is critical to rebuilding union membership rolls. This is a desperate ploy to save and revitalize unions, burdening businesses and keeping unemployment high.

So what kind of policies would the unions help Barack Obama and his allies push through? For answers, look no further than Andy Stern, the president of the Service Employees International Union, who was briefly mentioned in this book's introduction as one of the contributing architects of President Obama's blueprint.

Explaining how unions like his could remake America, Stern said, "There are opportunities in America to share better in the wealth, *to rebalance the power*. And unions and government are part of the solution."[17]

Rebalance the power. Share the wealth. Sound familiar?

Card check is the single most sought-after piece of legislation for unions in decades, as it would reverse their slumping fortunes. And it would empower Democrats to win elections where right now they don't stand a chance.

Undercutting Congress through NLRB

The Left wants card check badly enough that they're willing to break the law to get it. Remember in chapter 3 that we saw Obama is willing to violate Article I of the Constitution by using administrative regulations to make new laws.

The National Labor Relations Board (NLRB) was created by the National Labor Relations Act (aka, the Wagner Act, referenced in the previous section). The NLRB consists of five members who are nominated by the president and confirmed by the Senate. (You'll remember that whole theme from chapter 1.)

Among other things, the NLRB has the power to interpret the Wagner Act. When issues come up, the NLRB acts in a quasi-judicial capacity, interpreting the Wagner Act in different circumstances. (This is the kind of agency action that we saw in chapter 3, which is on shaky constitutional ground.)

Card check legislation is on the ropes. It's not going anywhere right now in Congress.

But if Craig Becker has his way, it won't matter. He's President Obama's nominee for an open seat on NLRB (and as of this writing, is being blocked by Republicans).[18] He is also associate general counsel at Andy Stern's SEIU, whom we met previously.

So what's the problem with the Becker nomination? There are several issues that we won't go into, such as evidence that he may have perjured himself by lying under oath during his Senate confirmation hearings, answering a direct question from Senator John McCain by saying that he had never performed legal work for ACORN, despite ACORN records showing that he did.[19]

We won't go into that because that's a character issue for the Senate. For the purposes of this book, we're more worried about Becker's published writings on unions.

When Becker was a law professor at UCLA, he wrote an article in the prestigious *Minnesota Law Review* in which he expresses some very interesting ideas about how labor issues should be handled. Among these ideas are the following: Employers shouldn't be allowed to attend NLRB hearings concerning union elections; unionizing votes should be held at a location other than the workplace (where employers can see what's going on); these votes can also just be done by mail; and employers should be barred from having observers watching the election. He's got lots of other "creative" ideas just like these.[20]

What's key about his theories, and most alarming, is that he believes that most or all of these things can be done *without legislation*. He believes that NLRB can accomplish these things through rulemaking or other executive action.

This would short-circuit the democratic process, and be unconstitutional to boot. The actions he thinks the NLRB should do unilaterally essentially amount to card check, only without congressional authorization. This is exercising legislative power, which the Constitution only permits Congress to do, as under the separation of powers lawmaking is something that the executive can never do.

So here, Obama wants to build his legions of political foot soldiers. If Congress—even with a Democrat majority—will not give that to him, then he just wants to appoint executive officials that will give it to him anyway.

POLITICIZING THE CENSUS: 1, 2, 3, 9 . . . SOME VOTERS COUNT MORE THAN OTHERS

Regardless of how much of his agenda President Obama manages to pass, there should be surges of voter backlash in both the 2010 midterm election and also the 2012 presidential election. To help shield him and his allies from being ejected from office, the Obama blueprint calls for him to put his thumb on the scales of democracy: Barack Obama's plan dictates that he politicize the census.

Although at first "politicize the census" may sound wonkish and bureaucratic, it's anything but. The census determines how many congressmen each state has in the U.S. House. It determines how the congressional districts are drawn within each state, and how every state legislative district is drawn. And it also determines how many Electoral College votes each state gets in the presidential election.

If you can change the way the census works, you can change the political landscape in this country, and with it, who gets elected to what office . . . including the presidency.

One of your authors (Blackwell) was co-chairman of the 2000 Census Oversight Monitoring Board. This is something we know, including knowing how the census can be manipulated to aid an unconstitutional power grab.

Census Basics

The Constitution requires a census to be held in the United States once every ten years.[21] The Bureau of the Census conducts the census of the American population. The Census Bureau is part of the Commerce Department, so federal law makes the secretary of commerce responsible for carrying out the census.[22] The commerce secretary gives the totals for each state to the president.[23] Then the president sends it to Congress.[24] Then the clerk of the House sends a certificate to each of the fifty governors,[25] telling them how many congressional seats they are entitled to for the next five congressional elections based on the population numbers.

The census was originally carried out by marshals, who also had the power to swear in assistants to help them.[26] These marshals went to households to get a head count, and could only accept an answer as to how many people lived there from a person who was at least sixteen years old.[27] Within a few years, federal law specified that the only legal ways to count people were either through speaking with the head of a household or physically visiting every home.[28]

The Danger of Statistical Sampling

The Census Clause of the Constitution provides that seats in the U.S. House of Representatives "shall be apportioned among the several States . . . according to their respective Numbers" and further calling for an "actual Enumeration."[29]

This clause has been controversial in several respects over the years. That clause provided that all free persons (including indentured servants) would be counted, but that a slave only counted as three-fifths of a person. That was explicitly changed after the end of slavery, when the Fourteenth Amendment modified the constitutional census command to read, "Representatives shall be apportioned among the several States according to their numbers, counting the whole number of persons in each State, excluding Indians not taxed."[30]

But this count can be corrupted by using computer models to "fill in the gaps" to account for supposed human error or lack of responsiveness to census takers. Previous administrations acknowledged that sampling would violate the Census Act. It wasn't until 1994 that the Clinton administration reversed this long-held position,[31] which is being embraced by many within the Obama administration.

No Supreme Court Case Stops Sampling

There is a common misperception that the Supreme Court held that sampling is unconstitutional. The Court did no such thing. In the 1999 case, *Department of Commerce v. U.S. House of Representatives*, the Supreme Court was presented with questions of whether statistical sampling violated the federal law governing the 2000 census, called the Census Act, and separately, whether sampling violated the Census Clause in the Constitution. The Court held that a provision in the federal statute prohibited sampling.[32]

Under the doctrine of constitutional avoidance, a court will not decide a constitutional question presented by a case unless absolutely necessary.[33] So if a court can decide a case on statutory or regulatory grounds, then it will do so, and never reach the constitutional question. That's what happened in *Department of Commerce*. The Court held that the federal statute barred sampling, and so never considered whether sampling would also be unconstitutional.

This means that all it takes to implement sampling is a simple change in the current census statute. Barack Obama holds large majorities in both houses of Congress. Such a change could happen at any time.

Not only that, but the Supreme Court's holding in 1999 that statistical sampling cannot be used was limited to using sampling to reapportion congressional seats between states.[34] The Court's holding was limited to reapportionment: taking House seats away from one state and giving them to other states. That leaves open the question of whether the Constitution would allow sampling in drawing congressional and state legislative district lines within each state.

So even without a change in statute, there is nothing standing in the way of the White House ordering the Census Bureau to use sampling for redistricting. The statute itself only bars sampling from being used for reapportionment.[35]

Some could say that there's no reason to worry about redistricting, because it's the states that redraw district lines. While it's true that states determine district lines, either through legislation or through an independent commission, sampling can still change the results. The Supreme Court required that within each state, the population in each congressional district must be precisely equal (which seems impossible, but it's still the requirement), and the population for each state legislative seat must be as close to equal as is practical. The Supreme Court has also held that, "because the census count represents the best population data available . . . it is the only basis for good-faith attempts to achieve population equality."[36] Those pushing for sampling insist it's necessary to get a more-accurate count.

On top of all that, the current form of the Census Act requires the commerce secretary to use statistical sampling for issues other than reapportionment, "if he considers it feasible."[37] Putting all that together, it means Team Obama can argue that they have no choice, and shed crocodile tears as they encourage their far-left surrogates to put together lawsuits trying to compel the states to use statistical sampling in their redistricting. After all, they can argue, under the Constitution's Supremacy Clause, whenever federal law conflicts with state law or a state constitution, the federal law prevails.

These lawsuits could arise because redistricting plans can be challenged in federal court, so once the green light is given for sampling, it's possible that federal judges could use them to impose new lines on states.

This may all sound pretty technical and seem like it belongs more in a law school textbook. But the reality is that statistical sampling estimates from the Commerce Department could be used to change how many congressmen each state gets, instead of districts being drawn based on the number of people actually counted in the census. Then within each state, the estimates could be used to redraw districts to elect more Democrats. (State Senate and House districts can be manipulated the same way.)

But as with so many things, the big enchilada is the White House. The president is elected by the Electoral College.[38] The number of Electoral College votes each state has is the sum of the number of congressmen that state has, plus its two senators. If you falsely reallocate congressional seats, you change how many votes each state gets in the Electoral College. Out of 538 Electoral College votes, if you shift five votes away from red states into blue states, you have a net change of ten votes in favor of Obama. With that shift alone,

Obama could stand to lose a midsize midwestern state such as Iowa or Wisconsin. Move a few more votes, and he could afford to lose yet another state, and still hold on to his power.

The critical point is supplied by several Supreme Court justices. Four justices explain that, even if sampling would produce a more accurate number, the purpose of a person-by-person enumeration of the census is that it's "the most accurate way of determining population with minimal possibility of partisan manipulation."[39] If Congress could use sampling, then the majority would pick the sampling method and statistical equations they believe most likely to skew the numbers in their direction, "to give the party controlling Congress the power to distort representation in its own favor."[40]

The Founders knew and accepted that the census numbers would never be accurate.[41] But they still deliberately refused to use any sampling methods, some of which were available in those years (methods that didn't require computers, obviously), because they knew that such methods could be twisted for political purposes.

Human nature hasn't changed since 1789 when the original Constitution was adopted, and we would do well to follow the Framers' example by adhering to the Constitution they gave us.

Counting Illegal Aliens?

Another question that needs to be asked is this: When we conduct the census, who are we counting? We know that may seem like a silly question, but the answer may surprise you.

The way it is conducted now, the census counts persons. That means persons, not American voters. For that matter, it means persons instead of American citizens.

In other words, right now we are counting aliens, including illegal aliens, in the census, and it affects how many political representatives we all get as American voters.

As big of a problem as this could be, it may also be part of the solution, as explained below.

Asking the Wrong Questions

Before touching on the solution, though, we'd like to make two points regarding the questions that are asked on the census. Current federal law, as amended in 1976, authorizes the secretary of commerce to determine the content of the census survey and to collect information beyond the number of people in the house.[42]

It's true that the census has been asking questions beyond the constitutional mandate since before 1960. In fact, until Congress changed the law in 1964, when personal "enumerators" came to your house, they were required to press for answers to every question they had.

There's nothing inherently wrong with asking those questions, so long as they're voluntary. But it becomes quite a different matter when the government threatens to fine you $5,000 for not answering the questions.

The first point is that while there may not be anything inherently wrong about asking questions, such questions are counterproductive. One basic law of economics is that the more expensive you make something, the fewer people obtain it. Expense doesn't just apply to money; it also applies to whatever your costs are in any form. In addition to price, costs such as time and effort factor into your decision.

The census is no different. The more questions you put on the census, the longer it takes to fill out. The more questions you ask, the more you make someone uncomfortable by prying into their privacy. So the more questions asked on the census, the fewer people will fill it out. Thus, the more questions the government asks, the less accurate of a count the government gets from the census.

The whole point of conducting the census is to get an accurate population count. Factoring in that goal, the important thing to note is that the more questions the government asks on matters that are not essential to the census, the less reliable are the resulting numbers for the only thing the census needs to be counting.

The second point is that the census does not ask one of the two questions that it should ask. The first that it asks—and should—is how many people live at that location. But as we look back to the language of the Constitution, what's clear is that the census numbers are meant to allocate political representation. This means that the census should be counting *American citizens*, not just all people. Both parties haven't pushed this point for fear of alienating certain ethnic groups, but it's time to set those fears aside and do the job that the Supreme Court declares the Constitution requires.

The census should ask more than how many people are in each house. It should also ask how many of those people are American citizens, because elected representatives are not elected to fight for the interests of foreigners; our elected leaders are elected to represent Americans. If a state legislative district or U.S. congressional district is half comprised of Americans and half comprised of aliens—whether legal or illegal—then according to Court precedent American citizens are getting shortchanged by that district.

Solution: Sue

Our best hope is to look to the courts to vindicate the rule of law on these census issues. There are four federal lawsuits that should be brought to try to save the census, and one is already under way. This current suit involves a group of Texas voters who are suing over the fact that the census's counting of persons—rather than citizens— is depriving them of equal political representation.[43] (This case has been brought to light by one of America's top election law experts, Hans von Spakovsky, former commissioner on the Federal Election Commission and a senior legal fellow at the Heritage Foundation.[44])

This case, *Lepak v. City of Irving*, involves an issue that's been kicking around for decades. Irving, Texas, is governed by a city council. The voting districts for a city council are drawn according to population. But while Irving is 40 percent Hispanic, it appears that 60 percent of those Hispanics are illegal aliens. Those illegal aliens are concentrated in a couple of districts. Since those aliens are not allowed to vote, that means that there are far fewer eligible citizen voters in the heavily alien districts than in the other districts. For example, one heavily alien district has only 13,000 eligible voters, while the neighboring district has 23,000 eligible voters. This means that the voters in the heavily alien district have much more voting power, because each of their votes has more of an impact on who wins a seat on the city council each election.

The *Lepak* case may be about a city council, but it presents a problem that everyone acknowledges plays out in every congressional election and state legislative election in the country. And again, because the census determines how many Electoral College votes each state has, this issue also impacts who wins the White House every four years.

In *Wesberry v. Sanders* and *Gray v. Sanders*, the Supreme Court declared that the Constitution lays down the rule of "one person, one vote" when it comes to congressional elections.[45] In other words, it means everyone gets an equal vote. In *Reynolds v. Sims*, the Supreme Court extended that principle to state and local elections, saying that voting is a federal right under the Constitution, and that "one person, one vote" applies to every election in our representative system of government.[46] The Court based its holding on the idea that elected officials represent people, not trees or acres, and therefore, the vote of every voter should carry equal weight in electing a public official.[47]

If you think about that, then, the proper rule we should take away from those cases isn't "one human being, one vote"; instead, it's "one citizen, one vote." The *Lepak* case is driving that issue now. Although there won't be any final decision by the time the 2010 census is complete—we won't even have a decision until later this year, and you can be sure that there will be an appeal no matter which way this case goes at the trial-court level—we should at least have a decision from the U.S. Court of Appeals for the Fifth Circuit before 2012. Indeed, this issue may go all the way to the Supreme Court before the 2012 elections.

If so, this could have a huge impact on the new congressional districts in 2012, and maybe even the allocation of Electoral College votes for the 2012 presidential election. Even if it doesn't, though, it could have a lasting impact going forward, and *Lepak* could turn out to be a historic case.

But we need more lawsuits on the other issues we've looked at here.

First, if any sampling is used in redistricting, a suit should immediately be filed in federal court. To bring such a suit, we first need a plaintiff with standing. It could be harder to find a plaintiff here than it was with the Supreme Court case that held sampling unconstitutional when used in reapportionment. There, a member of Congress was able to file suit because it was clear that with statistical sampling, the state of Indiana was going to lose one congressional seat.[48] This both endangered the members of Indiana's U.S. House delegation (as they were about to have to play musical chairs, with one less seat than the number of current congressmen) and also Indiana's voters, who would have less representation in Congress.

Federal law at the time allowed any person aggrieved by the effects of sampling to sue. That statutory help could be removed at any time. But so long as such provisions exist, good lawyers should be able to design a suit to litigate any use of sampling, and we need to be ready to do so.

Second, although ACORN is now disgraced and discredited, if any ACORN-type organization, or rebranded version of ACORN, is involved in collecting data, a lawsuit should be filed to challenge the data submitted. States have standing to sue if they are challenging some aspect of the census that results in that state's losing a congressional seat that the state would otherwise have had for the next decade.[49] If left-wing organizations submit numbers that are clearly suspect and that boost a state that goes Democratic in presidential elections and creates a solidly Democratic House district, then whichever state loses the seat in question could sue.

The constitutional duty to count the population in the census must include the duty to certify only result totals that are honest and untainted by fraud. The courts have never had to wrestle with this question before, but then again, there's no record that any previous administration has ever contracted with an organization with a clear record of criminal activity to corrupt our election system. The Supreme Court has stated that the census certificates that go to each governor, telling the governor how many congressional seats the state now has, can be revised if there is a serious error.[50]

Third, a lawsuit should be used to stop the Census Bureau from asking any questions aside from how many people live in the home and how many of them are U.S. citizens or legal residents, or at least to throw out penalties for refusing to answer those questions. There have been lawsuits brought in the past (and there is one under way in Texas right now), but what the courts have said there is, frankly, not encouraging.[51] The courts have held that the Commerce Department has wide latitude on how to conduct the census.

However, the silver lining in these cases is that, in the most recent one to go all the way to the Supreme Court, *Wisconsin v. City of New York*, the Court specifically held that the Commerce Department has this broad discretion over the census insofar as it is in keeping with guaranteeing "the constitutional goal of equal representation."[52] If the plaintiffs manage to show how more questions lead to a less-accurate count, then there would be a possibility of getting the Court to consider it.

D.C. VOTING RIGHTS ACT (DCVRA)

The next piece in Team Obama's puzzle for shifting electoral outcomes is to give the District of Columbia representation in both houses of Congress.

Our nation's capital of Washington, D.C., is not a state—it's a city (and a very liberal one, at that). It's a special city, in that it's not part of any state. It's created directly by the U.S. Constitution, and put under exclusive congressional control.[53] (This explains a lot of its problems.)

But D.C. is not a state. The Constitution itself acknowledged this when the Twenty-Third Amendment was adopted in 1961, saying that D.C. would henceforth have the number of Electoral College votes that it "would be entitled to if it were a state."[54] Thus, the Constitution makes it crystal clear that D.C. is not a state.

Yet Barack Obama wants to give them a congressman in the U.S. House of Representatives through a piece of pending legislation called the D.C. Voting Rights Act (DCVRA).[55] This legislation is bogged down at the moment, because the good people at the National Rifle Association managed to get a provision inserted in the bill that would expand gun ownership rights in D.C., and this has become a poison pill that too many liberal Democrats just can't swallow. (If they truly believe that the people of D.C. are being disenfranchised, it's sad that these antigun members of Congress are still so hostile to the Second Amendment that they'd sell out the voting rights of some people to keep them from also being able to have guns.)

But don't expect President Obama and his Democrats to give up. And why is that? Look no further than the current nonvoting delegate that D.C. has in the House, Eleanor Holmes Norton. Delegate Norton is one of the most wide-eyed reactionary liberals in the House. D.C. is a purely urban jurisdiction, with no rural or suburban culture, no industrial base, no agricultural base, and no distinct marks of statehood. As such, its politics are purely liberal-city politics. Democrats would love to add one more committed liberal vote for every issue that comes up in Congress.

They can't have a congressional seat because such a seat would be unconstitutional. Article I of the Constitution says, "The House of Representatives shall be composed of members chosen every second year by the people of the several states."[56] Thus, only "the people of the several states" can vote for a congressman. D.C. isn't a state; therefore, its citizens don't get to vote for Congress. Period.

And don't be deceived when Team Obama and their allies suggest that their push to remake Congress would stop with a House seat. As soon as they had that, taking the House from 435 members to 436, then they'd go for the big prize: two U.S. senators. Each state gets two senators. Therefore, once D.C. has a House seat, they could argue that the people of D.C. are considered "people of the several states." They could then say that this implies that D.C. is effectively a state, so it should have two seats in the Senate. This would take the Senate from 100 senators to 102, and if Delegate Norton is any indication, it would be two far-left senators, forever shifting the entire body.

D.C. protests that it is entitled to congressional representation because the people living there are American citizens. That's hardly fair. Puerto Rico has no representation in Congress. Neither does Guam or American Samoa. That's because those federal territories aren't states. For that matter, none of them have any votes in the Electoral College, either. The Left already achieved a partial power grab by giving D.C. Electoral College votes in 1961, but at least they did it the legal way, by passing a constitutional amendment.

They're welcome to pass another constitutional amendment to give D.C. a congressman, and even two senators. But they can't do it with a federal statute. Such a law would be unconstitutional, making it fit in with many other parts of President Obama's blueprint.

VOTER REGISTRATION SCAMS
Part and parcel of the election section of Obama's power-grab blueprint are two things to look out for involving voter registration.

One Day Only: Same-Day Registration
The first is same-day registration. This bill has been introduced by Senator Russ Feingold and Congressman Keith Ellison, both far-left politicians.[57] It would require, by federal law, that every state allow people to register on Election Day and cast a vote that very

same day. It would be a process for unprecedented and unfathomable voter fraud.

As your two authors wrote at length in the *Yale Law & Policy Review*, the Constitution vests primary authority over elections in the states, not the federal government.[58] The states are free to design whatever election system they see fit, so long as it conforms to the requirements of the U.S. Constitution and federal law regarding the times, places, or manner of elections. These elections are then administered by the secretary of state for each state. (Your author Blackwell served as Ohio's secretary of state from 1999 to 2007.)

Each state has different laws to protect against voter fraud. But this federal legislation would not just be run-of-the-mill fraud—it would completely subvert the electoral process.

Every state requires you to be a citizen of that state in order to vote there on Election Day. Some states require you to register thirty days before an election. Some require more than that. You're a citizen of a state if you reside in that state with the intent to remain there indefinitely.[59]

If this Feingold-Ellison bill were to become law, then liberal activists would flood by the hundreds of thousands—maybe more—to swing states on Election Day 2012. If they live in New York or Massachusetts, they know that state will go for Barack Obama. If they live in Utah or Oklahoma, they know that state will vote Republican. So countless activists would go to swing states such as Ohio, Pennsylvania, or Florida, show up at a polling location, declare themselves to live in that state, fill out a registration form, and cast a vote.

The state would have no time to check residence. The state would have no time to see if that person was a convicted felon, making them ineligible to vote in many states. If this is done on the scale of hundreds of thousands, it would take many months to check all of those November same-day registrations. By that time the new president would be sworn into office, along with the new Congress. The deed would be accomplished.

Come One, Come All: Universal Registration

A related problem would be universal registration. This would require every state to take everyone on the unemployment rolls, the welfare rolls, and all these various government lists and automatically register them to vote. The official justification is that this would "modernize" voter rolls to make them current and more accurate.

The reality is that universal registration is nothing but crass political partisanship. Team Obama and its congressional allies know that most government lists are social welfare lists. That means many people on those lists have little or no income. Statistically, low-income and no-income people are far more likely to vote Democrat than Republican. It's just making it easier to shuttle those people to the polls. Many of these people would be more susceptible to buyoffs and other inducements to get them to vote a particular way, and would be more likely to vote for the person who promises new entitlements and services, paid for by middle-class voters.

A Few Bad Apples

To be sure, the vast majority of Americans, both left and right, wouldn't do any of these things because they know it's dishonest and dishonorable, as well as illegal. But many would. Over the past four cycles, there have been a number of House and Senate races that have been decided by thousands, or even just hundreds, of votes out of millions cast. And if you think back to Florida in 2000, it's clear that just a few votes can make the difference in who wins the White House.

Elections are sacred in a democratic republic. It's how we choose our leaders. It's how we choose our destiny as a people, and our future as a nation.

We must resist every aspect of President Obama's election power grab.

CHAPTER 7

GUNFIGHT

*Do you support state legislation to ban the manufacture, sale
and possession of handguns? Yes.*
— BARACK OBAMA, ANSWER TO CANDIDATE
QUESTIONNAIRE, SEPTEMBER 10, 1996

*The City of Chicago has gun laws; so does Washington, D.C.
... The notion that somehow local jurisdictions can't initiate
gun safety laws ... isn't borne out by our Constitution.*
— BARACK OBAMA, FEBRUARY 15, 2008

*It's better to have a gun and not need it than to need a gun
and not have it.*
— CLARENCE (CHRISTIAN SLATER),
IN *TRUE ROMANCE* (1993)

No power grab could ever be complete without one thing: taking
away your guns. President Barack Obama will, if you give him the
chance.

If there is one issue that separates the political Left and Middle America, it's guns. This is not a left-right issue. Even before the
Supreme Court weighed in on this issue in 2008, over 70 percent
of Americans believed that they had a constitutional right to own a
gun. That huge majority means that this is an issue where moderates
and independents side very heavily with the Right, and even some
liberals do as well. That's why there are 90 million gun owners in
America, with almost 200 million guns.[1]

The Second Amendment secures the right of every law-abiding and peaceable American citizen to keep and bear arms.[2] It is the right to purchase, keep, and use a gun for any lawful purpose, whether it's hunting, self-defense, or even protecting your liberty.

Leftists' Antigun Delusions on the Big Screen

The Left was euphoric as 1993 began. In November 1992, Democrats had won the White House for the first time in twelve years (although Bill Clinton sold himself as a moderate, not a liberal). And the Democrats maintained a majority in both houses of Congress. It was the first time since the 1970s that America had a unified Democrat government.

So, in 1995, several leftist Hollywood heavyweights produced *The American President*, a film about a young liberal Democrat president. President Andrew Shepherd—a widower—struggles to balance a blossoming romance with an environmental lobbyist who's pushing Congress to pass a bill to stop global warming (because back in the 1990s, most people didn't know that man-made global warming was a myth) alongside the president's signature legislative priority: banning guns. Toward the end of the movie, Shepherd makes a deal to kill the global warming bill (which would have been the highlight of his presidency) in exchange for the votes he needs to pass a watered-down gun-ban bill that only bans "assault weapons."

Finally, at the end of the movie, the president comes back to his liberal roots. He holds a press conference and announces that he's junking his gun-ban bill because it doesn't go far enough, and will instead put all his weight behind a ridiculous job-killer of a cap-and-trade-style carbon emissions control law.

But he's not giving up on gun control. Instead, he says of his gun-control bill:

> *As of today, it no longer exists. I'm throwing it out. I'm throwing it out and writing a law that makes sense. You cannot address crime prevention without getting rid of assault weapons and*

handguns. I consider them a threat to national security, and I
will go door to door if I have to, but I'm gonna convince Ameri-
cans that I'm right, and I'm gonna get the guns.

Ah, the nostalgic delusions of yesteryear. The Left really thought they could kill the Second Amendment, and in a fitting display of effete liberal snobbery, that quote shows a man surrounded by people (the Secret Service) with guns to protect his life, who believes that ordinary Americans having them to protect their own lives are so stupid and incompetent that those gun owners amount to a threat to national security.

That was before America's gun owners, mobilized by the National Rifle Association as the tip of the spear, rocked the Leftist world by taking back Congress by huge numbers in 1994 after Democrats passed their Brady Act and their Assault Weapons Ban. Then, the Right drove them from power altogether in 2000.

It wasn't until 2008 that antigun forces were back in the driver's seat.

But now the antigun Left has a new problem. Because now the United States Supreme Court is involved in the Second Amendment right to bear arms.

The Fight over Guns

There really was no organized antigun movement in this country before the 1960s. Even though there were scattered gun-control politicians, none of them ever took the reins of power to determine American policy. Presidents of both parties, from Ulysses Grant to Teddy Roosevelt, from Harry Truman to Jack Kennedy, were NRA members. (Just imagine a Democratic president who joined the NRA in the current political climate!) In fact, after Ulysses S. Grant finished his time as commanding general of the Union armies in the Civil War and then served two terms as president in the White House, he went on to become president again—this time as president of the NRA.

But with the rise of modern liberalism in the 1960s, with its strong peacenik element and counterculture mentality, the antigun movement became a real presence in American politics. This movement saw the worst antigun law in American history, the Gun Control Act of 1968, become law under Democrat Lyndon Johnson and a liberal Democrat majority in Congress.

The gun-control movement swept across the nation. This antigun tide was what forced the NRA to become involved in politics in the 1970s in order to protect the Second Amendment, creating its political and legislative arm, the Institute for Legislative Action. In an epic fight for the Second Amendment, these pro–gun rights forces took the helm of the NRA in 1977, and grew and transformed the NRA into a political juggernaut that would shape the destiny of a nation.

The NRA's political apparatus became full-fledged in 1980, and that was the first year that the NRA endorsed a political candidate for president: NRA Life Member Ronald Reagan. The next quarter-century saw gun-rights policies swing back and forth, with big wins under Reagan and George W. Bush, but also with setbacks under Bill Clinton.

The NRA helped carry the day in the 2000 election, as Bill Clinton admitted on national television that the NRA likely cost Al Gore Arkansas, West Virginia, and even Gore's home state of Tennessee (the first time in a generation that a candidate lost his own home state), and with those, the presidency.[3] And John Kerry was also hurt by his opposition to gun rights, which contributed to his loss of the state of Ohio.

Most Antigun President in American History

But as bad on the Second Amendment as Bill Clinton, Al Gore, and John Kerry were, none compare to Barack Obama when it comes to opposing guns. Bill Clinton came from a strong gun state, and for reasons of political expediency had actually been supportive of gun owners as governor of Arkansas in the 1980s. (If he were openly antigun, he never could have been elected in that state.) It wasn't until he was on the national stage that Clinton showed his true colors.

The fact that Gore and Kerry showed their true colors before running for president is what kept them out of the White House. But even then, Gore came from a pro-gun state, and for most of his life, fit in with the moderate culture and politics of Tennessee. And Kerry, though from antigun Massachusetts, had grown up with guns and knew his way around a rifle from his years in Vietnam.

Then we have Barack Obama. Our current president came from a radically antigun jurisdiction. For starters, Illinois is one of the worst antigun states in the nation. Within Illinois, no place is half as antigun as the city of Chicago. Obama got elected in a city with one of the most draconian gun bans in the country. He supports the Chicago gun ban, as well as every other gun-control measure to be brought before him.

Unlike Clinton, Gore, and Kerry, Obama is perfectly consistent in his 100 percent antigun record. He's voted to: ban common ammunition; allow people to sue gun makers if a gun is used by a criminal; increase federal taxes on guns and ammo; force every gun owner to get a license; and to force everyone to register their guns. He wants to outlaw concealed carry. He voted for the government to be able to keep secret records on gun owners. And the list of antigun ideas he espouses goes on.[4]

More frightening than all of those facts, Barack Obama also supported the complete ban on Washington, D.C., guns that kept Americans in our nation's capital defenseless.

But then Obama tried to pull a fast one when the Supreme Court's 2008 gun decision came down. As one of your authors (Klukowski) explained in a Fox News op-ed:

When the Supreme Court handed down its landmark decision, District of Columbia v. Heller, *on June 26, 2008—holding that the Second Amendment secures an individual right for private citizens to keep and bear firearms—then-Senator Obama decided to play some politics. Despite his long-standing record of denying gun rights, Obama said that he supported the Heller decision.*

Obama knew that he couldn't win the presidency without getting a good number of votes from America's 90 million gun owners. He had locked up the Democratic nomination, and was now focused on the general election. So he did a 180 on his long-held beliefs, and announced that the Court made the right decision in Heller.

He couldn't help himself, however, from slipping in a covert antigun statement. In his remarks on Heller, Obama added that he still supported Chicago's gun law, saying that, "I know that what works in Chicago may not work in Cheyenne." As a Chicago politician, Obama had always supported the Chicago gun ban, saying as he did in his 2008 statement that the Second Amendment is "subject to reasonable regulations enacted by local communities to keep their streets safe."

Those of us who work and litigate in gun rights were pulling our hair out, because we knew that Chicago has essentially a complete ban on all guns, just like D.C. We all knew that this wasn't a "reasonable regulation." Just like the District of Columbia, Chicago doesn't allow people to have guns at all, even in their own homes.[5]

And just a few months earlier, he had voiced his support for both Chicago's gun ban and D.C.'s gun ban, saying, "The City of Chicago has gun laws, so does Washington, D.C. . . . The notion that somehow local jurisdictions can't initiate gun-safety laws . . . isn't borne out by our Constitution."[6]

Well, let's see later in this chapter what the Supreme Court has to say about that.

But the smoking gun on Obama's gun-control beliefs comes from a 1996 candidate questionnaire, where he was in a race for the Illinois State Senate and thought he had nothing to fear from being honest. On question 35 of this questionnaire, Obama was asked, "Do you support state legislation to ban the manufacture, sale and possession of handguns?" His answer was unusually blunt and direct for someone who is so loquacious and prefers to give such expansive answers. With one word, he said, "Yes."[7]

NRA Eternally Vigilant against Elaborate Gun-Control Schemes

In the midst of all of this, the National Rifle Association of America has stood tireless and vigilant, and has never been fooled by the smooth talk of our silver-tongued president, just like the NRA was not fooled by his antigun predecessors.

Vigilance is especially needed in the current environment, because some of the current leaders of the Left, both in the White House and in Congress, have learned that a frontal assault on gun rights is a one-way ticket to political oblivion, thanks in no small part to the massive voter education and mobilization structure that the NRA has built over the past thirty-five years.

The dangers facing America's gun owners right now are more subtle. Although an examination of modern gun-control politics would take an entire book in its own right, here are the highlights.

Legislatively, laws have been proposed to get all ammunition stamped with a unique serial number to help law enforcement trace bullets used in crimes. The reality is that this technique, called micro-stamping, would make a box of ammunition so expensive that many people wouldn't be able to afford much ammunition, making their guns useless. There's also legislation to force gun owners to register their firearms. As benign as that sounds, that's always been the bane of gun ownership, and something that can never be allowed. There's also legislation proposed—yet again—to ban certain models or types of firearms, always using scary words like "assault weapons," but always banning weapons that are operationally identical to common hunting rifles and shotguns in terms of range, power, and accuracy.

From a regulatory perspective, there are countless issues that sound so wonkish and technical, such as the Bureau of Alcohol, Tobacco, Firearms and Explosives (ATF) making it hard for gun stores to get or renew their licenses. All of that is important, but it doesn't quite capture the imagination.

Instead, the second-greatest threat that gun owners face right now is from international law.

There is a treaty pending at the United Nations called the Inter-American Convention Against Illicit Manufacturing of and Trafficking in Firearms (CIFTA). This 1997 treaty is the latest incarnation of a treaty that the Bush administration refused to join because it would set up a global enforcement body to regulate all ownership of handguns and many long guns, including privately owned firearms in the United States. Every gun owner in America would have to be licensed with a UN-affiliated international body, and would have to register every firearm with this UN body.

Each of your authors wants to answer that ridiculous treaty with the same five words, which President Obama had better listen to and heed: "From my cold, dead hands!"

For many people, the first time they heard of Ambassador John Bolton was when Bolton was the undersecretary of state for arms control during the first term of George W. Bush, and Bolton announced to the international community that the United States would never join such a treaty because it violates our Second Amendment.

The Left hated him from that day forward, and that's why Democrats blocked his confirmation as the U.S. ambassador to the United Nations Security Council.

We saw in chapter 3 how President Obama would try to use international law to impose foreign ideas on America. This small-arms treaty is the perfect example. We must oppose CIFTA. If Obama signs it, then it must be blocked from being ratified by the Senate. The NRA has been working on all these fronts, including at the UN.

We know what we're talking about when it comes to the National Rifle Association. We're more than just NRA members. Blackwell serves on the NRA board of directors, and sits on several of its committees. Klukowski worked for several years as an aide and advisor to one of the greatest presidents the NRA has ever had, Sandy Froman, who since completing her term continues to serve the NRA on its board of directors, and was elected to a lifetime seat on the NRA's executive council.

It's often said that the price of freedom is eternal vigilance. That's as true for the Second Amendment right to bear arms as it is for any right enshrined in our Constitution. That's why the NRA stands vigilant on the political ramparts, protecting the Second Amendment.

Armed by Right

In the past few years, the fight over gun rights in America has shifted to a place that we all knew it would have to go eventually: the Supreme Court of the United States. That means that henceforth, the single greatest threat to the Second Amendment is also its single greatest potential protector.

Almost everyone has now heard of the 2008 case, *District of Columbia v. Heller,* and most have now also heard of the case that was argued in March 2010, with a decision expected to come down in June, *McDonald v. Chicago.*

But there's been some revisionist history that should be set straight. While it's beyond the scope of this book to get into all the details of how these historic cases came about, the cases themselves are at the heart of how we fight to protect our right to keep and bear arms against President Obama and his allies.

First, though, we'd like to share where the Second Amendment—which the NRA correctly refers to as America's First Freedom—actually comes from.

Origins of America's First Freedom

The Second Amendment was proposed in 1789, and was ratified by the necessary number of states in 1791 to become part of our Constitution with the rest of the Bill of Rights. Like many provisions in the Constitution, it had its origins both in English common law and also in the experiences of the Founding Fathers, from the years before and during the Revolutionary War.

The right to bear arms has its origins in the ancient past. Greek philosophers such as Plato referenced the right to arms as a means of defense. The Middle Ages were full of such works as well, such as a 1360 book on dueling as part of resolving interpersonal conflicts.

Then in the sixteenth, seventeenth, and eighteenth centuries, many books were written about a person's right to defend himself, both against lawless individuals and also against lawless government. Famous political writers such as Montesquieu and Barclay wrote extensively about the right of the individual to defend himself against even his own government, if that government ever turned against him. And William Blackstone, the foremost authority on the unwritten English Constitution, also wrote about the right of self-defense.

Of all these writers, however, none had more of an influence on the Founders than John Locke. Some of the language that Thomas Jefferson used in the Declaration of Independence is found almost verbatim in Locke's *Second Treatise on Government*. Lockean thought, as it's called, is also found in Thomas Paine's *Common Sense*, and also in *The Federalist Papers*. It's even found in the Constitution's Preamble.

The heart of Locke's theory was that when any outside actor violates your rights, he's at war with you. That actor can be a person, a group, or even a government—including your own government. (That's a jarring thought, but it's one that a lot of Americans are thinking in 2010.) When it's the government violating your rights, at some point it can become so bad that it ceases to be a legitimate government and is simply an unjust assailant. Every person has the right to defend themselves against unjust assault, and to use force if necessary to defend themselves against menacing force from others.

All the Founders were well versed in Locke, just as they were in Blackstone and the others that we've mentioned. The writings of these fellows formed part of the political theory that justified the Glorious Revolution in England in 1688. This revolution resulted in the English Bill of Rights of 1689 that was the first true limit on national authority in Britain since the Magna Carta was signed in 1215. The Founders' education as young men included all of this philosophy and history. And of course, the Founders were increasingly mindful of the fact that many of the first settlers on the North American continent had come here to escape a government that they considered unfriendly to certain rights, mostly the right of religious liberty.

All this informed their thinking as they grappled with increasing British hostility. Then on July 4, 1776, the Continental Congress declared independence and launched a war that resulted in the United States becoming an independent nation. As we learned in chapter 2, many of the provisions that would later be codified in the Bill of Rights or the original body of the Constitution were inspired by abuses that the colonists had experienced in the 1760s, 1770s, and early 1780s.

The right to keep and bear arms is no exception. The colonists believed in a right to bear arms. There was a provision in the English Bill of Rights of 1689 that declared a right to bear arms, albeit much more limited than ours. It was the attempted violation of this right that launched the Revolutionary War, and this incident must inform any assessment of what the Second Amendment right to keep and bear arms really means.

The First American Gun Grab

On April 19, 1775, the Shot Heard 'Round the World was fired on Lexington Common. Seven Americans lay dead after the shooting. Word of British soldiers firing on civilian colonists spread like wildfire, and anger reached a critical mass among the American people. The colonists decided that the split with the British couldn't be mended, and that war was inevitable. Historians point to this incident as the straw that broke the camel's back, and you doubtless heard some reference to the Shot Heard 'Round the World when you were in school as a kid.

What fewer people know, however, is what the British were doing that day. They were marching to Concord, Massachusetts, on orders from Lieutenant General Thomas Gage, who was in charge of the growing unrest in Massachusetts, to seize the firearms and ammunition kept in an armory at Concord. The act that sparked the American Revolution was an attempt by the government to take away our guns.

So when the Constitution was ratified and the Founders resolved to amend the Constitution to include a Bill of Rights (without promises for which the Constitution would never have been ratified), the right to keep and bear arms was among the specific rights enumerated in the amendments.

The Second Amendment reads, "A well regulated militia, being necessary to the security of a free state, the right of the people to keep and bear arms, shall not be infringed."

By and large, there were no significant Supreme Court cases on firearm rights until the 1900s. (There were a couple of cases that touched on the Second Amendment, but they never really looked at what the amendment meant.)

Mr. Miller Goes to the Supreme Court

Then in 1939 the Court took the case of *United States v. Miller.* The opinion is very short. Two defendants were indicted for transporting an unregistered sawed-off shotgun across state lines. This violated the National Firearms Act of 1934. They fought back, challenging that law on Second Amendment grounds. The Court made several statements regarding gun rights, noted that the record was too spotty to determine whether a short-barreled shotgun has "some reasonable relationship to the preservation or efficiency of a well regulated militia," and remanded the case back to a lower court for more hearings.

It's funny that some gun-control advocates say that *Miller* implicitly rejects the idea that the Amendment secures a private right to bear arms. That's just wrong. The primary antigun argument presented by the government in *Miller* was that the Second Amendment does not apply to individuals. The Court didn't accept that argument, and instead chose to explore the backup argument of what relationship a short-barreled shotgun might have to militias. But when the case was sent back to the lower court, criminals being what they are, Mr. Miller managed to get himself killed, so the case never made it back to the Supreme Court.

Miller was useless. Courts described it with words like "cryptic," leaving scholars to try to salvage something from it. No one ever did. It's important to note that plaintiff Miller did not even have a lawyer at the Supreme Court. The only party present was the government.

Three-Way Argument over the Meaning of the Second Amendment

After that case, three competing schools of thought evolved regarding the Second Amendment.

The first is the *individual-right model*. The individual-right model of the Second Amendment is the conservative view. It says that the Second Amendment guarantees an individual right to law-abiding and peaceable adult citizens to have firearms for any lawful purpose. Its supporters point to the fact that the Second Amendment exists to secure a fundamental right to personal protection, derived from both natural law and English common law. In addition to ordinary purposes (such as self-defense, target shooting, hunting, or collecting), the Second Amendment also provides a last resort against tyranny.

On the opposite end of the scale is the *collective-right model* of the Second Amendment. The collective-right model is what the Far Left believes, including President Obama's allies. It argues that the purpose of the Second Amendment was to provide for an armed military force, while taking into account the Founders' apprehension about the government having standing armies in our country. This theory says that the Second Amendment conveys no individual right whatsoever; it's only intended to prevent federal interference with state militias.

Believe it or not, this model was the dominant school of thought from the 1960s until as recently as the turn of the century. Some considered it to be such a consensus view that former Chief Justice Warren Burger, in a PBS interview after he had retired from the Supreme Court, said about the individual-right view we mentioned above:

> *[That view is] one of the greatest pieces of fraud, I repeat the word "fraud," on the American public . . . that I've ever seen in my lifetime. The real purpose of the Second Amendment was to ensure that state armies—the militia—would be maintained for the defense of the states. The very language of the Second Amendment refutes any argument that it was intended to guarantee every citizen an unfettered right to any kind of weapon he or she desires.*

But then several people wrote law review articles laying out evidence for an individual right. In 1983 Don Kates published an article in the elite *Michigan Law Review*, laying out compelling evidence for an individual right. This was followed in 1984 by a book written by Stephen Halbrook, and in 1987, with an *Alabama Law Review* article by Nelson Lund, a constitutional law professor at George Mason who currently holds the only endowed professorship of Second Amendment studies. (For full disclosure, Klukowski wants to add that Lund was one of his professors in law school.)

These works forced the legal community to talk about the mounting evidence for an individual right. There emerged liberals who admitted they didn't like what they were finding, but that they had to admit the truth. The best example of this is a 1989 *Yale Law Journal*

LEADING UP TO *HELLER*

With all this going on, it was only a matter of time before the Second Amendment would go to the federal judiciary. Previous cases had merely looked to *Miller*, but now there was scholarship examining the underlying facts and arguments surrounding the adoption of the Second Amendment itself.

The first big case was *United States v. Emerson*, in 2001. In this case, Charles Cooper (former head of the Justice Department's elite Office of Legal Counsel (OLC), and again Nelson Lund (who had served under Cooper at OLC)) submitted a massive analysis of the Second Amendment, arguing for an individual right. The Fifth Circuit held in a 2–1 decision that there was such a right, in a long, scholarly opinion by Judge Garwood embracing the individual-right view.

The following year, the Ninth Circuit decided *Silveira v. Lockyer*. In an opinion written as a rebuttal to *Emerson*, liberal lion Judge Reinhardt wrote a long opinion embracing the collective-right model.

Then in 2005, the D.C. Circuit decided *Seegars v. Gonzales*, challenging the constitutionality of the D.C. gun ban. A divided panel dismissed the case for lack of standing, over the dissent of now-Chief Judge David Sentelle (another law professor of Klukowski's from George Mason).

article entitled, "The Embarrassing Second Amendment," by Sanford Levinson. In a footnote, Levinson admitted that he had heard a lecture by Professor Lund during Lund's visit to the University of Texas Law School, and that Levinson was won over, to his own regret.

So antigun scholars started casting about for a theory to account for this growing evidence. This led to the third school of thought on the Second Amendment, the *sophisticated collective-right model*. This view says that the Second Amendment secures a right for individuals to keep and bear arms, but only to the extent that they're serving in a state-run militia like the National Guard.

Practically speaking, this model is no different from the standard collective-right model. But it did provide a way to give lip service to the idea of an individual right while still trying to deny that everyday citizens could use that right in their private lives.

The Real Story of District of Columbia v. Heller

Some cities based complete gun bans on these theories that denied an individual right.

Our nation's capital, Washington, D.C., had the most severe gun ban in America (an embarrassing fact all by itself). This ban completely barred all handguns, even in the home, even if the gun was broken. It also banned standard long guns (rifles and shotguns), unless those guns were kept unloaded, and either disassembled or bound with a trigger lock, with any ammunition kept separate.

In 2003, a group of libertarians decided to bring a test case to challenge the D.C. gun ban, and filed suit under the name *Parker v. District of Columbia*.

The trial court dismissed the case, stating that there is no right to own a gun. The U.S. Court of Appeals for the D.C. Circuit reversed in an outstanding 2–1 decision authored by Judge Larry Silberman in 2007. The circuit court held that the Second Amendment guarantees an individual right to keep and bear arms, and therefore, that the D.C. ban was unconstitutional. The Supreme Court took the case under the name *District of Columbia v. Heller*.

(The suit was renamed *District of Columbia v. Heller* because Dick Heller was the only plaintiff that the D.C. Circuit found to have standing. The only reason that even Dick Heller had standing was because his friend, pro-gun D.C. lawyer Dane von Breichenruchardt, had given Heller legal advice that he needed to attempt to get a gun permit from the D.C. government, so that Heller could cite the city's denying of his application as a personal injury that he suffered. It worked. Dane is one of the unsung heroes in the *Heller* case, since without his idea, the case would never have made it to the Supreme Court. The lead lawyer in the *Heller* case sent Dane a letter admitting that fact, and thanking Dane for his brilliant idea. Beyond that, some say that it was Dane's idea to bring a legal challenge against the D.C. gun ban to begin with.)

The question presented in *Heller* was whether the relevant sections of the D.C. Code violated an individual right under the Second Amendment to keep and bear arms unconnected to service in a state militia.

In a 5–4 decision, the Supreme Court affirmed the D.C. Circuit, holding that there is an individual right for private citizens to keep and bear arms, and holding therefore that the D.C. gun ban was unconstitutional in a lengthy opinion written by Justice Scalia for himself, Chief Justice Roberts, and Justices Thomas, Alito, and Kennedy as the swing vote. In *Heller*, the Court examined the meaning of the words of the Second Amendment in 1791, exploring English and American history.

What's amazing about this opinion is that Justice Scalia did not go with any of the parties' arguments. He did not adopt the *Heller* team's arguments, instead developing his own from the various amicus briefs that were filed in the case.

In fact, it's likely that one of those amicus briefs won the case. During argument (all of which is found on the Court's public transcript), Justice Kennedy noted that there was an argument as to how the Court could uncouple the first clause in the Second Amendment (referencing a militia) from the second clause (referencing a right to bear arms), and

Kennedy added that he was not taking this argument from the *Heller* team's brief.[8] The only brief filed in the case that made such an argument was from Nelson Lund, Klukowski's former law professor, who is considered by many to be the foremost scholar in America on the Second Amendment.[9] Various other constitutional scholars, including leading scholar David Kopel and some law professors, all acknowledge that it was Professor Lund's argument that won over the decisive fifth vote to save the Second Amendment.[10]

The Court in *Heller* held that the Second Amendment extends to all arms that can be borne by individuals; found that the Second Amendment right includes a right to self-defense against both public and private violence; and that handguns are the instrument of choice for most Americans for self-defense. The Court also found that handguns are particularly important to some people, who may have a rough time handling long guns such as shotguns or rifles.

Justice Scalia went on in the opinion to say that the *Heller* opinion should not be read to cast doubt on existing laws barring firearms from felons or mental defectives, from sensitive areas such as schools and government buildings, or laws restricting unusually dangerous firearms.

The four dissenters—Justices Stevens, Souter, Ginsburg, and Breyer—all joined two dissenting opinions. One was by Justice Stevens, arguing that the proper interpretation of the Second Amendment is the sophisticated collective-right view. (Not one justice even tried to defend the traditional collective-right view that had been embraced by the Ninth Circuit as recently as 2002.) The other dissent was by Justice Breyer, arguing that even if there is an individual right, all gun laws should be upheld unless they're completely irrational.

There are plenty of aspects of the opinion that are problematic, but its core holding that the Second Amendment is an individual right is a huge step forward for the Constitution.

The *Heller* holding was narrow, so all sorts of questions remain open. Depending on how the Court's membership changes over the next few years, Second Amendment rights could become broad and robust, or they could be so narrowly construed that the Amendment only forbids absolute disarmament of handguns within the home, if the owner satisfies licensing and registration requirements imposed by local government. It's wide open at this point.

Chicago Gun Ban Going Down in McDonald v. Chicago

In 2010, the Supreme Court took the first follow-up case to *Heller* to see how the Second Amendment will develop. The Chicago gun ban that we looked at earlier in this chapter is now at the U.S. Supreme Court in the case *McDonald v. City of Chicago.*

After *Heller*, lawsuits were filed against Chicago's gun ban, which is essentially identical to the ban in D.C.. In September 2009 one of those cases, *McDonald v. City of Chicago*, was taken by the Court.

The question in *McDonald* is whether the Second Amendment right to bear arms applies to the states. When the Bill of Rights was adopted in 1791, it originally only secured rights against the federal government. Then, after the Civil War, when the Fourteenth Amendment was adopted in 1868, it extended most—but not all—of the Bill of Rights to also apply to the states. (This includes cities, because cities are political subdivisions of the sovereign states.) The legal term is that the Fourteenth Amendment "incorporates" certain provisions of the Bill of Rights against the states.

As the federal capital city, Washington, D.C., is directly under federal law. So *Heller* did not involve incorporation, leaving that issue for the *McDonald* case.

The pro-gun camp split on this case, with some groups that do not focus on Second Amendment rights trying to use this case to seize this issue for themselves. The traditional route for incorporating rights is through the Fourteenth Amendment Due Process Clause. Even though there are all sorts of serious constitutional problems with that approach—which is part of what is called the *doctrine of substantive due process*—the NRA (which was also a party in this case) wisely argued for this approach because it is the safest and surest approach to take.

But the libertarian activists arguing this case for Otis McDonald and his co-plaintiffs instead argued for the Court to incorporate the right to bear arms through the little-used Privileges or Immunities Clause of the Fourteenth Amendment. They argued that in doing so, the Court should overrule one of the biggest Supreme Court decisions of all time, the *Slaughter-House Cases*, from 1873. These activists admitted that they also support incorporation through the Due Process Clause, but devoted the vast bulk of their briefs and argument time to pushing Privileges or Immunities.

(There is a third argument—that it's possible to incorporate gun rights through the Privileges or Immunities Clause without over-ruling the *Slaughter-House Cases*—which your author Klukowski argued in an amicus brief that he wrote on behalf of the American Civil Rights Union, Let Freedom Ring, the Committee for Justice, and the Family Research Council. This approach would incorporate the Second Amendment without endorsing substantive due process—which gave us *Roe v. Wade*—or all the terrible things that could result from overruling *Slaughter-House*. In fact, the reason that the Family Research Council got involved is because overruling *Slaughter-House* could have opened the door to a radical antifamily agenda. But the Court focused on the two main arguments and never got around to ours.)

In the *Slaughter-House Cases*, some butchers sued in federal court over a Louisiana law granting a monopoly over butchering animals in and around New Orleans. In the days before refrigeration, slaughtering animals posed serious health risks, and so there were lots of laws heavily regulating butchering. The butchers here claimed that this state law violated their rights under the Privileges or Immunities Clause.

The Supreme Court rejected their argument. Nowhere does the Constitution declare any rights against monopolies, and as we saw in the introduction, public-health laws are part of the police power that states wield as sovereign entities. The Court held that only rights inherent in federal citizenship are incorporated to the states through

Privileges or Immunities, and that the Court would not invent the right that the butchers claimed.

This was a conservative decision. Had the Court decided *Slaughter-House* differently, declaring rights where the Constitution doesn't, and using those rights to strike down state laws, this would have been gross judicial activism.

There was excitement in some libertarian circles regarding the possibility of *Slaughter-House* being overruled, as this would open the door to all sorts of libertarian economic rights. (It should also be noted that many libertarians oppose overruling *Slaughter-House*, and that one of Klukowski's clients in the *McDonald* case is libertarian.) Lots of liberal scholars enthusiastically supported these libertarians, because they knew overruling the *Slaughter-House Cases* could lead to declaring all sorts of new constitutional rights, from government-run health care to environmental "rights" to abortion to same-sex marriage.

But any hopes for the Privileges or Immunities Clause were dashed during oral argument. In the very first minute of argument, Chief Justice John Roberts declared that the *McDonald* lawyers faced a heavy burden if they meant to convince the Court to overrule *Slaughter-House*, which had been on the books for 140 years and may be second only to *Marbury v. Madison* as the most far-reaching Supreme Court decision ever.

Then Justice Antonin Scalia came in with all guns blazing, asking why the *McDonald* lawyers were pressing such an argument on the Court. Scalia admitted that substantive due process is wrong, but that it's the way the Court had always done it. Why would the Court completely overhaul how constitutional rights are extended to the states?

Then former U.S. Solicitor General Paul Clement argued on behalf of the NRA, taking the conventional approach and smacking the ball over the fence with that argument. The liberal justices tried to trip up Clement, but the NRA proved that it had spent its money wisely, as Clement performed like a legal ninja master, never missing a beat.

Chicago's lawyer then argued that the Second Amendment isn't incorporated at all, and was promptly destroyed both by the conservative justices and by moderate Justice Kennedy, who told the Chicago lawyer that the right to keep and bear arms is a fundamental right, and that the Court must incorporate unless the Court could be convinced to overrule *Heller* after just two years. Chief Justice Roberts sealed Chicago's fate, adding that Chicago's argument "sounds an awful lot to me like the argument we heard in *Heller* on the losing side."

So as this book goes to print, it looks like a slam-dunk that the Second Amendment will be incorporated to the states through the Fourteenth Amendment, and that the Chicago gun ban will be struck down. The incorporation will likely happen through the Due Process Clause, as the Court will put an end to some activists' attempts to hijack the Second Amendment to advance their economic agenda, partly because the Court understands the unprecedented power it would give the courts to declare new constitutional rights and remake our society—in a liberal direction.

Those of us who are true to the Founders of our country who wrote our Constitution share their belief that the federal courts are not to be trusted or given more power than Congress or the president. Judicial activism is wrong, whether it advances big-government liberalism or freedom-enhancing libertarianism. Courts must confine themselves to the Constitution as it is written—not make up new rights or powers as they go along. To say judicial activism is okay when it advances freedom but bad when it grows government is to forfeit the high ground of a principled position for nothing more than personal gain and political expediency. That's no way to interpret the Supreme Law of the Land.

McDonald was a case about gun rights. The NRA was right to keep it about gun rights, and these activists were wrong to try to commandeer the Second Amendment to advance their own pet agenda. The Supreme Court didn't just shut the door in their faces; the Court slammed the door—loudly.

McDonald is only the second case presented over the Second Amendment. *Heller* was the first. There will likely be a dozen or so more over the next thirty years. And that's why the biggest battles over gun rights will now ultimately be won or lost in the U.S. Supreme Court.

The Real Purpose of the Second Amendment

Given that we've entered a whole new world when it comes to gun rights, we need to understand what the Second Amendment really means. It secures a right to firearms, which can be used for self-defense, hunting, collecting, and any number of purposes.

The Second Amendment is intended to serve two purposes: The first is to enable people to defend themselves against criminals. The second is to enable people to defend themselves against government, both foreign and domestic.

The fact that we've had two centuries of almost-unbroken domestic peace may make people think less of that concern, especially since the United States also has the most powerful military in history. But it was nonetheless foremost in the Framers' minds in 1791. An originalist interpretation of the Constitution includes their political philosophy, so this right is still part of the Constitution.

Early Americans were very concerned with the possibility of a tyrannical central government. They had just escaped an oppressive government, and so the fear of exchanging one oppressor for another was very much on their minds. That's why James Madison explained that if the federal government were to ever threaten the rights of American citizens, that government would "be opposed [by] a militia amounting to near half a million of citizens with arms in their hands."[11] This number refers to most of the able-bodied adult male population of the country at the time, which, by law, is what the militia was, and still is.[12] The idea of armed citizens as a safeguard against tyranny is why Madison described, as an advantage, citizens of this country "being armed, which the Americans possess over the people of almost every other nation."

Protecting liberty is both the right and the duty of citizens. The Second Amendment ensures that "the people" of the United States will always be able to act as guardians of their liberty, retaining supremacy over every level of government.

Some of the most respected federal judges on the bench understand this point clearly. Judge Diarmuid O'Scannlain is a well-respected Reagan-appointed judge on the U.S. Court of Appeals for the Ninth Circuit. Writing for that court in a 2009 gun-rights case, Judge O'Scannlain explained that the Second Amendment "right contains both a political component—it is a means to protect the public from tyranny—and a personal component—it is a means to protect the individual from threats to life or limb."[13]

Judge Janice Rogers Brown, whom we discussed in chapter 2, is one of the most-respected and most-capable judges in the country, serving on the U.S. Court of Appeals for the D.C. Circuit. (In fact, Judge Brown is a top contender to serve on the U.S. Supreme Court.) Before that, Judge Brown served as a justice on the California Supreme Court. In one gun case, Brown wrote, "Extant political writings of the [founding] period repeatedly expressed a dual concern: facilitating the natural right of self-defense and assuring an armed citizenry capable of repelling foreign invaders and quelling tyrannical leaders."[14]

And in *Heller*, the U.S. Supreme Court noted all of this as well, saying that the purpose of the Second Amendment was so that We the People could hold government accountable,[15] and specifically declaring that the right to keep and bear arms was intended as a "safeguard against tyranny."[16]

Chilling Words from Someone Who Knows

Perhaps the most powerful exposition we've ever read for the reason for the Second Amendment is the one written by Chief Judge Alex Kozinski of the Ninth Circuit.

For those who would dismiss his statements as fear-mongering or alarmist, know this: Kozinski was born in Romania, under communist tyranny. His parents were Holocaust survivors. So when he speaks of Jews being herded into cattle cars for mass extermination, he's not invoking some bogeyman; he's speaking of his own family.

His words are so profound that we have nothing to add; we'll just close with the insight he and his family have gained from their own nightmarish experience. Writing in dissent on the denial of rehearing the case *Silveira v. Lockyer*, which challenged the California assault weapons ban, Kozinski wrote:

> *[Some believe] that ordinary people are too careless and stupid to own guns, and we would be far better off leaving all weapons in the hands of professionals on the government payroll. But the simple truth—born of experience—is that tyranny thrives best where government need not fear the wrath of an armed people. . . .*
>
> *All too many of the other great tragedies of history—Stalin's atrocities, the killing fields of Cambodia, the Holocaust, to name but a few—were perpetrated by armed troops against unarmed populations. Many could well have been avoided or mitigated, had the perpetrators known their intended victims were [armed] . . . If a few hundred Jewish fighters in the Warsaw Ghetto could hold off the Wehrmacht for almost a month with only a handful of weapons, six million Jews armed with rifles could not so easily have been herded into cattle cars.*
>
> *[Many forget] these bitter lessons of history. The prospect of tyranny may not grab the headlines the way vivid stories of gun crime routinely do. But few saw the Third Reich coming until it was too late. The Second Amendment is a doomsday provision, one designed for those exceptionally rare circumstances where all other rights have failed—where the government refuses to stand for reelection and silences those who protest; where courts have lost the courage to oppose, or can find no one to enforce their decrees. However improbable these contingencies may seem today, facing them unprepared is a mistake a free people get to make only once.*

CHAPTER 8

A PRISON FOR YOUR MIND: INFORMATION

Speech is an essential mechanism of democracy, for it is the means to hold officials accountable to the people. . . . The right of citizens to inquire, to hear, to speak, and to use information to reach consensus is a precondition to enlightened self-government and a necessary means to protect it. . . . For these reasons, political speech must prevail against laws that would suppress it. . . . Premised on the mistrust of governmental power, the First Amendment stands against attempts to disfavor certain subjects or viewpoints. . . . By taking the right to speak from some and giving it to others, the Government deprives the disadvantaged person or class of the right to use speech to strive to establish worth, standing, and respect for the speaker's voice. The Government may not by these means deprive the public of the right and privilege to determine for itself what speech and speakers are worthy of consideration. The First Amendment protects speech and speaker, and the ideas that flow from each.

—CITIZENS UNITED V. FEDERAL ELECTION COMMISSION,
130 S. CT. 876 (2010).

One of big movies of the 1990s was *The Matrix*. At the point in the movie where the world gets turned upside down for the main character (Neo), an interesting dialogue takes place between Neo (aka, Mr. Anderson) and the man who will become his mentor and guide, the famous Morpheus.

They're sitting in large, leather chairs in a dark and foreboding room at night, with lightning flashing outside the window and thunder rumbling in the background as rain pours down. In answer to the question of what the Matrix is, the following exchange takes place:

Morpheus: The Matrix is everywhere. It is all around us. Even now, in this very room. You can see it when you look out your window, or when you turn on your television. You can feel it when you go to work . . . when you pay your taxes. It is the world that has been pulled over your eyes to blind you from the truth.

Neo: What truth?

Morpheus: That you are a slave, Neo. Like everyone else, you were born into bondage, born into a prison that you cannot smell or taste or touch. A prison for your mind. . . .

One of the critical tools used by overbearing governments is withholding information from its citizens. They control the flow of information and ideas.

When most people hear "control the flow of information and ideas," they think of totalitarian regimes such as North Korea, Cuba, or the former Soviet Union, where all media is for government propaganda purposes, and where no one is allowed to speak or write without government permission. Or at least people think of authoritarian regimes like China, where government freely censors news on any subject, as well as access to the Internet or e-mail.

But there are less-severe forms of control as well. You see it in Iran, where government cracks down on speech that it regards as un-Islamic. You see it in Venezuela, where the government yanks the broadcasting licenses of TV or radio stations that say things critical of the government.

That's why the Founders wrote the Free Speech Clause into the First Amendment—so that people could share what they learn and what they think. The First Amendment is to foster the free exchange and dissemination of thoughts and information. Free speech is meant to create a free "marketplace of ideas,"[1] where everyone can make their case and try to inform and persuade their fellow man, the goal being that the best ideas will win in the end.[2]

The First Amendment is a huge problem for President Obama. The United States is a center-right country, and if the country received all the information about what is happening and how it could affect them, there would be a serious backlash against his administration.

So President Obama's blueprint dictates that this information be censored. The blueprint includes discrediting media outlets that are critical of the president, and seeking to co-opt the rest. It includes barring dissenting opinion from the airwaves. It includes silencing even public officials who disagree with the president. And it includes shaping how your children are taught to think and believe.

The blueprint calls for keeping you from hearing and watching certain things. It calls for keeping things from being said that would jeopardize President Obama's agenda. The blueprint calls for building a prison.

A prison for your mind.

PRAVDA USA: CO-OPTING THE MEDIA

One of the tools that big-government regimes—including the one President Obama seeks to build—employ is the co-opting of the media. This is done through media figures who support the regime's agenda, through promises of access or other rewards, and through threatening media outlets critical of the regime.

There's a common misperception about the media that somehow the Free Press Clause gives its members more protection to speak out than the rest of us. Not true. The Supreme Court "has consistently rejected the proposition that the institutional press has any constitutional privilege beyond that of other speakers,"[3] and reaffirmed that principle as recently as the landmark *Citizens United v. FEC* case decided this year.

Free speech is free speech as far as the Constitution is concerned, regardless of the speaker. Fox News and the *Wall Street Journal* don't have any additional First Amendment protection to speak than you do.

What makes the media different is that they have bigger platforms, and more people deliberately seek out certain media outlets to inform them. All of the major media outlets are massive corporations with vast financial resources that they use to project their images across the world. Such powerful resources pose a serious threat when a government is trying to do something that the people would reject.

Fortunately for President Obama, he has a lot of media people in his pocket. Bernie Goldberg's book, *A Slobbering Love Affair*, recounts plenty of the pathetic instances of Obama media coverage that was ridiculously biased, such as reporters openly saying that they were so excited about Obama that they couldn't stay objective, or MSNBC's Chris Matthews talking about getting a tingle up his leg listening to Candidate Obama.

But that was 2007 and 2008, and the first few months of Obama's presidency in 2009. Although much of the media is still in the tank for Barack Obama, the bloom is off the rose. Every day sees media coverage that is still biased; it's just not as blinded by love as it was in the first half of 2009.

Too many in the media are still a problem. They are cheerleaders for President Obama. (We chuckle to think of how a Robert Gibbs press briefing would look if the mainstream media felt the same way about Obama that they did about Bush.) Because the media has not covered many of the issues we've discussed in this book, too many Americans haven't been informed as to how serious these issues are.

The War against Fox News

Then you have Fox News.

Of all the television networks, only the Fox News Channel has consistently carried the names and voices that provide the other side of the story. With the News Corp family—including the *New York Post*, the *Wall Street Journal*, and now, the new Fox Business Network (which has very quickly fielded a superb lineup)—there is a strong alternative voice for America to get the facts on every story, and to hear opinions on both sides of every issue.

That's a problem for Team Obama. And so they launched a war against Fox News.

President Obama's defenders deride this concept of a war, implying that those saying such things are paranoid, just playing for ratings, or shilling for the Republican Party. But when you see three top White House advisors simultaneously using the same language, coupled with White House decisions regarding press access, the truth becomes clear.

First you had Anita Dunn, former White House communications director. She was also the senior White House aide who said on camera that one of her two favorite political philosophers was Chinese Communist Chairman Mao Zedong, who mass-murdered tens of millions of Chinese during his tyrannical reign of China. (Saying you admire Mao is really shocking, seeing as he killed more people than either Adolf Hitler or Josef Stalin.)

Dunn fired the first shot, saying that Fox News is "opinion journalism masquerading as news."[4] Asked about it during a later interview, she responded, "[I]f you were a Fox News viewer in the fall election, what you would have seen would have been that the biggest stories and biggest threats facing America were a guy named Bill Ayers and something called ACORN. The reality of it is that Fox News often operates almost as either the research arm or the communications arm of the Republican Party."[5] Dunn also said, ". . . what is fair to say about Fox and certainly the way we view it is that it is really more a wing of the Republican Party."[6]

Then you had Rahm Emanuel, the White House chief of staff known for walking naked around public showers to confront congressmen, sending dead fish to critics, and dropping the F-bomb so frequently in conversation that parents wouldn't want their kids to be within earshot. Emanuel said, ". . . the way we, the president looks at it, we look at it is it's not a news organization so much as it has a perspective . . . more importantly is not have the CNNs and the others in the world basically be led and following Fox. . . ."[7]

Next there was David Axelrod. This is the White House senior advisor who runs the message and political shop. Axelrod said that the country's most-watched news station is "not really a news station," because the news it reports is "not really news."[8] Okay.

And finally you have the president himself. Although presidents generally don't lower themselves to get involved in such petty disputes, President Obama seems unconcerned that such antics are not befitting his office. So in an interview, he said, "I've got one television station entirely devoted to attacking my administration."[9] When asked if he meant Fox News, Obama responded yes, and that, "Well, that's a pretty big megaphone . . . you'd be hard-pressed, if you watched the entire day, to find a positive story about me. . . ."[10]

All these add up to the head of state and his personal advisors going after a news outlet critical of his policies. It was an attempt to discredit his critics as not being real journalists, saying that somehow, a twenty-four-hour cable news outlet was not at all news.

In President Obama's America, dissent will not be tolerated.

Solution: Media Rising
The solution to this war on Fox came from the media itself. To its credit, other media outlets rallied to Fox's side. They had enough professional concern for the integrity of their profession and the vital role that they play in our democratic republic that they called out the White House on this disturbing big-government heavy-handedness, and forced the White House to retreat.

A perfect example of that came when the White House had an event in which the networks were involved as part of the press pool, but Fox News was deliberately excluded. The rest of the networks dug in their heels, saying that the pool functioned for all news organizations, and that if Fox couldn't participate, then none of them would.

The White House caved, and with it ended the first battle against a free news outlet. But this fight is far from over, because the blueprint still calls for silencing and discrediting whoever criticizes the president.

KILLING THE MESSENGER: TALK RADIO

As part of this silencing of the media, President Obama's power grab must also seek to silence talk radio.

Talk radio has come to play a vital role in America's dialogue over the issues of the day. Hosts like Glenn Beck, Sean Hannity, Laura Ingraham, Hugh Hewitt, Mike Gallagher, Bill Cunningham, Bill Bennett, Martha Zoller, Dennis Prager, and Mark Levin—along with dozens of others—speak to millions of people each day.

Most talk-radio voices are conservative, since the intellectual and reason-based arguments of conservatives are more conducive to a voice-only presentation than the emotionalism and illogic of the Left. But this isn't just about conservative shows. Some radio hosts defy stereotyping, such as the wildly independent Don Imus.

Of all these talk-radio personalities, the reigning king is Rush Limbaugh, and so it should be no surprise that the White House launched a war against Rush Limbaugh in its desperate attempt to silence these valuable voices. The White House tried for several weeks to label Rush the leader of the Republican Party, hoping to recast the GOP as something other than a political party.

This war on Rush was not only pushed by left-wing outlets such as *Salon*,[11] and liberal mainstream newspapers like the *Los Angeles Times*.[12] That accusation was made by—again—Chief of Staff Rahm Emanuel.[13]

But all this started with President Barack Obama himself. Within a couple days of taking office, the president criticized the Republican Party by saying, "You can't just listen to Rush Limbaugh and get things done."[14] It was only later revealed that this otherwise-inexplicable single-person attack by the president arose from confidential data researched by Democratic pollsters, finding that casting Rush as the head of the GOP would help the White House drive a wedge between the Republican Party and moderate voters.[15]

So in other words, the White House is willing to single out private citizens by name to press a partisan advantage, all the while saying that we need to get past partisanship to work together. Amazing.

Fairness Doctrine Killed
The way that the White House is trying to silence talk radio, however, goes far beyond attacking talk-radio hosts; they'd like to drive them off the air altogether with regulations by bringing back some version of the falsely labeled Fairness Doctrine.

The Fairness Doctrine was an old requirement for obtaining or keeping a broadcast license from the Federal Communications Commission (FCC). A station could not get or keep a license unless it agreed to abide by the government's policy on what material could be broadcast. Without a license, a station would be shut down.

In the 1940s when broadcast media was young, some people were concerned about how quickly the limited broadcast spectrum would be eaten up by various outlets. Some were concerned that there could only be a limited number of stations, and that if those stations all represented one perspective, then the American people wouldn't have access to competing viewpoints and contrary information.

So the FCC adopted the Fairness Doctrine in 1949. This regulation required broadcasters to give "fair coverage" to public issues. The term "fair" was never defined, but was always considered to mean that lots of broadcast time must be given to opposing arguments; some suggested that the ideal was a straight fifty-fifty division in order to give equal time to opposing voices on all issues. In reality, it was a censorship regime, with government telling private media outlets what they needed to say on their own programming.

In 1987, Ronald Reagan's FCC abolished the Fairness Doctrine. Congressional Democrats held the majority in both chambers for the following eight years. During that time they passed bills in 1987 and 1991 to reinstate this censorship regime. President Ronald Reagan vetoed the 1987 bill, and President George H. W. Bush vetoed the 1991 bill.

Supporters of the Fairness Doctrine note that it has been upheld by the U.S. Supreme Court. That's true. In 1969 the Court upheld the Fairness Doctrine in *Red Lion Broadcasting v. FCC*.[16] The Court held that public airwaves are scarce, and so the government can impose restrictions and conditions on those seeking to reserve their own exclusive channel by securing the rights to a particular frequency on the radio dial or TV tuner.

The first thing that needs to be said is that *Red Lion* may not even be good law (a legal phrase for enforceable law) any longer. Several years later, in 1974, the Court struck down a similar restriction on a newspaper in *Miami Herald v. Tornillo*. While it's possible to distinguish newspapers from broadcast media, the Court did not explain how its decision in *Tornillo* could be reconciled with *Red Lion*.

Commentators and courts have tried without success to determine what the current law is after those two cases. Some say that *Tornillo* simply created a newspaper exception to the *Red Lion* rule. Others note that *Red Lion* raised a challenge under the Free Speech Clause of the First Amendment (which applies to every private person or organization), while *Tornillo* was based on the Free Press Clause of the First Amendment (which applies only to the media), and that somehow press freedoms receive stronger constitutional protections. (That statement doesn't square with what the Supreme Court has said about the press.)

Regardless of the explanation, the current Supreme Court is not the Warren Court that decided *Red Lion*, or even the Burger

Court that decided *Tornillo*. The current Roberts Court is friendly to free expression, and takes a dim view of the federal government regulating private speech—especially speech that carries the connotation of educating the public and stirring public debate on current issues.

Also, everyone knows that informational sources are no longer scarce. There are hundreds of radio and television stations, not to mention online sources. The entire scarcity rationale for the Fairness Doctrine and the *Red Lion* decision is completely obsolete.

Fairness Doctrine Resurrected

But President Obama plans on bringing back a new form of Fairness Doctrine under new names. There are calls for "diversity," meaning something to compete against conservative radio. There are also talks about the need for "local control." What that means is that the FCC would issue regulations to create local boards (heavily dominated by inner-city "community leaders") that would be able to insist on content that reflects the "views" and "needs" of their communities.

This too is a weapon against talk radio, because many of the big conservative names are national in audience, and dozens more cover whole states or regions. Requiring "local control" would allow these left-wing groups to insist on half of the programming coming from their liberal perspective.

To implement all this, President Obama has appointed a "diversity czar," first mentioned in chapter 1. His name is Mark Lloyd, and officially, he is the FCC diversity officer.

You could write a whole book on Czar Lloyd; in fact, a great deal has already been written by the American Civil Rights Union's Peter Ferrara and the Media Research Center's Seton Motley.[17] Lloyd has also been covered by Fox's Glenn Beck. Rather than go on at length, just look at what this radical czar has to say about oppressive communist dictator Hugo Chavez of Venezuela—a perfect illustration of countless statements Lloyd has made:

In Venezuela, with Chavez, is really an incredible revolution—a democratic revolution. To begin to put in place things that are going to have an impact on the people of Venezuela.

The property owners and the folks who then controlled the media in Venezuela rebelled—worked, frankly, with folks here in the U.S. government—worked to oust him. But he came back with another revolution, and then Chavez began to take very seriously the media in his country.[18]

These statements are important when you consider that Chavez has shut down more than two hundred radio stations that aired content critical of his policies, passed legislation to financially destroy the rest, and seized control of other outlets.[19]

Mark Lloyd loves Hugo Chavez. And Barack Obama loves Mark Lloyd enough to put him in charge of our radio and TV stations. That should worry you.

If the Fairness Doctrine were brought back, stations would either have to go half-liberal (according to the government, surely meaning "mostly liberal" to be "fair"), or just dump their talk shows altogether and play music.

Either way, talk radio would be dead.

Solution: Save the First Amendment

It's pretty clear that Congress has no stomach to pass legislation enacting any form of Fairness Doctrine. But as we saw in chapter 3, Team Obama is big on using administrative regulations to do things that the Constitution only allows to be done through Congress.

So we have a two-part solution.

The first is that if any new regulations are passed, then they need to be challenged under the Administrative Procedure Act, which we also learned about earlier in this book. They could be challenged both on the grounds that the legal interpretation allowing Congress to muzzle talk radio is faulty, and also that the factual basis for such rationing and censorship is false, because there are countless media outlets, and thus, no scarcity.

Aside from that, the second solution is to sue on First Amendment grounds. The Fairness Doctrine violates the Free Speech Clause. As referenced above, the scarcity rationale the Supreme Court used in *Red Lion* is utterly obsolete. The current Court has five votes to overrule *Red Lion* and strike down any version of the Fairness Doctrine. We need to be ready to push for exactly that.

SILENCING DISSENT FROM PUBLIC OFFICIALS

The Obama blueprint even calls for silencing public officials who disagree with the president—and that's exactly what Team Obama and their supporters are doing.

You Can't Say That, Congressman!

A perfect example of this political censorship is what happened with Congressman John Carter (R-TX) over the summer of 2009. Opposing President Obama's plan for a government takeover of health care, Congressman Carter was sending a letter to his constituents, explaining the policy debate and where Carter stood on the issue as their representative.

Members of Congress (only the House, not the Senate) enjoy what's called the "franking privilege," whereby the U.S. Postal Service delivers letters from a congressman to his constituents without charge; no postage is required. Allowing congressmen to inform their constituents about important issues is seen as a service to the country.

This can only be used for policy purposes, not campaigns. A congressman cannot say, "Vote for me," or "Vote Republican." He also can't use it to ask for campaign contributions, or to tell his constituents, "Call Congressman Smith at 202-555-0000 and tell him to vote for my bill." But aside from those purely political purposes, the congressman can use his franking privilege to raise awareness about whatever issues he chooses to raise, and to describe them as he sees fit.

To separate campaign letters from bona fide legislative-policy letters, an entity called the Franking Commission reviews letters before they can be franked and sent out without postage.[20] This entity isn't supposed to interfere with the content beyond the low bar of ensuring that it's not campaign-type literature.

Now Democrats control it, and they've told Congressman Carter that he can't send his letter. Why? Did he ask for campaign money? Did he say, "Vote for me to stop the Obama agenda?" No, nothing like that.

He did two things. First, he calls the Obama plan "government-run health care." The Franking Commission insists that he call it the "public option," the Democrats' nice little euphemism for their socialist takeover of medicine. Second, he referred to this plan as the "Democratic" plan. The commission insists he refer to it as the "majority" plan.

This is the censoring of political speech. It is the majority abusing its power to shut down the political opposition.

A related example comes from a chart. Congressman Kevin Brady (R-TX) developed a flowchart showing the bureaucratic monster being pushed by Team Obama and the Pelosi-Reid Democrats to take over American health care. Some members of Congress wanted to use this chart as an illustration when sending letters to their constituents explaining why these congressmen opposed the Obama-Pelosi-Reid plan.

Once again, the Franking Commission said no.[21] This is an eye-opener, given that when Republicans made a similar flowchart when opposing Hillarycare, there was no objection to the franking privilege covering those mailings.

Unfortunately, there's no legal remedy here. First, there is no First Amendment protection. The Free Speech Clause only protects private persons, such as American citizens or private organizations. It doesn't protect government. And Congressman Carter is speaking as an elected official, not a private citizen.

Second, there is no constitutional entitlement to franking. Congress made a policy judgment that House members should be able to send information to their constituents free of charge. This is a narrow privilege limited to those serving in the House; senators have no franking privilege, nor do others in government. So these congressmen can't sue to force the franking.

This is just a gross power grab to keep people from learning the truth. It's transparency and openness, Obama-style.

Absolute Loyalty Demanded from Democrats

We should also note that not all of these threats are reserved for Republicans. Occasionally, Democrats who are foolish enough to think for themselves also get into trouble.

Take, for example, Representative Pete DeFazio (D-CA). DeFazio is one of those sincere and consistent liberals. He's unapologetically far-left, and is often as happy to sound the liberal trumpet against Democrats who fail to track on a far-left agenda as he is going after Republicans.

DeFazio has become an outspoken liberal critic of President Obama, usually for not taking an ultra-left stance to further damage national security or to go after corporate America with higher taxes and more regulation to ensure that we strangle these economic engines to death.

President Obama himself let DeFazio know in front of witnesses that disloyalty will not be tolerated. "Don't think we're not keeping score, brother," Obama menacingly warned at a closed-door meeting of the House Democratic Caucus.[22]

In other words, in President Obama's America, you can freely promote and be true to your beliefs . . . unless those beliefs don't agree with his beliefs, in which case you will be targeted for retribution if you don't betray your own beliefs to do as you're told.

That's tolerance in President Obama's world. He'll tolerate you so long as you slavishly obey, and don't dare voice any thoughts that are contrary to his.

The Fired Inspector General

Most people understand that government shouldn't be trusted. Even though most Americans know someone in government who they trust and respect, they have a healthy distrust for government institutions as a whole.

This clear-eyed perspective has been a hallmark of American democracy since the Founders. George Washington famously said of government: "[L]ike fire, it is a dangerous servant and a fearful master."[23] Our constitutional systems of separation of powers and checks and balances are designed to protect us as citizens from an overly powerful government.

This understanding of the nature of government also led us to create the post of inspector general for various government agencies. An inspector general (IG) is an official who acts as an ombudsman for the public and for congressional oversight. An IG holds his agency accountable and reports on problems or irregularities, and his role is "to more effectively combat fraud, abuse, waste and mismanagement" in the agency where he serves.[24] IGs are intended to keep government honest, avoiding egregious abuses by providing transparency and accountability.

These are official whistleblowers. Because their job requires them to call other government officials onto the carpet, including high-ranking political appointees, an IG needs to be protected from political retaliation. They can't do their job unless they don't need to worry about losing their job.

So Congress has passed laws over the years to protect IGs from political backlashes. The latest version is the Inspector General Reform Act of 2008.[25] This law requires that a president cannot remove an IG unless he notifies Congress thirty days before removal.[26] It also requires that Congress be given a full written explanation for the removal thirty days before removal.[27]

But then we have the case of Gerald Walpin, the inspector general for the Corporation for National and Community Service (CNCS), the federal agency overseeing AmeriCorps. Walpin was fired on June 10, 2009, after determining that AmeriCorps funds were misused by Kevin Johnson, the mayor of Sacramento, a good friend and political ally of President Obama. Senator Charles Grassley (R-IA) has sent a letter to CNCS, demanding all records on this matter and—interestingly—demanding to know what role First Lady Michelle Obama may have had in it.[28]

Walpin has now filed a federal lawsuit challenging his firing.[29] The suit alleges that there was no thirty-day notice, nor was any written explanation given to Congress. All the administration said is that Walpin seemed incoherent and not fully in command of his mental faculties. Since Walpin is both a talented lawyer and seventy-seven years old, he's decided to throw a separate age-discrimination count into the lawsuit as well. (Those comments are code for saying that Walpin is senile, which is absurd to anyone who spends any time speaking with this very intelligent, well-spoken, and sharp-witted attorney.) The suit is ongoing as this book goes to print.

Limited Solutions but Signs of Hope: Citizens United

Thankfully, however, everyone should take heart. We're already fighting back against attempts to take away our free speech.

On January 21, 2010, the U.S. Supreme Court handed down its decision in *Citizens United v. FEC*.[30] At issue was part of the Bipartisan Campaign Reform Act (BCRA), better known as McCain-Feingold, making it a federal felony—punishable by five years in prison—for a corporation to use any of its funds to criticize a candidate for federal office within thirty days of a primary election, or sixty days of a November general election.

The group Citizens United made a documentary about Hillary Clinton during the 2008 campaign that wasn't very flattering. The Federal Election Commission did not allow it to be distributed, and David Bossie, president of Citizens United, decided to fight back.

The case went to the Supreme Court. During argument, the Obama administration's lawyer, Solicitor General Elena Kagan, made wild claims about the extent to which government can censor its critics, outlawing books, movies, and other methods of informing the public. Her opponent, former Solicitor General Ted Olson, pushed back hard, pointing to the terrible power that this gives the government against private citizens.

The Supreme Court agreed that such power is frightening. In an opinion written by moderate Justice Anthony Kennedy, the Court noted that decades ago the Court upheld regulations on corporate speech, on the theory that corporations could amass vast sums of money to drown out ordinary citizens, distorting public debate.

The Court overruled that earlier case, *Austin v. Michigan Chamber of Commerce*, and also part of a 2003 case involving BCRA, *McConnell v. FEC*, finding the earlier cases' reasoning "unconvincing and insufficient" to justify government censorship of political speech. Instead, the Court noted that ordinary people often need to pool their money into an organization they support, to use those pooled funds to get their message out on issues they care about when elections are approaching. Rather than drown out the little guy, such an option allows groups, be they Citizens United, the National Rifle Association, the American Civil Rights Union, or the Family Research Council, to be a megaphone for the little guy, informing the voters of what's at stake.

The Court's opinion went on to note that the government's theory—that it should be able to censor an organization that speaks to the public simply because that organization is a corporation with the ability to accumulate money—would enable the government to go after the media. Every major press outlet is a corporation, and all have vast sums of money. The government's argument could be used to justify censorship of the press.[31] When that happens, the First Amendment dies.

The Left has long pushed for legislation to get government's foot in the door to censor the press. In *Citizens United* the Court quoted from Justice Clarence Thomas's dissenting opinion in the first challenge to McCain-Feingold, *McConnell v. FEC*, where Thomas reacted to the Court's upholding government power to silence any corporate entity by saying, "The chilling endpoint of the Court's reasoning is not difficult to foresee: outright regulation of the press."[32]

The Supreme Court that handed down *Citizens United* is the Court we have today. And we should press our case before this Court.

FAMILY MATTERS: SCHOOL CHOICE AND RELIGIOUS LIBERTY

Although there isn't space to go into detail, there are two other issues that need to be considered regarding this insidious part Obama's blueprint.

Sweet Child of Mine

The first issue is about controlling children's minds.

Often, if you can control what a child is taught when he's young, you can dictate much of what he will believe as an adult. The blueprint relies on this simple principle of childrearing.

For that reason, Team Obama seeks to push all children into public schools. This administration's policies are hostile to private schools, charter schools, and homeschooling. Look no further than Washington, D.C., itself, where President Obama destroyed the charter-school voucher program for D.C. children, a program that gets them out of failing schools, over the objections of even the liberal Democrat government in D.C. that begged—and protested—to keep that program alive.

But President Obama wants our children in his schools. He wants them in public schools, where public school unions have proven to be devoted disciples of his programs, sharing his vision of a monstrously massive central government, and teaching our children to think as they think. (You might have even seen the disturbing and chilling videos online of children singing religious-style hymns of praise to President Obama, even using phrases such as that children are "all equal in his sight," which is a line out of "Jesus Loves the Little Children.")

Team Obama wants schools that teach that biblical faith is ignorant, and that it's wrong to make judgments about sexuality. Schools that teach life choices are about what feels good and makes you happy, instead of doing what is right even when it's hard or painful. Schools that teach there's no such thing as right and wrong, only opinions. Schools that teach that individuals must sacrifice for "the common good," that capitalism is selfish and destructive, and that we're more enlightened today than the Founding Fathers, so we need to take their Constitution with a grain of salt. These would be schools that teach Barack Obama's version of history, of politics, of civics, of everything.

They want schools designed by President Obama's "safe schools" czar, Kevin Jennings, a radical and militant homosexual activist and author of *Queering Elementary Education*, who seeks to remake American education. Jennings's activism and professional neglect is well documented by groups such as the Family Research Council, including the idea that homosexuality should be taught to children as early as kindergarten.[33]

Parents have the right to keep children out of toxic learning environments, and to provide educations that reflect those parents' values. President Obama wants Kevin Jennings to educate your children instead.

These controls don't stop with elementary education. One huge item slipped into the Obamacare medical takeover law was a federal takeover of all student loans in this country. Although it has nothing to do with health care, the government will take over all federal loans to U.S. college students. Where such loans previously came from private banks, they'll now come directly from the federal government.

Part of the reason for skyrocketing tuition costs is the government floods the college market with extra money, so schools keep jacking up prices. Now President Obama will be in a position to say that he'll forgive one year of tuition loans per year of government service. He'll do this to funnel tens of millions of young people into goverment service, to condition them to support big government and possibly keep millions more people in lifetime government service. A "free" college education is never free.

You've Got to Have Faith

On no line of thought is Obama's takeover more dangerous than religious faith, which is the second issue.

President Obama seeks a militantly secular culture. In such a culture, government is the highest authority. There is no law higher than that which our imperial president gives us. The state defines right and wrong for us. That is why people of conservative faith—including devout Catholics and Mormons, but most especially Evangelical Christians—are shuttered out of any public event.

A perfect example is when Family Research Council President Tony Perkins was supposed to speak at a prayer breakfast at Andrews Air Force Base in early 2010. Perkins is a former U.S. Marine and a former police officer, and is now an Evangelical Christian minister. Along with millions of Americans and many of our servicemen, Perkins opposes the president's attempted repeal of don't-ask-don't-tell.

Simply for disagreeing with President Obama, Tony Perkins was disinvited from the prayer breakfast. The breakfast had nothing to do with the policy on gays; Perkins was going to speak and pray about faith, not any policy issue. And Perkins's beliefs come from his own personal Evangelical faith. Yet for disagreeing with President Obama, even from sincerely held religious beliefs, the government shut him out of a religious event on public land.

Instances like this are happening across the nation, from our increasingly secular schools to our increasingly secular public squares. Conservative religious faith, especially anything arising from the Holy Bible, is at odds with parts of the Obama blueprint, and so that blueprint calls for silencing such voices.

In the Bible, the Lord Jesus Christ says that "the truth shall set you free."[34] Truth would indeed free us from the prison that the Obama blueprint plans for us, and especially for our children. This prison would hold our children all their lives, along with the rest of us. A prison for our minds.

CONCLUSION:
A New Birth of Freedom

It is important . . . that the habits of thinking in a free country should inspire caution in those entrusted with its administration, to confine themselves within their respective spheres; avoiding in the exercise of the powers of one department to encroach upon another. The spirit of encroachment tends to consolidate the powers of all the departments in one, and thus to create, whatever the form of government, a real despotism.
—PRESIDENT GEORGE WASHINGTON,
FAREWELL ADDRESS, SEPTEMBER 17, 1796

It is rather for us to be here dedicated to the great task remaining before us . . . that this nation, under God, shall have a new birth of freedom; and the government of the people, for the people, by the people, shall not perish from the earth.
—PRESIDENT ABRAHAM LINCOLN,
GETTYSBERG ADDRESS, NOVEMBER 19, 1863

We've now shown you the blueprint that Barack Obama has developed to subvert the safeguards the U.S. Constitution provides for our liberty. In its place, Team Obama plans to establish a permanent liberal government led by an imperial president.

This blueprint calls us to action: We must inform our fellow citizens. We must force candidates for office in 2010 to address these issues, so that the next Congress is compelled to freeze the legislative parts of this blueprint. We need presidential candidates for the Republican Party to address these issues so that they can be committed to reversing and repealing all the parts of President Obama's blueprint that make it into law by 2013. We need to press lawsuits against the parts of this blueprint for which we have shown the courts to be the answer. And for the issues where the damage is permanent, we must know what was wrong with what happened to this country, and pledge to our children that we will not let it happen again.

But you can't fight something with nothing. In addition to the various solutions we've given throughout this book, the Republican Party needs a conservative resurgence to restore our Constitution and the Founding Fathers' vision of America.

And it must be the Republican Party. America is a two-party system, and has been for 150 years. The idea of a third party is sheer folly. The single greatest hope that Barack Obama has for winning a second term in 2012, or that Democrats have for continuing to hold the House and Senate in 2010 and 2012, is for a third party to arise on the right, pulling votes away from the Republicans by splitting the anti-liberal vote. We can count on Team Obama working hard to fuel a third party on the right in a cynical attempt to divide the opposition and hold on to all the levers of power to complete their subversion of the Constitution.

That Republican Party must be a conservative party. A moderate Republican Party will not fix the enormous challenges facing this country. Our challenges are very real, and are of epic proportions. The rise of a third party would derail the hopes of overcoming these problems, but so would a Republican Party that does not staunchly adhere to conservative principles.

Key Elements to Conservative Resurgence

As we mentioned in the introduction, more than a hundred conservative leaders, including both of your authors, signed the Mount Vernon Statement in February 2010, which makes the case that the three parts of the Reagan Coalition—economic conservatives, national security conservatives, and social conservatives—are all absolutely essential in order for America to live up to its constitutional principles, and for all Americans to enjoy the blessings of liberty and happiness to the fullest.

In order to mobilize and energize the Reagan Coalition in the twenty-first century, there are five elements necessary for a resurgence of conservatism in America. Each of these five may appeal to some Americans more than others, but all five are necessary if we are to halt construction on what Team Obama is trying to build and take America back. All five must be upheld by the Republican Party and its leadership and presidential candidate if the GOP is to lead America in recapturing our nation's constitutional promise.

Element 1: Jobs

America needs an economy in which jobs are created at a robust pace. Jobs are essential for people to be able to support themselves and their families, as well as to be able to help others. Jobs keep people from depending on the government for help. Unless you're a student, a homemaker, a retiree, a person with special needs, or independently wealthy, you can't be part of the solution unless you are doing your part by working at a job.

Everyone knows that America has lost a lot of jobs over the past couple of years, including over a million jobs lost under President Obama. But the reality is far worse than the 9.7 percent or so unemployment that we see on the television screen.

Those numbers are masked by three facts. First, hundreds of thousands of jobs that President Obama has "created" are government jobs. That means every single one of them is a burden on the taxpayer, not a source of economic wealth. Although certain government positions, such as the military or law enforcement, play a vital role in our country, we need to always remember that each of those jobs consumes scarce taxpayer resources, and so we must shrink the size of government, not expand it, and send many of those workers that do not serve a vital function back into the private sector.

Second, the unemployment rate does not take into account the underemployed rate. For millions of Americans, they've scrambled to find a job and managed to do so, but it's not the kind of job that they need. It's only a part-time job, or a job without the benefits that their family needs, or it's a job that only pays them half of what their education or experience should demand. It's forcing millions of Americans to settle for jobs suited to a teenager just starting out while in high school, or for a person without a developed skill set. In this environment, many experienced professionals have to take or keep low-level professional jobs, making it hard for new college graduates to get their first big job to get rid of student debt and start building their own financial security.

And third, the unemployment rate doesn't count discouraged workers. These are millions of people that haven't been able to find jobs, and have given up looking for one. Unfortunately, President Obama's expansion of the Nanny State has also removed much of the incentive for many of these people to find jobs, with some of them instead just adjusting their lifestyle to live for the foreseeable future off welfare and public assistance, which simply means additional burdens on businesses and taxpayers.

All these things considered, the "real" unemployment rate is around 16 percent, a disturbingly high number. The horrific debt that Barack Obama is piling on continues to keep that number high, just as threatened tax increases keep businesses from hiring.

We need to cut taxes, jettison countless regulations, shrink government, and give businesses incentives to be able to create real jobs in the private sector.

Element 2: Ownership Culture

Once people have money from a job, they need to be able to use it in a way that will put them in charge of the well-being of their family, instead of looking to the government or to the community.

We need an ownership society. Although that term is associated with President George W. Bush—who laid out a number of good principles for such a culture of ownership—it didn't start with him. It comes from conservative principles embraced by Ronald Reagan, but it didn't start with him either. Instead, the principles for owning the major assets needed for a self-sufficient lifestyle, caring for family, and planning for the future go to the very origins of America as a free country.

The American Revolution was largely fought over property rights. As we saw earlier in this book, in many European monarchies, only the king held permanent title to land. The colonists believed no one could be truly free without property ownership, especially owning your own home and other essentials of life. The idea of having rights regarding your own family, home, and personal possessions has always been at the heart of the American Dream.

America needs policies that embody that principle. People need to own their own retirement, health care, education, and capital assets, such as a house.

Element 3: God and Family

Life is about more than jobs and a roof over our heads, even if we all need those things to make it through life. America is not only a culture of ownership—it's a culture of faith.

America was founded as a nation of faith. It was first settled by Christians who sought a new land in which they could worship according to the dictates of their conscience, without government interference. With them they brought a passion for what is right, a recognition that there are transcendent truths and moral absolutes, and an acknowledgment that every human life is created by Almighty God, from whom we all receive our daily blessings and to whom every one of us will one day have to give an account.

From this religious foundation, a virtuous and courageous people descended. Moral instruction, based in biblical text, was a mainstay of American education until the mid-1900s. Families worshipped together, spent time growing together, and were taught that faith, hope, and love are greater blessings than anything that is rooted in the uncertain and fleeting nature of our temporal world.

How far we have fallen. This isn't romanticizing about early America as a blend of Norman Rockwell and Thomas Kinkade paintings, nor is it wistfully looking back on earlier times as the glory years. Life has always been hard, and it used to be harder in terms of material needs.

But we've lost something. We've become a militantly secular culture, where anything that hints at unseen realities or eternal truths is violently chased away. More than just a culture of the here and now, fixated on the latest bells and whistles, we've become a culture in which large segments openly scorn those who speak of spiritual things.

Having created a secular culture where each person is taught to look out for number one, and to follow the credo, "It's all about what makes me happy," many are shocked to find that popping pills doesn't make them smile every day, and that spending those days seeking self-satisfaction leaves them unfulfilled. As families have fallen apart, more and more people return home from a long, stressful day to an empty house or apartment.

The role of religious faith and traditional values lies at the very root of American success. The spiritual vacuum in parts of Europe and elsewhere on the globe has contributed to the listlessness, lack of productivity, and casual existentialism that renders them unable to stir themselves as a nation to face countless threats, from Islamic radicalism to sky-high unemployment to declining population rates.

These foreign examples stand in stark contrast to America as it's been since the time of the Founders. Yet it creeps along here in America, led by zealots who seek to purge every reference of faith from our culture. And it is pushed by others who seek to undermine the central role of the family in our nation's life, putting government in the place of parents.

If we fix our economic and entitlement programs but fail to address these problems of the role of God and family in our society, then we will not build a secure and flourishing society.

There are things that are true and right and beautiful that fill the human heart with inspiration, courage, and joy. They motivate us to sacrifice for our children and even for strangers. They compel us to fight for what we know to be right.

We've lost much of that in this country, and we need to get it back. America needs policies that do not penalize families or people of faith, and judges that respect and uphold our Founders' provisions on both of those issues. Rather than shove social conservatives to the back of the crowd, any durable conservative resurgence will embrace Americans with such values and priorities.

Element 4: Federalism
One key aspect of the genius of the American system is federalism. It provides three critical benefits for us in this country as part of the Constitution's design, and so must be a part of a conservative comeback.

The first is what we saw before from Justice Brandeis's famous statement—that the states are the laboratories of democracy. There are fifty states, all inhabited by Americans with a shared culture and shared history, and with all the interstate moving these days, each state has the benefit of perspective from people who previously lived in other states.

That sets up laboratories for democratic experiments. Taking populations of people with similar lives, similar educations, and similar skill sets, we can allow them to go to different states to see what works best. Granted, sometimes differences in geography, natural resources, or other variables would mean that what works best in one state doesn't work best in all states. But it allows for people to try all sorts of solutions at the state level to problems that we all face. If one state finds the best solution, then other states can adopt it.

The second benefit of federalism was alluded to under the first point, and that is allowing for local solutions. On many issues, one size does not fit all. Sometimes what works on a particular issue in Phoenix, Arizona, doesn't work in rural Indiana, and neither works in suburban Ohio. Federalism allows states to find local solutions that reflect the needs of that state, best utilizing the resources of that state. And it does so in a way that reflects that state's values and priorities. People are welcome to live in a state that best suits their tastes.

The third advantage of federalism is that it protects us all from a too-large federal government. Government is dangerous. The bigger it is, the more dangerous it is. Federalism empowers the smaller state governments to handle all the matters that the Constitution doesn't vest in the federal government. (This is aside from whatever rights are held by the people that neither federal nor state governments can take away.) By maximizing the sovereignty of the states, allowing the federal government to handle the matters that only the federal government is capable of handling (and authorized to handle), we minimize the harm that the federal government can do.

Element 5: Courts

The final aspect that must be part of a conservative resurgence should be no surprise to anyone who has read even part of this book. It's the federal courts.

The Republican Party cannot be a conservative party again unless the party leadership—and, most especially, whoever the GOP presidential nominee is in 2012—is dedicated to putting the right people on the federal bench, and is willing to spend whatever political capital is necessary to make that happen.

As we've seen time and time again, whether any given action of the federal government is held to be constitutional versus unconstitutional is determined by what the judges deciding the case believe about the Constitution.

A liberal judge has a broad view of federal power, and under that view tends to read almost everything government wants to do as being authorized by the Constitution (unless those government actions advance a conservative idea; in those cases, it's apparently okay to strike them down). More precisely, a liberal judicial philosophy means that the judge feels free to interpret the Constitution in light of "evolving standards of decency," or with "due respect for a modern understanding" of certain issues, or "in accordance with the needs of modern times."

A conservative judge believes that he or she has no such power to depart from the constitutional text. Even a moderate judicial philosophy is at least *textualist*—meaning that when the Constitution (or any law) is being interpreted, it must be interpreted according to the words found in the text.

But judicial conservatism goes even further, in that it is *originalist*. This means that each term in the Constitution should be interpreted according to the ordinary meaning that a reasonably educated and aware citizen would have given that term at the time it was adopted. According to the philosophy of originalism, the Article II Appointments Clause of the Constitution means what a public-minded and intelligent person on the street in 1789 thought it meant. It means that "establishment of religion" in the First Amendment or "the right to keep and bear arms" in the Second Amendment means what such a person in 1791 thought it meant, and the same goes for the Fourteenth Amendment, adopted in 1868.

Only originalism is an effective tool for combating judicial activism. It forces courts to consult original sources, including dictionaries and legal treatises, to interpret the Constitution. Sure, there's still plenty of mischief for people to try. But it forces the whole debate over meanings into such a confined area that it stops all sorts of outrageous attempts to essentially rewrite the Constitution from the bench.

This will be a real challenge in 2012, one where GOP primary voters need to make sure that this issue is central to what the nominee stands for in the next presidential cycle. We don't mean that voters need to force the nominee to talk about it in every speech; not at all. But the courts aren't just deciding social issues. As we saw throughout this book, the courts are also deciding the reach of federal power into our lives, deciding economic policy issues like cap and trade, and deciding national security issues such as interfering with how our military detains foreign terrorists on foreign soil.

The entire shape of the Constitution, and the role that it permits the federal government to have in our lives, will be determined by the Supreme Court. We need good justices on the Court. We can't return to constitutional conservatism without an originalist Court, and we can't have good, conservative government without a good Supreme Court.

Self-Government Depends on Governing Self

In one sense, what America got with Barack Obama is what we should have expected from such a young and inexperienced politician, who at the same time had such a far-left view of the Constitution and big government.

To repeat one point from the introduction: We live in a constitutional democratic republic. Much of what it takes for that form of government to function relies upon self-restraint by each of the three branches of government. Each of the branches is more than capable of stretching and abusing its power to the breaking point, where it warps our constitutional system of government.

We see this from time to time. When Congress tries to micromanage a war, it violates the Constitution's commitment of our military to the president, who alone is the commander in chief. When the president tries to make substantive public policy through rulemaking and regulations, he violates the Constitution's commitment of the lawmaking power to our Congress, which alone is our legislative body for federal matters. When the Supreme Court declares a right not found in the Constitution or ignores a right that is there, it usurps the power of We the People, which alone has the authority to amend the Constitution.

To take politics out of the equation, consider one example that has nothing to do with any current controversy in this country—at least, not at the time of this writing! The Constitution empowers only Congress with the authority to declare war, and also only Congress can create military units, pay them, or equip them. At the same time, only the president is commander in chief of the military. Only the president can order troops into battle or make strategic military decisions for the national security of the United States.

Either branch could go to the extreme in military matters. It's possible that the president could see a pressing need to send military power overseas to protect the country, but Congress could be so opposed that it votes to de-fund the military for such purposes. Without any fuel or bullets, the military couldn't move or fight. On the other hand, the president could order massive unprovoked air strikes on another country without Congress authorizing war, but now that America has engaged in a massive act of war against that country, we'd be thrust into war regardless.

So each branch of government understands it must act in a self-restrained manner with due respect for the coequal branches of government. It's accepted that the president has inherent authority as commander in chief to order military action on a certain level to deal with certain threats or immediate dangers without congressional approval. It's also accepted that launching military might on a massive scale, or attacking another nation where there is no imminent threat to American lives or our homeland, is an act of war that requires Congress to declare war through an authorization of military force.

At the core of President Obama's power grab to build an imperial presidency is his rejecting these constraints and refusing to restrain himself and his allies. He forces administrative action that can only properly be done by Congress. He proposes legislation that tramples the Constitution, and will use any legislative trick to cram it through. He seeks to pack the courts with judges who will rubber-stamp whatever he wants to do. He seeks to avoid accountability by changing how elections are done. He seeks to keep the American people from knowing the truth by muzzling the media and limiting the information that we're able to access. And in countless ways, he ignores the traditions and self-constraints that all three branches have developed over more than two centuries to keep our republic running.

Beware All Government

These concerns about government don't just apply to President Obama and his blueprint. All government must be watched carefully. Government is power, and all governments include people who think they are better qualified to run your life than you are. As one leading political philosopher of the twentieth century explained:

> *If we attend carefully to the psychology of the persons who manifest such an eagerness to serve us, we shall find that they are even more eager to control us. What one discovers, for example, under the altruistic professions of the leaders of a typical organization for humanitarian crusading . . . is a growing will to power and even an incipient terrorism. . . .*
>
> *On the pretext of social utility they are ready to deprive the individual of every last scrap and vestige of his freedom and finally to subject him to despotic outer control. No one, as Americans of the present day are only too well aware, is more reckless in his attacks on personal liberty than the apostle of "service." He is prone in his furtherance of his schemes of "uplift" not only to ascribe unlimited sovereignty to society as against the individual, but also to look on himself as endowed with a major portion of it, to develop a temper, in short, that is plainly tyrannical.*[1]

Great conservative leaders throughout American history have understood this truth. As Ronald Reagan famously said, "Government is not the solution to our problems. Government *is* the problem." The only thing different about Barack Obama's blueprint is that he takes this problem to a level never seen before in the United States.

Paradigm Shift

We need to mention one final concern inherent in this issue of limited government versus an overbearing government controlled by an imperial president, and that's the fork in the road that we as a country have encountered in terms of our national paradigm.

A paradigm is a worldview. That is to say, a paradigm is the prism through which we filter everything. It's the framework through which we understand the world in which we live.

The blueprint that President Obama and his allies are trying to force on all of us cannot last unless they change our paradigm. Much of what we've read about what they're trying to do right now is to force that change.

The blueprint calls on all of us to think of ourselves as parts of a collective, where we are all parts of a giant machine—where we make sacrifices for the "common good." These sacrifices include forfeiting our right to self-defense by giving up guns, because criminals can misuse guns. It includes forcing our children to go to public schools instead of redirecting our money to private or charter schools, or homeschooling, because the common good requires a robust public school system. It includes giving away vast amounts of our money in taxes to pay for cradle-to-grave entitlements in a Nanny State, because the good of society trumps property rights. It includes foregoing the best health care in order to provide everyone with "decent" health care through a nationwide government system, because the health of the population as a whole trumps the well-being of any one individual—even if that individual is your own child.

The blueprint requires Americans to think of rights as gifts from a benevolent government. It has us look to government as an all-wise, all-powerful, all-good provider for whom we work and to whom we owe our allegiance. The blueprint needs us to regard ourselves as the servant of the government.

The American paradigm is the exact opposite. We believe, as the Declaration of Independence proclaims, that each of us is created by Almighty God. We believe that our rights come from God— not from government—and that these rights cannot be justly taken away by any government. Government is our servant, not the other way around. Government exists to protect our rights and to perform such services as we command through the Constitution.

The American paradigm is also that we are a nation of individuals, not a collective. We designed a form of government to keep us free and independent, not safe and provided-for at the cost of losing our independence. We are free to govern our own lives, to think first of the well-being of our children, not a government system, and to chart our own course.

We look to God for our rights and for meaning in our lives, and we tolerate government—a *limited* government—as a necessary burden for those limited areas of life where only government can act.

We pledge allegiance to our republic, not to its government. As a sovereign people, we refuse to bow to our government. And as a sovereign nation, we refuse to bow to any world body or foreign nation.

Government is not God. We reject any paradigm that makes government our master, instead of servant, or that makes government the source of our rights, instead of existing to secure our God-given rights.

A Time for Choosing

We the People of the United States must choose whether we will allow our Constitution to be subverted. We need to choose whether President Obama's blueprint to reject and rewrite our Constitution will stand. We need to choose whether we will allow a permanent liberal government to emerge in this country, led by an imperial president of unprecedented power.

Such a blueprint cannot be implemented without subverting the Constitution. As one conservative icon said, "The administration has met the enemy, and it is the Founding Fathers of this country."[2] President Obama's blueprint is utterly at odds with the U.S. Constitution, which is the Supreme Law of the Land.

The stakes could not be higher, because once government takes something over, it's hard to take it back. Once you lose a right—any right—it's hard to reclaim it. Government tends to grow and consume, and the bigger it gets, the stronger it gets, and the harder it is to shrink it.

Often the only way to shrink government is to get to the point of such anger and frustration that you take an ax to the tree of big government and start hacking off limbs. Such actions always leave some people worse off in the short run, even though it leads to long-term benefits. The best course of action is to keep government from ever growing so large in the first place.

The federal government of the United States has become too big and too expensive. We are going bankrupt as a nation, and so radical change is needed in government spending and in our long-term entitlements. Our culture is under assault, and we need a robust revival of faith and family to rebuild our society from the ground up. We need more government issues to be handled by the states, not the federal government. We need people to keep the resources to make their own long-term decisions, to get government out of the Nanny State business, and to allow individuals and companies to suffer the consequences of selfish and irresponsible behavior. And we need courts that will interpret and uphold the Constitution of the United States as it is written.

We need these things because our continuing existence as a nation and a free people depends on it.

Although others have ended their books with a particular quote from Ronald Reagan, we will do so with two quotes, because they speak to what we need. President Reagan had such a profound grasp of the promise of America and just how precious a blessing liberty is. He had seen the Great Depression and served in World War II, and he was watching the 1960s when he said these words. As such, he could see the perils and the need for economic prosperity, national security, and a society built upon faith and strong families. Understanding that the course of a nation is shaped through who we give the powers of government to, President Ronald Reagan said:

You and I have a rendezvous with destiny. We will preserve for our children this, the last best hope of man on earth, or we will sentence them to take the last step into a thousand years of darkness.[3]

There was a reason that President Reagan made that statement. It was his understanding that formed the very foundation of conservative thought, and it was at the core of our Founding Fathers' beliefs about the very nature of government: It tends to expand on the backs of the people, consuming their resources and their rights, dominating ever more of their lives, unless the people constantly push back against it, to force it back into the narrow confines of the Constitution.

Aware of the danger of our own government, and the need for constant vigilance to protect our Constitution and our liberty, Reagan warned:

Freedom is never more than one generation from extinction. We didn't pass it on to our children in the bloodstream. It must be fought for, protected, and handed on for them to do the same, or one day we will spend our sunset years telling our children and our children's children what it was once like in the United States where men were free.[4]

APPENDIX: THE OBAMA BLUEPRINT

CZARS

What he's doing: President Obama is appointing dozens of czars—powerful executive officials reporting solely to him. They are not Senate-confirmed and are outside congressional oversight. Many of them are radicals, including avowed communists and socialists. These czars are strategically placed in critical positions of power to create a shadow government.

Is this constitutional? No. Under the Article II Appointments Clause, such powerful officials must be confirmed by the U.S. Senate.

The conservative response: For some of these czars, citizens who are directly impacted have legal standing to challenge the czars' constitutionality.

COURTS

What he's doing: President Obama is packing the courts with judges who share his far-left vision of the Constitution. He's also working to expand the lower courts to pack them with dozens of new judges, who would dominate the courts for a generation. Obama seeks a judiciary that will rubber-stamp his agenda as constitutional, and that will give him whatever he cannot get through the ballot box or Congress.

Is this constitutional? Yes. Congress can create additional judgeships whenever it wants, and the president has sole power to nominate all federal judges.

The conservative response: The proposed judgeship bill to expand the courts cannot be allowed to take effect until after the next presidential election. Beyond that, the only way to fix our nation's courts is to elect a president who is adamantly committed to appointing true originalists to the bench, and, most especially, to the Supreme Court.

UNCHECKED PRESIDENT
Executive Orders and Agency Actions

What he's doing: President Obama is seeking to enact sweeping changes in law through administrative rulemaking and executive orders.

Is this constitutional? No. Article I of the Constitution provides that only Congress can make laws, and administrative actions that are so broad they change public policy are instead considered lawmaking.

The conservative response: Conservatives need to flood the record with contrary evidence during the rulemaking process. Anyone at the receiving end of these executive actions can challenge them in court.

International Law

What he's doing: President Obama's blueprint calls for using foreign and international law to advance a policy agenda based on foreign values, instead of American culture and priorities.

Is this constitutional? Although the Constitution vests tremendous power in the president when it comes to foreign policy, President Obama cannot do through treaty or foreign law anything the Constitution does not allow to be done through legislation.

The conservative response: By retaking Congress, conservatives can undo by statute anything Obama does through a treaty or executive agreement—and any citizens injured by an unconstitutional treaty can sue in federal court.

Domestic Army

What he's doing: President Obama, his chief of staff, and the First Lady have all made bizarre statements about the president planning to create a civilian security force as large and well-funded as the U.S. military. This domestic army would answer to Obama alone.

Is this constitutional? Unsure, because no one knows any of the details of Obama's plan, but very likely unconstitutional.

The conservative response: We cannot do anything until we know more about what President Obama and his inner circle plan to do. Conservatives need to demand this information.

HEALTH CARE

What he's doing: President Obama seeks to take over the entire American health-care system.

Is this constitutional? Partly, no; key parts of Obamacare violate the Constitution, including the individual mandate and state-based insurance exchanges. Other parts are terrible policy but do not violate the Constitution, unless a court finds that the final passage vote does not meet constitutional requirements.

The conservative response: The parts of Obamacare that don't involve the Constitution can only be stopped by defeating the Obamacare bill, or preparing to repeal whatever passes. If the bill passes, then the unconstitutional parts could be defeated in court.

ECONOMY
Sovereign Fund

What he's doing: Through various bailouts, President Obama has converted the government stake in massive companies into voting shares of stock, taking over those companies and with it large parts of the U.S. economy.

Is this constitutional? Yes. These takeovers violate the American system of private property ownership and free enterprise, and they may violate federal laws, but the Constitution doesn't forbid every type of terrible policy.

The conservative response: Conservatives need to stop these bailouts and regain the levers of power to get the federal government out of the business of owning businesses.

Cap and Trade

What he's doing: President Obama is trying to push through a job-killing carbon emissions–control system to give the government enormous power over the entire economy. If he can't ram legislation through Congress, he may do it through executive action.

Is this constitutional? Yes. The Constitution doesn't forbid cap and trade, regardless of how harmful it is to the economy. Although constitutional, it would be illegal if President Obama does it through administrative action.

The conservative response: Conservatives must stop this legislation. If Obama enacts cap and trade through administrative rule-making, businesses should challenge it in court.

Stimulus

What he's doing: President Obama is using stimulus bills to spend money on liberal wish-list items. In doing so he's engaging in massive wealth redistribution by funneling over a trillion dollars from taxpayers and businesses to low-income individuals, and permanently growing government by creating countless new taxpayer-funded programs.

Is this constitutional? Yes. The Constitution does not stop redistribution of wealth.

The conservative response: There is no court remedy. The only conservative response is to elect truly conservative majorities to Congress, and retake the White House with a true fiscal conservative.

Taxes

What he's doing: President Obama is creating class warfare by shifting the tax burden to less than half of the population, so that a majority of the population has nothing to lose personally by supporting higher taxes. This tax code is then used to control and manipulate individual behavior.

Is this constitutional? Yes. The Constitution allows several types of taxation, including the income tax.

The conservative response: Conservatives must retake Congress and the White House to enact fundamental tax reform, creating a system that encourages business growth and does not penalize success.

ELECTIONS
Amnesty

What he's doing: President Obama's blueprint calls for granting American citizenship to every illegal alien in the United States, making them all voters with the expectation that they will vote for bigger government, paid for by higher taxes on others.

Is this constitutional? Yes. The Constitution allows Congress to make anyone a citizen.

The conservative response: Conservatives must stop this legislation. Unlike most legislative parts of Obama's blueprint, amnesty cannot be repealed. Granting citizenship is something that cannot be taken away.

Card Check

What he's doing: President Obama seeks to abolish secret ballots in businesses voting on whether to unionize. This system opens the door to massive intimidation to enormously increase the size of labor unions in America.

Is this constitutional? Maybe. This anti-business measure is constitutional if it's a bill. But if Obama tries to ram it through with administrative rulemaking, such regulations would be unconstitutional.

The conservative response: Republicans need to defeat this legislation. If card check is passed by executive action, then a court challenge is called for, and if such a challenge fails, then the legislation must be repealed and new elections held in recently unionized businesses.

Census

What he's doing: President Obama's blueprint calls for politicizing the census by using statistical sampling and politically charged vote counters to reallocate congressional seats, redraw legislative districts, and shift the number of Electoral College votes that each state has for president.

Is this constitutional? No. The Constitution requires an actual count of persons, and may even require the counting of citizens, not just persons.

The conservative response: Various lawsuits are required to keep the census honest and legal, and one of them is already under way.

D.C. Voting Rights Act

What he's doing: President Obama seeks to give the far-left city of Washington, D.C., a voting member of Congress and two U.S. senators.

Is this constitutional? No. The Constitution provides that congressmen are elected to represent only those Americans who live in states, and that only states also get two senators.

The conservative response: If this legislation passes, it must be defeated in court.

Voter Registration

What he's doing: President Obama's blueprint calls for nationwide same-day voter registration and "universal" registration of everyone on various welfare rolls, to open the door both to massive voter fraud and to skyrocket voter turnout among welfare recipients to vote for bigger government.

Is this constitutional? Yes.

The conservative response: This legislation must be defeated, because voting-rights legislation is difficult to fix afterward, regardless of how negative the results.

GUNS

What he's doing: President Obama's blueprint seeks to radically restrict gun ownership in the United States.

Is this constitutional? No. Most antigun actions that the blueprint calls for violate the Second Amendment right to keep and bear arms.

The conservative response: Gun owners must mobilize and vote for their rights. Beyond that, the Second Amendment is in a critical stage right now in the Supreme Court, making it a top priority to get a pro-gun president and pro-gun Senate to confirm judges and Supreme Court justices that faithfully uphold the Second Amendment.

INFORMATION
Co-opting the Media

What he's doing: President Obama is seeking to co-opt the media, both by planting friendly left-wing questioners in the press pool and also by launching a war on the only TV network that never toes the White House line—Fox News.

Is this constitutional? Yes. While the First Amendment guarantees free speech and a free press, government hostility must be severe before it violates the Constitution.

The conservative response: The media is rallying to protect itself, and conservatives must demand continued protection for the press and support outlets that provide the real news.

Talk Radio

What he's doing: President Obama's blueprint calls for destroying talk radio through new versions of the falsely named Fairness

Doctrine, passed either through legislation or administrative rule-making. The president has already launched a war against Rush Limbaugh.

Is this constitutional? No. The Fairness Doctrine was unconstitutional, and each variation being promoted now is a form of government censorship of the media, which violates the First Amendment.

The conservative response: If any form of the Fairness Doctrine is reenacted, the affected radio stations must fight it in federal court.

Silencing the Opposition

What he's doing: President Obama's administration and allies have been silencing public officials who oppose them in both the executive and legislative branches.

Is this constitutional? Yes. Such heavy-handed tactics do not violate the Constitution, although some executive-branch firings likely violate current federal law.

The conservative response: The muzzling efforts in Congress can only be fought by the Republicans retaking Congress, and executive-branch muzzling must be fought in court.

Education and Religion

What he's doing: President Obama is seeking to create a militantly secular society, in which the federal government controls every aspect of how our children are raised and what they are taught to believe.

Is this constitutional? No. The First Amendment protects people of faith and their religions from government interference, not the other way around. Parents have a fundamental right to make decisions regarding the upbringing of their children.

The conservative response: People of faith need to be more active as citizens and voters, and demand judges who are faithful in upholding the Constitution. We need a president, Congress, and judiciary that all welcome family rights and religious freedom.

NOTES

INTRODUCTION
Freedom in Crisis

1. Barack Obama, interview with editorial board of *San Francisco Chronicle,* January 17, 2008, in Sara Goss, "Obama Said He Would Bankrupt the Coal Industry," American Thinker, February 27, 2008, http://www.americanthinker.com/blog/2009/02/obama_said _he_would_bankrupt_t.html.

2. Barack Obama, Campaign speech in Roseburg, Oregon, May 17, 2008, in AFP, "Obama: 'We can't . . . eat as much as we want,' " *Free Republic,* May 18, 2009, http://www.freerepublic.com/focus/f-news/2017697 /posts.

3. Barack Obama, Transcript of town hall meeting in Johnstown, Pennsylvania, March 29, 2008, in David Brody, "Obama Says He Doesn't Want His Daughters Punished with a Baby," *The Brody File,* CBN.com, March 31, 2008, http://blogs.cbn.com/thebrodyfile/archive/2008/03/31/obama-says-he-doesnt-want-his-daughters-punished-with-a.aspx.

4. Interview of Barack Obama by Gretchen Helfrich on WBEZ Radio (Chicago), January 18, 2001, in "Obama Lamented Lack of 'Redistributive Change' in American Wealth," CNSNews.com, October 28, 2008, http://www.cnsnews.com/Public/Content/Article.aspx? rsrcid=38247. This interview is dealt with in more detail in chapter 2.

5. Charles Hurt, "Obama Fires a 'Robin Hood' Warning Shot," *New York Post,* October 16, 2008 (quoting Steven Joseph Wurzelbacher), http://www.nypost.com/seven/10152008/news/politics/obama_fires_a_robin_hood_warning_shot_133685.htm.

6. *Ibid.* (quoting Barack Obama).

7. *See* "General Election: McCain vs. Obama," RealClearPolitics, http://www.realclearpolitics.com/epolls/2008/president/us/general_election_mccain_vs_obama-225.html.

8. Chad Pergram and AP, contr., "Congress Passes $787B Stimulus Bill, Sends It to Obama for Signature," Fox News, February 14, 2009, http://www.foxnews.com/politics/2009/02/13/congress-readies-final-vote-b-stimulus/.

9. AP, "Biden Says 'Everyone Guessed Wrong' on Unemployment Numbers," Fox News , June 14, 2008, http://www.foxnews.com/politics/2009/06/14/biden-says-guessed-wrong-unemployment-numbers/.

10. 42 U.S.C. § 1395dd (2006).

11. Overview of EMTALA, Centers for Medicare and Medicaid Services, U.S. Department of Health and Human Services, http://www.cms.hhs.gov/emtala/.

12. *See* Barack Obama, Prime Time Press Conference on Health Care, July 22, 2009, http://www.realclearpolitics.com/articles/2009/07/22/obama_press_conference_health_care_transcript_97586.html.

13. Benjamin Franklin, "The Electronic Ben Franklin," Independence Hall Association, http://www.ushistory.org/franklin/quotable/quote71.htm.

14. Ken Klukowski, "Conservatives Come Together at Mount Vernon," *Fox Forum,* Fox News, February 18, 2010, http://www.foxnews.com/opinion/2010/02/18/ken-klukowski-mount-vernon-statement-conservatives-right-obama-pelosi/.

15. U.S. Const. art. I, § 8, cl. 18 (the Necessary and Proper Clause).

16. U.S. Const. amend. X.

17. *See Black's Law Dictionary*, 8th ed., s.v. "police power."

18. *Gonzales v. Oregon*, 546 U.S. 243, 270 (2006).

19. *McCulloch v. Maryland*, 17 U.S. (4 Wheat.) 316, 405 (1819).

20. *Hamilton v. Kentucky Distilleries & Warehouse Co.*, 251 U.S. 146, 156 (1919).

21. *Marbury v. Madison*, 5 U.S. (1 Cranch) 137, 177 (1803).

22. Ken Blackwell and Ken Klukowski, "Obamanomics," *Townhall*, November 3, 2008 (citing Barack Obama's 2001 interview on WBEZ radio in Chicago), http://townhall.com/columnists/KenBlackwell/2008/11/03/obamanomics?page=full&comments=true.

CHAPTER 1
All the President's Men: The Czars

1. Wikipedia, "Office of National Drug Control Policy," http://en.wikipedia.org/wiki/Office_of_National_Drug_Control_Policy.

2. *See* Office of National Drug Control Policy, http://www.whitehousedrugpolicy.gov/.

3. Pub. L. No. 108–458, 118 Stat. 3638.

4. "Former AID Atlanta Director Sandra Thurman Named Clinton's 'AIDS Czar,' " The Body, April 9, 1997, http://www.thebody.com/content/art32995.html.

5. U.S. Department of the Treasury, Organization, Treasury Officials, Herbert M. Allison, Jr., http://www.ustreas.gov/organization/bios/allison-e.html.

6. *Ibid.*

7. FCC, Office of General Counsel, Mark Lloyd, http://www.fcc.gov/ogc/lloyd.html.

8. Pub. L. No. 79–404, 60 Stat. 237 (1946), 5 U.S.C. § 551–559 (2006).

9. This power comes from the Appointments Clause. U.S. Const. art. II, § 2, cl. 2.

10. *Buckley v. Valeo*, 424 U.S. 1, 124–136 (1976).

11. *Morrison v. Olson*, 487 U.S. 654, 670–677 (1988).

12. *See* Nia-Malika Henderson, "President Obama Announces Another Czar, Ron Bloom," *Politico,* September 8, 2009, http://www.politico.com/news/stories/0909/26824.html.

13. Scott Ott, "Obama Forces GM Chief Out, Puts Reid, Pelosi on Leave," *Washington Examiner,* March 30, 2009, http://www.washingtonexaminer.com/opinion/columns/scottott/Obama-forces-GM-chief-out-puts-Reid-Pelosi-on-leave-42164352.html.

14. *See, e.g.,* Tom Granahan, "Pay Czar Feinberg Caps More Bank Salaries," Fox Business, December 11, 2009, reproduced at http://m.foxbusiness.com/quickPage.html?page=19453&content=28132555&pageNum=-1.

15. U.S. Const. art. II, § 2, cl. 2.

16. Letter from Robert Byrd to Barack Obama, quoted in "Byrd Questions Obama Administration on Role of White House 'Czar' Positions," Press Release from Office of Robert C. Byrd, February 25, 2009, http://byrd.senate.gov/2009_02_25_pr.pdf.

17. *Ibid.*

18. Chris Woodyard, "Ralph Nader Blasts Obama Automotive Task Force in Defense of Chrysler and its Dealers," *USA Today,* May 18, 2009, http://content.usatoday.com/communities/driveon/post/2009/05/66942327/1.

19. Joseph Abrams, "Obama's Science Czar Considered Forced Abortions, Sterilization as Population Growth Solutions," Fox News, July 21, 2009, http://www.foxnews.com/politics/2009/07/21/obamas-science-czar-considered-forced-abortions-sterilization-population-growth/.

20. Drew Zahn, "Obama Science Czar Holdren Called for Forced Abortions," *WorldNet-Daily,* July 11, 2009, http://www.wnd.com/?pageId=103707.

21. *See Congressional Record,* March 19, 2009, S3577–S3578.

22. Office of Management and Budget, "About OIRA," The White House, http://www.whitehouse.gov/omb/inforeg_administrator/.

23. Executive Order 12866.

24. John Van Ness, "Cass Sunstein Animal Rights Views: Should Activists Stop Him from Joining Obama Administration?" Examiner.com, September 9, 2009, http://www.examiner.com/x-2320-Baltimore-Hunting-and-Fishing-Examiner~y2009m9d9-Cass-Sunstein-animal-rights-views-Should-activists-stop-him-from-joining-Obama-administration.

25. Americans for Limited Government, Nominee Alert [Cass Sunstein], July 2009 (citing Cass R. Sunstein, *Radicals in Robes,* Basic Books, 2005), http://www.getliberty.org/files/NomineeAlert%20-%20Cass%20Sunstein%20-%20OIRA%20Administrator%20-%20OMB%2007_06_09.pdf.

26. Cass R. Sunstein, "Lives, Life-Years and Willingness to Pay," 104 *Columbia Law Review* 205 (2004).

27. Matt Cover, "Obama Regulation Czar Advocated Removing People's Organs Without Explicit Consent," CNS News, September 4, 2009, http://www.cnsnews.com/news/article/53534.

28. U.S. Senate, Roll Call Votes, PN323 [Cass Sunstein], http://www.senate.gov:80/legislative/LIS/roll_call_lists/roll_call_vote_cfm.cfm?congress=111&session=1&vote=00274.

29. Sam Theodosopoulos, "Fox News Notes Communist Past of the 'Green Jobs' Czar," NewsBusters, July 10, 2009, http://newsbusters.org/blogs/sam-theodosopoulos/2009/07/10/fox-news-notes-communist-past-green-jobs-czar.

30. *Ibid.*

31. Video of Van Jones, "Van Jones, in His Own Words," *The Glenn Beck Program*, Fox News, September 1, 2009, http://www.foxnews.com/story/0,2933,545360,00.html.

32. *Ibid.*, http://glennbeck.blogs.foxnews.com/2009/09/01/van-jones-in-his-own-words/.

33. Audio of Van Jones, "Even More Crazy Czar Audio," *The Glenn Beck Program*, Fox News, September 3, 2009, http://www.glennbeck.com/content/articles/article/198/30090/.

34. Glenn Beck, "Is Van Jones a 9/11 Truther?," *The Glenn Beck Program*, Fox News, September 4, 2009, http://www.foxnews.com/story/0,2933,546681,00.html.

35. Video of Valerie Jarrett, "Valerie Jarrett on Green Jobs Czar Van Jones," YouTube, http://www.youtube.com/watch?v=Ud_yNFnfrSI.

36. Ken Klukowski, "Our President Is Not Protecting Us," *Fox Forum*, Fox News, January 5, 2010, http://www.foxnews.com/opinion/2010/01/05/ken-klukowski-obama-christmas-terror-attack/.

37. *Ibid.*

38. Tony Romm, "Brennan: I Let Him Down," *The Hill*, January 7, 2010, http://thehill.com/blogs/blog-briefing-room/news/74861-brennan-i-let-him-down.

39. Jonathan Weisman and Siobhan Gorman, "Obama Orders Security Fix," *Wall Street Journal*, January 8, 2010, http://online.wsj.com/article/SB126287015166119561.html.

40. *See* NBC News, Transcript of John Brennan on *Meet the Press*, February 7, 2010, http://thepage.time.com/transcript-brennan-on-meet-the-press/.

41. *See* Transcript of Lindsey Graham, Interview with Chris Wallace, *Fox News Sunday*, February 14, 2010.

42. *See ibid.*

Chapter 2
Packing the Courts

1. Ronald Reagan's appointments during his second term were William Rehnquist (as chief justice) and Antonin Scalia in 1986, and Anthony Kennedy in 1987. Before Reagan, this many vacancies in one term hadn't happened since Richard Nixon. Nixon's appointments were Warren Burger (as chief justice) in 1969, Harry Blackmun in 1970, and Lewis Powell and William Rehnquist (as associate justices), both in 1971.

2. Abraham Lincoln had five appointments, William Howard Taft had five, Warren Harding had four, Franklin Roosevelt had five, and Richard Nixon had four.

3. David Lat, "Supreme Court Clerk Watch: More OT 2010 Hires," Above the Law, December 23, 2009, http://abovethelaw.com/2009/12/scotus_clerk_hiring_watch.php.

4. *See* "Biography of Oliver Wendell Holmes," Arlington National Cemetery, http://www.arlingtoncemetery.org/historical_information/oliver_wendell_holmes.html.

5. U.S. Const. art. II, § 2, cl. 2.

6. U.S. Const. art. III. §1, cl. 2.

7. U.S. Const. art. I, § 2, cl. 5 (Impeachment Clause); U.S. Const. art. I. § 3, cl. 6 (Impeachment Trial Clause).

8. Federal Judicial Center, "Impeachments of Federal Judges," Federal Judicial History, http://www.fjc.gov/history/home.nsf/page/topics_ji_bdy. It should also be noted, ironically, that as this book is being written, the U.S. House is considering the impeachment of Judge Thomas Porteous Jr., who would become the fifteenth judge ever to be impeached by the House, and then stand trial in the Senate. Congressional Desk, "House Judiciary Task Force on Judicial Impeachment of Judge Thomas Porteous Jr.," *American Chronicle,* February 5, 2010, http://www.americanchronicle.com/articles/view/140301.

9. Federal Judicial Center, *supra* note 8.

10. John G. Roberts, Jr., "2009 Year-End Report on the Federal Judiciary," *Supreme Court of the United States,* December 31, 2009, http://www.scotusblog.com/wp/wp-content/uploads/2009/12/Roberts-2009-report.pdf; *see also Caperton v. Massey Coal Co.*, 129 S. Ct. 2252, 2279 (2009) (Roberts, C.J., dissenting).

11. To be fair, we should explain that when a judge gives up his seat, it's often not for retirement. We mention "senior status" a couple of times in this chapter. Once a judge reaches the age of sixty-five, he can take what's called "senior status" after his age plus his years of service equals at least 80. 28 U.S.C. § 371(c) (2006). A senior judge is a part-time judge, usually with one-third to one-half of a regular judge's workload. There are dozens of senior judges that continue to sit on cases, especially appellate cases. So when a judge gives up his seat, giving the president a vacancy to fill, it doesn't always mean that the judge is completely out of the picture.

12. While all of the circuit courts are important, there is something of an unofficial hierarchy in that some circuits are considered more important than others. As noted in the text, the D.C. Circuit is considered the most important, followed by the Fourth Circuit. Aside from those, the Second Circuit, Sixth Circuit, and Ninth Circuit are usually considered the faster-paced and more consequential circuits.

13. Remarks of Mitch McConnell, Transcript, *State of the Union with John King,* CNN, http://www.washingtontimes.com/news/2008/nov/03/stark-differences-in-judicial-nominees-gain-little/. Invoking cloture is a motion to limit debate time on whatever is being considered on the Senate floor. A cloture motion requires sixty votes to pass. If it passes, then additional debate on the issue is limited to thirty hours, after which a vote for final passage occurs.

14. "Judicial Conference of the United States," U.S. Courts, http://www.uscourts.gov/ judconf.html.

15. *See* Judicial Improvements Act of 1990, Pub. L. No. 101–650, 104 Stat. 5089.

16. *See* Federal Judgeship Act of 2008, 110th Cong., 2nd Sess., S. Rep. No. 110–427, March 13, 2008, http://thomas.loc.gov/cgi-bin/query/D?c110:2:./temp/~c1103pcD58::.

17. *Ibid.*

18. U.S. Const. art. III, § 1. The Constitution literally says that judges hold their offices "during good behavior," but this has been understood since the Constitution was first adopted in 1789 that unless a judge commits a crime serious enough to warrant impeachment and removal from office by Congress, that the judge holds a lifetime tenure.

19. *Ibid.*

20. *See Carter v. Carter Coal Co.*, 298 U.S. 238, 299 (1936); *Railroad Retirement Board v. Alton Railroad Co.*, 295 U.S. 330, 368 (1935); *A. L. A. Schechter Poultry Corp. v. United States*, 295 U.S. 495, 548 (1935).

21. *See Youngstown Sheet & Tube Co. v. Sawyer* (*Steel Seizure Case*), 343 U.S. 579, 585–589 (1952).

22. It's important to note that the doctrine that the Constitution allowed for segregating people on the basis of race so long as the segregated facilities or services were of equal quality (which they never were) was itself created by an earlier Supreme Court case, the infamous *Plessy v. Ferguson*, 163 U.S. 537 (1896).

23. *Brown v. Board of Education*, 347 U.S. 483, 495, 497 (1954).

24. *Roe v. Wade*, 410 U.S. 113, 129 (1973).

25. *Massachusetts v. EPA*, 549 U.S. 497 (2007).

26. *Boumediene v. Bush*, 128 S. Ct. 2229, 2262, 2275 (2008).

27. Ken Klukowski, "Why Obama Was Wrong to Slap the Supremes," *Fox Forum*, FoxNews.com, January 29, 2010, http://www.foxnews.com/opinion/2010/01/29/ ken-klukowski-supreme-court-obama-alito/.

28. We say "her" because the leading names being considered to replace Stevens at the time of this writing are almost all women.

29. January 2006 is when Samuel Alito was confirmed as the successor to Sandra Day O'Connor. Whereas O'Connor was a moderate, Alito is a conservative, so the Court took a step to the right with Alito's appointment; nonetheless, it is still a moderate Court, with neither liberals nor conservatives having five votes.

30. U.S. Const. art. III, § 2, cl. 1.

31. The two words "case" and "controversy" are essentially interchangeable. We draw fine distinctions in the law on them, but they both involve a lawsuit being filed in a federal court, briefed and argued by the parties, and decided by a judgment. And all the rules of law that apply to one apply to the other as well. The only distinction is entirely theoretical, so you can think of them as the same thing.

32. *Clinton v. Jones*, 520 U.S. 681, 700 (1997); *Mistretta v. United States*, 488 U.S. 361, 385 (1989).

33. What that means is that the Constitution doesn't directly confer jurisdiction on specific matters to the courts. Instead, it creates zones where Congress is authorized to enact statutes that convey that jurisdiction. The Constitution creates the potential for jurisdiction; Congress doesn't use that potential to its furthest limits. For example, Article III allows for federal courts to have jurisdiction to hear lawsuits between citizens of two different states. But the federal statute on that issue, 28 U.S.C. § 1332, says that the parties must be from different states and the amount in controversy must exceed $75,000. So if you have someone from Indiana who wants to sue someone in Ohio for $50,000, the Constitution would allow it, but the federal courts still wouldn't have jurisdiction because there's no statute that allows it until the amount passes $75,000.

34. *Valley Forge Christian College v. Americans United* 454 U.S. 464, 471–472 (1982) (quoting in part *Flast v. Cohen*, 392 U.S. 83, 97) (1968)) (internal quotation marks omitted) ("The judicial power of the United States . . . is not an unconditioned authority to determine the constitutionality of legislative or executive acts. [It is limited] to those disputes which confine federal courts to a role consistent with a system of separated powers and which are traditionally thought capable of resolution through the judicial process.").

35. *United States v. Morrison*, 529 U.S. 598, 607 (2000); *United States v. Lopez*, 514 U.S. 549, 568, 577–578 (1995).

36. The U.S. Supreme Court is often referred to by the name of the chief justice presiding at that time. For example, from the years of 1987 to 2005, we had the Rehnquist Court, because William H. Rehnquist was chief justice of the United States during those years. We have been in the Roberts Court since 2005, under Chief Justice John G. Roberts, Jr. The Warren Court was from 1953 to 1969, under Earl Warren.

37. Interview of Barack Obama by Gretchen Helfrich on WBEZ Radio (Chicago), January 18, 2001, in "Obama Lamented Lack of 'Redistributive Change' in American Wealth," CNSNews.com, October 28, 2008, http:// www.cnsnews.com/Public/ Content/Article.aspx?rsrcid=38247.

38. *Ibid.*

39. *E.g., Carter v. Carter Coal Co.*, 298 U.S. 238, 299 (1936); *Railroad Retirement Board v. Alton Railroad Co.*, 295 U.S. 330, 368 (1935); *A. L. A. Schechter Poultry Corp. v. United States*, 295 U.S. 495, 548 (1935).

40. The Court was originally six justices, and at one point was even larger than it is now.

41. This change in attitude toward President Roosevelt's economic legislation became known as "the switch in time that saved nine," meaning that two members of the Court switched their views of congressional power to allow the feds to take a much larger role in running the country's affairs, and that this switch saved those nine justices from becoming a Supreme Court of fifteen instead of nine. But again this seems to be a myth, because the American voters' opposition to this power grab had already put the court-packing legislation on the road to oblivion. The Court could have held its ground and won.

42. Pat Leahy, quoted in UPI, "Reagan Gets Near-Win; He's Close to Near-Loss," *Ellensburg Daily Record*, August 18, 1986, page 6, http://news.google.com/newsp apers?nid=860&dat=19860818&id=HCgQAAAAIBAJ&sjid=bY8DAAAAIBAJ &pg=5291,3615514.

43. President Reagan had four vacancies, but only added three people to the Court. He appointed Sandra Day O'Connor to replace Potter Stewart in 1981. He then elevated Associate Justice William Rehnquist to chief justice when Warren Burger retired from that office in 1986, and appointed Antonin Scalia to take the associate justice seat that Rehnquist vacated to become chief. Then, in 1987, Robert Bork was nominated to replace the retiring Lewis Powell.

44. Senate Democrat Strategy Memos, http://www.cfif.org/htdocs/legislative_issues/ federal_issues/hot_issues_in_congress/confirmation_watch/judiciary_memos.pdf, at "P. 15" in upper-right corner (emphasis added). *See also* "Democrat Memogate: The Beginning of a Political Scandal," Center for Individual Freedom, http://www.cfif .org/htdocs/freedomline/current/in_our_opinion/democrat_memogate.htm

45. Roberts had a phenomenal résumé: He was a top graduate of Harvard Law School, where he was an editor of the *Harvard Law Review*. (He also got his undergrad from Harvard.) He then clerked for the well-respected Judge Henry Friendly on the Second Circuit (who was himself considered Supreme Court–caliber), and then Justice William Rehnquist on the Supreme Court (when Rehnquist was an associate justice, before he became chief justice). Roberts then served as an advisor to the U.S. attorney general, then as an associate White House counsel to Ronald Reagan, then went on to private practice. He later returned during the Bush 41 years, serving as chief deputy solicitor general, arguing on behalf of the United States before the Supreme Court. He was originally slated for a federal judgeship by Bush 41, but when Bill Clinton was elected president those plans were scuttled, and Roberts went on to become a top lawyer at the major law firm, Hogan & Hartson. When Bush 43 became president, the Democrats blocked Roberts for two years, but when Republicans retook the Senate in 2002 Bush re-nominated Roberts to the U.S. Court of Appeals for the D.C. Circuit, and Roberts was confirmed in 2003. This was a picture-perfect résumé for a Supreme Court nominee.

46. Alito's résumé was almost as impressive as Roberts. He received his undergrad from Princeton, and then earned his J.D. at Yale Law School, where he was an editor of the *Yale Law Journal*. He clerked for Judge Leonard Garth on the Third Circuit, then served as a federal prosecutor in New Jersey. He then went on to serve as an assistant solicitor general in the Reagan Justice Department, and then became the deputy assistant attorney general of the elite Office of Legal Counsel at the Justice Department when Ed Meese was attorney general. Reagan appointed Alito as the U.S. attorney for New Jersey in 1987, and then Bush 41 appointed Alito to the U.S. Court of Appeals for the Third Circuit in 1990. He served as a judge on the Third Circuit until his Supreme Court confirmation on January 31, 2006.

47. Remarks of Barack Obama on confirmation of John Roberts, http://obamaspeeches .com/031-Confirmation-of-Judge-John-Roberts-Obama-Speech.htm.

48. Stephen Dinan, "Differences in Judicial Nominees Gain Little Notice," *Washington Times*, November 3, 2008, http://www.washingtontimes.com/news/2008/nov/03/ stark-differences-in-judicial-nominees-gain-little/.

CHAPTER 3
The Unchecked President

1. U.S. Const. art. II, § 1, cl. 1. This provision, called the Vestiture Clause, is what empowers the president to exercise the executive power of the federal government.

2. U.S. Const. art. I, § 1, cl 1. It should be noted that this clause is a little different from its counterparts, because it begins, "All legislative powers herein granted." The others refer simply to "executive power" or "judicial power." The Constitution could have just conferred all "legislative power," but instead the Framers of the Constitution chose to only confer whatever legislative powers are "herein granted." Without getting too much into the legal weeds, just know that some scholars note this could mean that some legislative power is denied to Congress, and in fact denied to the federal government altogether. It's beyond the scope of this book to explore what that means, but suffice it to say that it was yet another example of our Founding Fathers making sure that they did everything possible to limit the powers of government. If they were passionate about limiting the power of a large and diverse group of leaders elected by states and congressional districts, just imagine how much more concerned they would be about such power being held by one single man.

3. U.S. Const. art. III, § 1, cl. 1.

4. *Marbury v. Madison*, 5 U.S. (1 Cranch) 137, 177 (1803).

5. U.S. Const. art. VI, cl. 2.

6. Case law is also called "decisional law," but we've never met a non-lawyer who uses that term.

7. So, for example, a decision of the U.S. District Court for the Southern District of Ohio may be the law in southern Ohio, but a decision of the U.S. Court of Appeals for the Sixth Circuit, which includes not only Ohio but also Michigan, Kentucky, and Tennessee, becomes the law for all of those states. The Supreme Court, of course, has jurisdiction over the entire country.

8. For example, if the Seventh Circuit appeals court decides a case involving the Second Amendment right to keep and bear arms, then that decision is the authoritative meaning of the Second Amendment in Illinois, Wisconsin, and Indiana, which are the three states in the Seventh Circuit.

9. The U.S. Supreme Court has jurisdiction over the entire country and is the highest court in the land, so it can never be reversed. If the Court is interpreting a federal statute or regulation, then that decision can be overcome by Congress passing a new statute. But when the Court decides a constitutional question, Congress can do nothing to change it. Only the Supreme Court can change Supreme Court case law when it overrules its own precedent, which it only rarely does.

10. U.S. Const. art. II, § 3.

11. Ronald A. Cass, Colin S. Diver, and Jack M. Beerman, *Administrative Law: Cases and Materials* (5th ed., 2006), New York: Aspen, p. 3 (quoting Act of July 31, 1789, 1 Stat. 36).

12. For example, Abraham Lincoln created the Department of Agriculture, although it was not a Cabinet-level agency. And Woodrow Wilson created the Department of

Labor as a Cabinet agency, and elevated the Agriculture Department to Cabinet status while he was at it.

13. Career civil servants that were not political appointees and could not be fired when a new president took over were created by the Pendleton Civil Service Reform Act of 1883, 22 Stat. 203.

14. *FTC v. Ruberoid Co.*, 343 U.S. 470, 487 (1952) (Jackson, J., dissenting).

15. Administrative Procedure Act of 1946 (APA), 60 Stat. 237, codified as amended at 5 U.S.C. §§ 551 *et seq.* (2006).

16. *National Petroleum Refiners Association v. FTC*, 482 F.2d 672 (D.C. Cir. 1973), *cert. denied*, 415 U.S. 951 (1974).

17. "Cap and trade" is a shorthand phrase referring to legislation to curb carbon emissions in this country, on the increasingly discredited notion that the earth is getting warmer and such emissions are responsible for this increase in temperatures (more in chapter 5).

18. *See* Molly Henneberg, "EPA's Endangerment Finding Inflames Climate Change Bill," Politics, Fox News, February 17, 2010, http://www.foxnews.com/politics/2010/02/17/epa-endangerment-finding-inflames-climate-change-debate/ . To be completely fair, we must note that the first round of regulating carbon came from the Bush administration. *See* U.S. Environmental Protection Agency, Advance Notice of Proposed Rulemaking: Regulating Greenhouse Gas Emissions under the Clean Air Act, EPA-HQ-OAR-2008-0318, July 11, 2008, http://www.epa.gov/climatechange/anpr.html. But as wrong as that was, it's important to realize that this move was compelled by a liberal Supreme Court decision in *Massachusetts v. EPA*, 549 U.S. 497 (2007), which we discuss more in chapter 5.

19. To be completely accurate, we need to mention two things: First of all, these senior government officials that head up departments and other agencies are—as we saw in chapter 1—what the Constitution calls *principal officers*, and so they are actually nominated by the president, and then must be confirmed by the U.S. Senate. *See* U.S. Const. art. II, § 3. Second, although Cabinet-level agencies are all headed by officials that serve at the pleasure of the president and thus can be removed at any time (and so are almost always replaced when a new president takes office), in some of the entrenched boards, commissions, and other agencies in the government, the top officials serve for a certain number of years, and can only be removed for good cause before their term expires. Thus, many of these people hang on long after a new president takes office.

20. U.S. Const. art. I, § 8, cl. 1.

21. U.S. Const. art. I, § 7, cl. 1.

22. Congressional Review Act of 1996, 5 U.S.C. §§ 801–808 (2006).

23. U.S. Const. art. I, § 1, cl. 1.

24. *Field v. Clark*, 143 U.S. 649, 692 (1892) ("That Congress cannot delegate legislative power . . . is a principle universally recognized as vital to the integrity and maintenance of the system of government ordained by the Constitution.").

25. *Cf. The Brig Aurora*, 11 U.S. (7 Cranch) 382 (1813).

26. *Hampton & Co. v. United States*, 276 U.S. 394, 409 (1928).

27. *Panama Refining Co. v. Ryan*, 293 U.S. 388, 430 (1935).

28. *A.L.A. Schechter Poultry Corp. v. United States*, 295 U.S. 495 (1935).

29. *Chevron U.S.A., Inc. v. NRDC*, 467 U.S. 837 (1984).

30. *Citizens to Preserve Overton Park v. Volpe*, 401 U.S. 402 (1971).

31. This standard only applies in the context of formal rulemaking (where APA §§ 556 and 557 are involved), which is rarely the case because formal rulemaking is a painstaking process and so informal rulemaking is normally used instead. But the substantial-evidence standard is still a legal standard that can be applied in the right context.

32. John Winthrop, "A Model of [Christian] Charity," from *Winthrop Papers* 1623–1630 (Boston: Massachusetts Historical Society, 1931), vol. II, p. 295, excerpted in William J. Federer, ed., *America's God and Country Encyclopedia of Quotations* (St. Louis: AmeriSearch, 1990), p. 700.

33. Ronald W. Reagan, Farewell Address to the Nation, Oval Office, January 11, 1989.

34. James Kirchick, "Squanderer in Chief," *Los Angeles Times*, April 28, 2009, http://articles.latimes.com/2009/apr/28/opinion/oe-kirchick28.

35. *United States v. Curtiss-Wright*, 299 U.S. 304, 319 (1936) (quoting Annals of Cong., 6th Cong., col. 613, March 7, 1800 (remarks of John Marshall)).

36. *Made in the U.S.A. Foundation v. United States*, 56 F. Supp. 2d 1226 (N.D. Ala. 1999) (quoting *Head Money Cases*, 112 U.S. 580, 599 (1884)), *aff'd on other grounds*, 242 F.3d 1300 (11th Cir. 2001).

37. *Dames & Moore v. Regan*, 453 U.S. 654 (1981); *United States v. Pink*, 315 U.S. 203 (1942).

38. Alister Bull, "U.S. to Push for New Economic World Order at G20," Reuters, September 21, 2009, http://www.reuters.com/article/topNews/idUSTRE58G34Z20090921?sp=true.

39. The American Non-Governmental Organizations Coalition for the International Criminal Court, "Status of the U.S. Signature of the Rome Statute of the International Criminal Court," http://www.amicc.org/docs/US_Signature.pdf.

40. *Ibid.*

41. *Ibid.*

42. *Whitney v. Robertson*, 124 U.S. 190, 194 (1888).

43. *Reid v. Covert*, 354 U.S. 1, 18 (1957).

44. *Medellin v. Texas*, 552 U.S. 491 (2008).

45. *Goldwater v. Carter*, 444 U.S. 997 (1979).

46. Rahm Emanuel, "After Words," C-Span2, August 21, 2006, *The Glenn Beck Program*, Fox News, July 28, 2009.

47. U.S. Const. amend. XIII. The Thirteenth Amendment, which was passed after the Civil War to outlaw slavery, specifically prohibits "involuntary servitude" except as a punishment for a criminal conviction. The Supreme Court subsequently explained

that the Thirteenth Amendment outlaws the "badges and incidents" of slavery. *The Civil Rights Cases*, 109 U.S. 3 (1883). The Constitution allows that the nation can institute a military draft when our national security requires it. But compelling people to give a time of service to the state as civilians, not military and not for national security, looks like it would violate the Thirteenth Amendment.

48. Michelle Obama, Speech at UCLA, February 18, 2008.

49. *Ibid.*, in *The Glenn Beck Program*, Fox News, July 28, 2009.

50. Barack Obama, Video of Speech at Heartland Democratic Presidential Forum, You-Tube, Beltway Blips, December 1, 2007, http://beltwayblips.dailyradar.com/video/obama_caught_saying_acorn_and_friends_will_shape_his/.

51. Community Reinvestment Act of 1977, Pub. L. No. 95–128, 91 Stat. 147, codified at 12 U.S.C. §§ 2901 *et seq.*

52. Most of the material on the Apollo Alliance here was best summarized in an interview. Interview of Phil Kerpen by Glenn Beck, *The Glenn Beck Program*, Fox News, July 28, 2009.

53. "Oaths of Enlistment and Oaths of Office," U.S. Army Center of Military History, http://www.history.army.mil/faq/oaths.htm.

54. Posse Comitatus Act of 1878, 20 Stat. L., 145, codified at 18 U.S.C. § 1385 (2006); *see also* 10 U.S.C. § 375 (2006).

Chapter 4
Health Care

1. One of the changes to the legislation that Team Obama may make to help push the bill through is to remove the criminal penalties. If they make that change, it won't affect our main point at all. The federal government can't force you to buy insurance, whether or not there's a criminal penalty attached to refusing to buy it.

2. Orrin G. Hatch, J. Kenneth Blackwell, and Kenneth A. Klukowski, "Why the Health-Care Bills are Unconstitutional," *Wall Street Journal*, January 2, 2010, http://online.wsj.com/article/SB10001424052748703278604574624021919432770.html.

3. Ken Klukowski, "Health Insurance Isn't Car Insurance, Mr. President," *Washington Examiner*, December 17, 2009, http://www.washingtonexaminer.com/opinion/columns/OpEd-Contributor/Health-insurance-isnt-car-insurance-Mr-President--79575592.html; Ken Klukowski, Open Letter to Nancy Pelosi and Robert Gibbs, *Fox Forum,* Fox News, October 30, 2009, http://www.foxnews.com/opinion/2009/10/30/ken-klukowski-open-letter-pelosi-gibbs-constitution-individual-mandate/; Ken Klukowski, "Individual Mandate Insurance is Unconstitutional," *Politico,* October 20, 2009, http://www.politico.com/news/stories/1009/28463.html.

4. Interview with Barack Obama, Jake Tapper, ABC News, November 9, 2009, http://blogs.abcnews.com/politicalpunch/2009/11/interview-with-the-president-jail-time-for-those-without-health-care-insurance.html.

5. *See* Klukowski, *Washington Examiner, supra* note 3.

6. To be fair, we must note that the federal government could require car insurance for drivers within the District of Columbia, since under the District Clause of the Constitution, Congress has complete legislative authority over the roughly seventy square miles that make up the nation's capital city. *See* U.S. Const. art. I, § 8, cl. 17. Thus, Congress can exercise police power in D.C. itself because it acts as a state government would. Congress has delegated most of these matters by a federal statute called the Home Rule Act to the D.C. City Council, Pub. L. No. 93–198, 87 Stat. 774 (1973).

7. *Saenz v. Roe*, 526 U.S. 489, 500–502 (1999); *Kent v. Dulles*, 357 U.S. 116, 125 (1958); *Crandall v. Nevada*, 73 U.S. (6 Wall.) 35, 44 (1868).

8. *See Reitz v. Mealey*, 314 U.S. 33, 36 (1941) ("The universal practice is to register ownership of automobiles and to license their drivers. Any appropriate means adopted by the states to insure competence and care on the part of its licensees and to protect others using the highway is consonant with due process."). We know that there are others out there who make contrary comments on this point. The reality is that the U.S. Supreme Court has said there is no federal right to use a car without a license, and the state courts of every state have held that it's within the states' police power to require licenses and registration to use an automobile. So that is the current state of the law, regardless of what other authorities may have said in earlier times.

9. U.S. Const. art. I, § 8, cl. 3.

10. *Carter v. Carter Coal Co.*, 298 U.S. 238, 299 (1936). The Court had also struck down two other New Deal laws the previous years because they exceeded the limits of Congress's power under the Commerce Clause. *See Railroad Retirement Board v. Alton Railroad Co.*, 295 U.S. 330, 368 (1935); *A. L. A. Schechter Poultry Corp. v. United States*, 295 U.S. 495, 548 (1935).

11. *Wickard v. Filburn*, 317 U.S. 111 (1942). This was not itself a change in course for the Court. Democrat Franklin D. Roosevelt had finally appointed enough Supreme Court justices that shared his big-government philosophy, and the Court was concerned enough about FDR's court-packing scheme (explained in chapter 3) that 1937 was the year of the immense leftward shift in the Supreme Court's jurisprudence governing the Constitution's limits on the scope of power of the federal government. Among the cases that heralded this tectonic shift in the Supreme Court that year was a Commerce Clause case in which the law was upheld under an expansive view of Congress's power to regulate interstate commerce. *See National Labor Relations Board v. Jones & Laughlin Steel Corp.*, 301 U.S. 1, 31 (1937). But although *Jones & Laughlin* signaled this profound expansion of Congress's power under the Commerce Clause, which was also then seen in *United States v. Darby*, 312 U.S. 100, 118 (1941) (upholding the Fair Labor Standards Act), it was not until *Wickard* that the country saw the extreme lengths to which this newfound power could be extended.

12. *Wickard*, 317 U.S. at 114.

13. *Id.* at 125.

14. *Heart of Atlanta Motel v. United States*, 379 U.S. 241, 252–253, 255–258 (1964).

15. *Katzenbach v. McClung*, 379 U.S. 294, 299–301 (1964).

16. *United States v. Morrison*, 529 U.S. 598, 627 (2000) (Thomas, J., concurring).

17. *United States v. Lopez*, 514 U.S. 549, 567–568 (1995).

18. *Id.* at 567.

19. *United States v. Morrison*, 529 U.S. 598, 602 (2000).

20. *See id.* at 617–618.

21. *Lopez*, 514 U.S. at 564.

22. U.S. Const. art. I, § 8, cl. 1.

23. See *Steward Machine Co. v. Collector of Internal Revenue*, 301 U.S. 548, 581–582 (1937) (quoting *Pollock v. Farmers' Loan & Trust Co.*, 158 U.S. 601, 622, 625 (1895)).

24. U.S. Const. art. I, § 8, cl. 1.

25. U.S. Const. art. I, § 9, cl. 4.

26. U.S. Const. amend. XVI.

27. *Pollock v. Farmers' Loan & Trust Co.*, 157 U.S. 429 (1895).

28. *Id.* at 558.

29. *Id.*

30. *License Tax Cases*, 72 U.S. (5 Wall.) 462, 471 (1866).

31. *Pollock*, 157 U.S. at 583.

32. U.S. Const. art. I, § 8, cl. 1. (The General Welfare Clause is a specific phrase in the broader Taxing and Spending Clause.)

33. Matt Cover, "Hoyer Says Constitution's 'General Welfare' Clause Empowers Congress to Order Americans to Buy Health Insurance," CNSNews, October 21, 2009, http://www.cnsnews.com/news/article/55851.

34. U.S. Const. art. I, § 8, cl. 1.

35. *United States v. Butler*, 297 U.S. 1, 64 (1936) (quoting Joseph Story, *Commentaries on the Constitution of the United States*, 5th ed., vol. 1, § 907)).

36. *E.g.*, Rick Klein, "The $100 Million Health Care Vote?," *The Note*, ABC News, November 19, 2009, http://blogs.abcnews.com/thenote/2009/11/the-100-million-health-care-vote.html.

37. Gail Russell Chaddock, "Healthcare's dealbreakers: Mary Landrieu likes her $300 million," *Christian Science Monitor*, November 24, 2009, http://www.csmonitor.com/USA/Politics/2009/1124/healthcares-dealbreakers-mary-landrieu-likes-her-300-million.

38. Jonathan Karl, "The $100 Million Health Care Vote," *The Note*, ABC News, November 19, 2009, http://blogs.abcnews.com/thenote/2009/11/the-100-million-health-care-vote.html.

39. Greg Hitt and Janet Adamy, "Sen. Nelson Holds Up Health Bill," *Wall Street Journal*, December 19, 2009, http://online.wsj.com/article/SB126108229914495975.html.

40. Trish Turner and AP, contr., "Nelson Accused of Selling Vote on Health Bill for Nebraska Pay-Off," Fox News, December 20, 2009, http://www.foxnews.com/politics/2009/12/20/nelson-accused-selling-vote-health-nebraska-pay/.

41. Susan Davis, with Doug Belkin and Janet Adamy, contrs., "Heat Rises on Nebraska's Nelson," *Wall Street Journal*, January 2, 2010, http://online.wsj.com/article/SB126239070215313011.html.

42. *Butler*, 297 U.S. at 64–68; *see also Helvering v. Davis*, 301 U.S. 619, 640 (1937).

43. *United States v. Lopez*, 514 U.S. 549, 568–583 (1995).

44. *Gonzales v. Raich*, 545 U.S. 1 (2005).

45. *Steward Machine Co. v. Collector of Internal Revenue*, 301 U.S. 548, 581 (1937).

46. *Id.* at 578–583.

47. U.S. Const. amend. X.

48. *National League of Cities v. Usery*, 426 U.S. 833, 852–855 (1976).

49. *Id.* at 842.

50. *Garcia v. San Antonio Transit Authority*, 469 U.S. 528, 547 (1985).

51. *New York v. United States*, 505 U.S. 144, 162 (1992) (citing *Coyle v. Smith*, 221 U.S. 559, 565 (1911)).

52. *Printz v. United States*, 521 U.S. 898, 933 (1997).

53. It's somewhat ironic that this problem exists. This provision was in the Senate version of the bill, while the House version contained a national insurance exchange run directly by the federal government. The thing is that the White House revealed on February 22, 2010, that the Senate version of this provision is the one in Barack Obama's version of the bill, which the White House is beginning the big push for as this book is being edited. Had the White House gone with the House version it could have avoided this problem. The irony is that the House version is a much more severe government takeover, with a heavy-handed statist dynamic to it, yet even though it would have been worse from a policy standpoint, it might not have been subject to a constitutional challenge on Tenth Amendment grounds.

54. Study by RTI International (Health Affairs, July 2009), in AP, "Nearly 10% of Health Spending Due to Obesity, Report Says," *Wall Street Journal*, July 27, 2009, http://online.wsj.com/article/SB12486934021 7883455.html.

55. Interview with Greta Van Susteren, *On the Record*, Fox News, July 23, 2009.

CHAPTER 5
"We're All Socialists Now": The Economy

1. *See* Socialist Party USA: America's Vote for Democratic Socialism, http://www.sp-usa.org/.

2. Jean-Claude Trichet, interview in *Le Monde* [The World] (French newspaper), September 21, 2009, in Alister Bull, "U.S. to Push for New Economic World Order

at G20," Reuters, September 21, 2009, http://www.reuters .com/article/topNews/idUSTRE58G34Z20090921?sp=true.

3. Smoot-Hawley Tariff Act of 1930, Pub. L. No. 71–361.

4. *See* Milton Friedman and Anna Jacobson Schwartz, *A Monetary History of the United States 1867–1960* (New Jersey: Princeton University Press, 1971).

5. Remarks of Ben Bernanke, Federal Reserve Board, November 8, 2002.

6. *See generally* Burt Folsom, *New Deal or Raw Deal: How FDR's Economic Legacy Has Damaged America* (New York: Simon and Schuster, 2008).

7. Revenue Act of 1932, 47 Stat. 169.

8. Mike Allen and Josh Gerstein, "GM CEO Resigns at Obama's Behest," *Politico,* March 30, 2009, http://www.politico.com/news/stories/0309/20625.html.

9. Reuters, "GM Global Sales Fall 22 pct in first half of 2009," CNNMoney.com, July 22, 2009.

10. *See* Hugh Son, "AIG Posts Loss Tied to Rescue, Reserves; Shares Fall," Bloomberg, February 26, 2010, http://www.bloomberg.com/apps/news?pid=20601087&sid=aOZm4lKzImYE.

11. Alan Rappeport, Tom Braithwaite, and David Oakley, "Goldman Role in Greek Crisis Probed," *Financial Times*, February 25, 2010, http://www.ft.com/cms/s/0/ca979904-2216-11df-98dd-00144feab49a.html.

12. Community Reinvestment Act of 1977, Pub. L. No. 95–128, 91 Stat. 147, codified at 12 U.S.C. §§ 2901 *et seq.*

13. Review & Outlook, "Barney the Underwriter," *Wall Street Journal,* June 25, 2009, http://online.wsj.com/article/SB124580784452945093.html.

14. Jeff Jacoby, "Frank's Fingerprints are All Over the Financial Fiasco," *Boston Globe*, September 28, 2008, http://www.boston.com/bostonglobe/editorial_opinion/oped/articles/2008/09/28/franks_fingerprints_are_all_over_the_financial_fiasco/.

15. Dawn Kopecki, "Fannie Seeks $15.3 Billion in U.S. Aid After 10th Straight Loss," Bloomberg, February 26, 2010, http://www.bloomberg.com/apps/news?pid=20601087&sid=alet_UTqF04M.

16. Dawn Kopecki, "Obama May Prohibit Home-Loan Foreclosures without HAMP Review," Bloomberg, February 25, 2010, http://www.bloomberg.com/apps/news?pid=20601087&sid=ahuuwBS8KYq8.

17. *See Indiana State Police Pension Trust v. Chrysler LLC*, 129 S. Ct. 2275 (2009).

18. Ian Talley, "U.S. Court Orders Records Unsealed in Cap-And-Trade Fraud Case," Dow Jones Newswires, December 24, 2009, http://www.nasdaq.com/aspx/stock-market-news-story.aspx?storyid=200912171847dowjonesdjonline000636&title=us-court-orders-records-unsealed-in-cap-and-trade-fraud-case.

19. *Ibid.*

20. Margot Wallstrom (former environmental minister of the European Union), Speech in 2000, *The Glenn Beck Program*, Fox News, July 13, 2009.

21. Fox News, "Obama: Climate Change an 'Irreversible Catastrophe' If Not Addressed," Politics, Fox News, September 23, 2009, http://www.foxnews.com/politics/2009/09/22/obama-climate-change-irreversible-catastrophe-addressed/.

22. Barack Obama, Address to the United Nations, September 23, 2009.

23. *Ibid.*

24. Jacques Chirac, Speech at The Hague, November 20, 2000.

25. Harry Dunphy, AP, "Head of IMF Proposes New Reserve Currency," ABC News, February 26, 2010, http://abcnews.go.com/Business/wireStory?id=9958995.

26. Gregory Viscusi, "French Constitutional Court Rejects Carbon Tax (Update1)," Bloomberg, December 30, 2009, http://www.bloomberg.com/apps/news?pid=2060 1092&sid=aY9Dhj8qZZZE.

27. If you remember back to chapter 3, there's a strong argument to be made that agencies shouldn't be making public policy decisions at all, because that amounts to lawmaking, which only Congress can do.

28. President Bush spent $152 billion in the Economic Stimulus Act of 2008. Adam Levine, contr., "Bush Sings Stimulus Bill; Rebate Checks Expected in May," CNN, February 13, 2008, http://www.cnn.com/2008/POLITICS/02/13/bush.stimulus/.

29. Sandra Fabry, "Happy Birthday, 'Stimulus'!? One Year by the Numbers," Americans for Tax Reform, February 18, 2010, http://www.atr.org/happy-birthday-stimulus-one-numbers-a4546.

30. Jeff Poor, "FNC's Kelly: What Happened to Eased Unemployment Promised with Obama Stimulus?," Business and Media Institute, May 26, 2009, http://www.businessandmedia.org/articles/2009/20090526101952.aspx.

31. Video of Christina Romer, ABC News, in RealClearPolitics, October 22, 2009, http://www.realclearpolitics.com/video/2009/10/22/romer_stimulus_will_contribute_little_to_growth_in_2010.html.

32. Fabry, *supra* note 29.

33. Andrew Roth, "100 Stimulus Projects," Club for Growth, June 16, 2009, http://www.clubforgrowth.org/perm/?postID=11082.

34. *Ibid.*

35. *E.g.*, Renee Williams, "$700 Million in Stimulus Money Running Out," ABC News 4, January 10, 2010, http://www.wciv.com/news/stories/0110/694642.html; "Stimulus Money for Education Running Out," WCVB TV 5 Boston, http://www.theboston channel.com/news/21765224/detail.html.

36. U.S. Const. art. I, § 8, cl. 12.

37. *Helvering v. Davis*, 301 U.S. 619, 640 (1937); *United States v. Butler*, 297 U.S. 1, 64 (1936).

38. *Helvering*, 301 U.S. at 640.

39. James Rosen, "Obama Administration Steers Lucrative No-Bid Contract for Afghan Work to Dem Donor," Fox News, January 25, 2010, http://www.foxnews.com/

politics/2010/01/25/obama-administration-steers-lucrative-bid-contract-afghan-work-dem-donor/.

40. "The 2008 Scorecard—House," Club for Growth, http://www.clubforgrowth.org/projects/?subSec=13&id=642.

41. *See* "NTU Rates Congress, 111th Congress, First Session (2009)," National Taxpayers Union, http://www.ntu.org/on-capitol-hill/ntu-rates-congress/p10-02-18-ntu-rating-final-pages.pdf.

CHAPTER 6
Barack the Vote: Elections

1. "More Immigrants Take to Streets to Protest Proposed Laws," Politics, Fox News, April 11, 2006, http://www.foxnews.com/story/0,2933,191142,00.html.

2. Steven A. Camarota and Karen Jensenius, "Trends in Immigrant and Native Employment," Center for Immigration Studies, May 2009, http://www.cis.org/FirstQuarter-2009Unemployment.

3. "Justice Dept. Figures on Incarcerated Illegals," NewsMax.com, March 27, 2006, http://archive.newsmax.com/archives/ic/2006/3/27/114208.shtml. *See also* Center for Immigration Studies, Panel Discussion: Immigration and Crime, November 2009, http://www.cis.org/Transcripts/ImmigrationAndCrimePanel.

4. *Ibid.* (quoting Steven Camarota of the Center for Immigration Studies regarding report from Urban Institute).

5. *See, e.g.*, U.S. Immigrations and Customs Enforcement, News Release, "15 Illegal Aliens Allegedly Used Fake Documents to Gain Work at Stewart Airport," December 17, 2009, http://www.ice.gov/pi/nr/0912/091217newburgh.htm.

6. *See* Roxana Hegeman (AP), "Illegal Immigrants Turn to Identity Theft," MSNBC, January 8, 2008, http://www.msnbc.msn.com/id/22562690/.

7. Center for Immigration Studies, cited in *The Glenn Beck Program*, Fox News, October 9, 2009.

8. *INS v. Chadha*, 462 U.S. 919, 940 (1983) (citing U.S. Const. art. I, § 8, cl. 4.).

9. We have to say "almost certain" here. There has never been a case that we know of where someone was granted American citizenship under whatever law was in effect at the time and then had that citizenship rescinded by a later change in the law. It's possible in theory. The Constitution specifies that anyone born on U.S. soil is a U.S. citizen, and so Congress can never pass a law stripping citizenship from natural-born citizens. But the Constitution doesn't explicitly say that changes in naturalization law cannot be made retroactive. However, citizenship is a sacred status in the American system, conveying all sorts of special rights and benefits to those who are blessed with the privilege of being called Americans. So it is very unlikely that the courts would uphold and enforce any law stripping recently minted citizens of their citizenship. It is far more likely the courts would hold that once a person has become a U.S. citizen under our laws, citizenship status *cannot* be taken away.

10. Immigration Reform and Control Act of 1986 (Simpson-Mazzoli), Pub. L. No. 99-603, 100 Stat. 3359.

11. James Walsh, "Immigration Reform: What Will the New Year Bring?," Newsmax.com, November 23, 2009, http://newsmax.com/JamesWalsh/immigration reform/2009/11/23/id/336384.

12. One of the best examinations we found of EFCA, which is also endorsed by the Club for Growth; see Andrew Roth, "All You Need to Know About Card Check," Club for Growth, March 10, 2009, http://www.clubforgrowth.org/perm/?postID=10554 (done from the Heritage Foundation). *See* http://www.heritage.org/Research/Labor/bg2175. cfm; http://www.heritage.org/Research/Labor/wm2334.cfm. An abbreviated version is found here: http://blog.heritage.org/2009/03/10/employee-no-choice-act-increasing-the-feds-role-again/. We cite some of the statistics and findings of this report through this section of chapter 6.

13. National Labor Relations Act of 1935 (aka, Wagner Act), Pub. L. No. 93–360, 88 Stat. 395.

14. Richard M. Eberling, "Obama Thanks His Friends: Government Spending and Union Support," American Institute for Economic Research, June 8, 2009, http://www.aier.org/research/briefs/1550-obama-thanks-his-friends-government-spending-and-union-support.

15. U.S. Department of Labor, Economic News Release, "Union Members Summary," Bureau of Labor Statistics, January 22, 2010, http://www.bls.gov/news.release/union2.nr0.htm.

16. *Ibid.*

17. Video of Andy Stern, "We Love You Too, Van Jones," *The Glenn Beck Program*, Fox News, March 1, 2010, http://www.foxnews.com/story/0,2933,587705,00.html (emphasis added).

18. Review & Outlook, "Andy Stern's Go-To Guy," *Wall Street Journal*, May 14, 2009, http://online.wsj.com/article/SB124226652880418035.html.

19. Don Loos, "Obama NLRB Nominee Craig Becker's Smoking Gun?," Big Government, February 9, 2010, http://biggovernment.com/dloos/2010/02/09/obama-nlrb-nominee-craig-beckers-smoking-gun/.

20. "Andy Stern's Go-To Guy," *supra* note 18.

21. U.S. Const. art. I, § 2, cl. 3.

22. 13 U.S.C. § 141(a).

23. *Id.* § 141(b).

24. 2 U.S.C. § 2a(a).

25. *Id.* § 2a(b).

26. Act of Mar. 1, 1790, § 1.

27. *Id.* § 6.

28. Act of March 26, 1810, § 1, 2 Stat. 565–566.

29. U.S. Const. art. I, § 2, cl. 3.

30. U.S. Const. amend. XIV, § 2.

31. Memorandum for the Solicitor General from Assistant Attorney General Dellinger, p. 1. (October 7, 1994).

32. *Dept. of Commerce v. U.S. House of Representatives*, 525 U.S. 316, 334 (1999) (citing 13 U.S.C. § 195).

33. *Id.* at 343 (quoting *Spector Motor Service v. McLaughlin*, 323 U.S. 101, 105 (1944)).

34. *Id.* at 316.

35. *See* 13 U.S.C. § 195.

36. *Karcher v. Daggett*, 462 U.S. 725, 738 (1983).

37. *Dept. of Commerce*, 525 U.S. at 316, 341 (1999).

38. U.S. Const. art. II, § 1, cl. 2.

39. *Dept. of Commerce*, 525 U.S. at 348–349 (1999) (Scalia, J., concurring in part).

40. *Id.* at 348.

41. *Utah v. Evans*, 536 U.S. 452, 464 (2002) (Thomas, J., concurring in part and dissenting in part) (quoting 31 Writings of George Washington 329 (J. Fitzpatrick ed. 1931); 8 Writings of Thomas Jefferson 229)).

42. 13 U.S.C. § 141(a), (g).

43. *Lepak v. City of Irving*, No. 3:10-cv-00277-P, (N.D. Tex. filed February 11, 2010).

44. *See* Hans A. von Spakovsky, "Left's Pernicious Redistricting Strategy," The Corner, *National Review*, February 17, 2010, reproduced by Townhall.com, http://liberalslie .blogtownhall.com/2010/02/17/lefts_pernicious_redistricting_strategy.thtml; Hans A. von Spakovsky, "Re: One Person, One Vote," The Corner, *National Review*, February 19, 2010, http://corner.nationalreview.com/post/?q=ZTg0YTRiNmNjODljNm QyNmM4YTQxNzliNDY2NGVhNmY=.

45. *Wesberry v. Sanders*, 376 U.S. 1 (1964); *Gray v. Sanders*, 372 U.S. 368, 381 (1963).

46. *Reynolds v. Sims*, 377 U.S. 533, 568–576 (1964).

47. *Id.* at 561–568.

48. *Dept. of Commerce*, 525 U.S. at 328–329. The state of Utah had standing for the same reason—that it was going to lose a congressional seat as a result of the statistical sampling at issue. *Evans*, 536 U.S. at 452–453 (2002).

49. *Evans*, 536 U.S. at 464 (2002).

50. *Id.* at 462.

51. *Wisconsin v. City of New York*, 517 U.S. 1 (1996), *Legal Tender Cases*, 79 U.S. 457, 536 (1870); *United States v. Moriarity*, 106 F. 886, 891 (S.D.N.Y. 1901);

52. *Wisconsin*, 517 U.S. at 15 (quoting *Franklin v. Massachusetts*, 505 U.S. 788, 804 (1992)).

53. U.S. Const. art. I, § 8, cl. 17 (District Clause).

54. U.S. Const. amend. XXIII.

55. District of Columbia Voting Rights Act of 2009, 111th Cong., 1st Sess., H.R. 157, S. 160.

56. U.S. Const. art. I, § 2, cl. 1.

57. Same Day Registration Act, 111th Cong., 1st Sess., H.R. 3957, S. 1986 (2009).

58. *See generally* J. Kenneth Blackwell and Kenneth A. Klukowski, "The Other Voting Right: Protecting Every Citizen's Vote by Safeguarding the Integrity of the Ballot Box," 28 *Yale Law & Policy Review* 107–123 (2009).

59. *Perry v. Pogemiller*, 16 F.3d 138, 140 (7th Cir. 1993); *Anwo v. INS*, 607 F.2d 435, 437 (D.C. Cir. 1979).

CHAPTER 7
Gunfight

1. Kenneth A. Klukowski, "Citizen Gun Rights: Incorporating the Second Amendment Through the Privileges or Immunities Clause," 39 *New Mexico Law Review* 195, 195 & n. 5 (2009) (citing various sources).

2. *District of Columbia v. Heller*, 128 S. Ct. 2783, 2799 (2008).

3. Bill Clinton interview, *60 Minutes II*, CBS, December 19, 2000, http://www.nrawinningteam.com/0012/moretodo.html.

4. "On the Second Amendment, Don't Believe Obama," National Rifle Association, http://www.nraila.org/obama/.

5. Ken Klukowski, "Why is Obama Hiding Under His Desk?," Fox News, March 2, 2010, http://www.foxnews.com/opinion/2010/03/02/ken-klukowski-obama-chicago-gun-ban-supreme-court-hiding-desk/.

6. Remarks of Barack Obama, quoted in Jan Crawford Greenburg, "Obama and Guns," *Legalities,* ABC News, February 15, 2008, http://blogs.abcnews.com/legalities/2008/02/obama-and-guns.html.

7. IVI-IPO General Candidate Questionnaire, September 10, 1996, reproduced in *Politico,* http://www.politico.com/static/PPM43_080328_obama_iviquestionaire_091096.html.

8. *See* Transcript of Oral Argument 5–6 (comments of Kennedy, J.), *District of Columbia v. Heller*, 128 S. Ct. 2783 (2008) (No. 07–290), http://www.supremecourt.gov/oral_arguments/argument_transcripts/07-290.pdf. Justice Kennedy refers to an argument for decoupling the two clauses of the Second Amendment, and specifies that this argument is not found in the "red brief" (each type of brief in the Supreme Court has a different-color cover, and red is the color of the merits brief for respondents).

9. *See generally* Brief for the Second Amendment Foundation as Amicus Curiae Supporting Respondent, *Heller*, 128 S. Ct. 2783 (No. 07–290) (written by Professor Nelson Lund of George Mason).

10. David Kopel, "Oral Argument in *D.C. v. Heller*: The View from the Counsel Table," The Volokh Conspiracy, March 31, 2008, http://volokh.com/2008/03/31/oral-argument-in-dc-v-heller-the-view-from-the-counsel-table/; Michael P. O'Shea, "The Right to Defensive Arms after *District of Columbia v. Heller*," 111 *West Virginia Law Review* 349, 363–366 (2009). *See also* Kenneth A. Klukowski, "Incorporating Gun Rights: A Second Round in the Chamber for the Second Amendment," *Engage*, Vol. 9, November 2009, at p. 10.

11. *The Federalist* No. 46.

12. That was the militia under the first federal law. Act of May 8, 1792, ch. 33, 1 Stat. 271. It's also the militia under current federal law. 10 U.S.C. § 311(a) (2006).

13. *Nordyke v. King*, 563 F.3d 439, 451 (9th Cir. 2009).

14. *Kasler v. Lockyer*, 2 P.3d 581, 602 (Cal. 2000) (Brown, J., concurring).

15. *District of Columbia v. Heller*, 128 S. Ct. 2783, 2801 (2008).

16. *Id.* at 2802.

CHAPTER 8
A Prison for Your Mind: Information

1. *Keyishian v. Board of Regents*, 385 U.S. 589, 605–606 (1967).

2. *Abrams v. United States*, 250 U.S. 616, 630 (1919) (Holmes, J., dissenting).

3. *Citizens United v. FEC*, 130 S. Ct. 876, No. 08–205, slip op. at 36 (January 21, 2010) (quoting *Austin v. Michigan Chamber of Commerce*, 494 U.S. 652, 691 (1990) (Scalia, J., dissenting)) (internal quotation marks omitted).

4. Anita Dunn, in Michael Scherer, "Calling 'Em Out: The White House Takes on the Press," *Time*, October 8, 2009, http://www.time.com/time/politics/article/0,8599,1929058,00.html.

5. Anita Dunn in CNN interview, in "White House Escalates War of Words with Fox News," Politics, Fox News, October 12, 2009, http://www.foxnews.com/politics/2009/10/12/white-house-escalates-war-words-fox-news/.

6. Anita Dunn in interview, *Reliable Sources*, CNN, October 11, 2009.

7. Rahm Emanuel, Interview in State of the Union, CNN, in Noel Sheppard, "Rahm Emanuel: Fox Isn't a News Organization Because it Has a Perspective," NewsBusters, October 18, 2009, http://newsbusters.org/blogs/noel-sheppard/2009/10/18/rahm-emanuel-fox-isnt-news-organization-because-it-has-perspective.

8. David Axelrod, interview in *This Week*, in Mike Allen, "Fox 'Not Really News,' Says Axelrod," *Politico*, October 18, 2009, http://www.politico.com/news/stories/1009/28417.html.

9. Barack Obama, in CNBC interview, in Jake Tapper, "In CNBC Interview, President Obama Attacks Fox News Channel," *Political Punch*, ABC News, June 17, 2009,

http://blogs.abcnews.com/politicalpunch/2009/06/in-cnbc-interview-president-obama-attacks-fox-news-channel.html.

10. *Ibid.*

11. *See, e.g.*, Thomas Schaller, "Rush Limbaugh Is the Leader of the Republican Party," *Salon,* March 1, 2009, http://www.salon.com/news/feature/2009/03/01/limbaugh/.

12. *See, e.g.*, Faye Fiore and Mark E. Barabak, "Rush Limbaugh Has His Grip on the GOP Microphone," *Los Angeles Times,* February 8, 2009, http://articles.latimes.com/2009/feb/08/nation/na-rush8.

13. Interview of Rahm Emanuel on *Face the Nation*, CBS, in Sam Stein, "Rahm on Rush: He's The Voice, Energy and Intellect of the GOP," *Huffington Post,* March 1, 2009, http://www.huffingtonpost.com/2009/03/01/rahm-on-rush-hes-the-voic_n_170854.html.

14. Barack Obama, quoted in *New York Post*, in "Obama: Quit Listening to Rush Limbaugh if You Want to Get Things Done," Fox News, January 23, 2009, http://www.foxnews.com/politics/2009/01/23/obama-quit-listening-rush-limbaugh-want-things/.

15. Paul Bedard, "Democratic Poll: Rush Limbaugh Is a Drag on the Republican Party," Washington Whispers, *U.S. News & World Report,* March 11, 2009, http://www.usnews.com/blogs/washington-whispers/2009/03/11/democratic-poll-rush-limbaugh-is-a-drag-on-the-republican-party.html.

16. *Red Lion Broadcasting Co., Inc. v. FCC*, 395 U.S. 367, 386–401 (1969).

17. *E.g.*, Seton Motley, "Video: FCC 'Diversity' Czar on Chavez's Venezuela: Incredible . . . Democratic Revolution," NewsBusters, August 28, 2009, http://newsbusters.org/blogs/seton-motley/2009/08/28/video-fcc-diversity-czar-chavezs-venezuela-incredible-democratic-revol.

18. Mark Lloyd, Remarks at National Conference for Media Reform, June 10, 2008, in Motley, *supra* note 17.

19. Motley, *supra* note 17.

20. The Franking Commission operates under the Committee on House Administration in the U.S. House of Representatives. It was created by Pub. L. No. 93–191.

21. Press Release from House Minority Leader John Boehner, "Boehner Blasts Censorship of Chart Detailing Democrats' Government-Run Health Care Labyrinth," July 28, 2009.

22. *See* Walter Alarkon, "Pelosi, Rahm Do Not Scare Rep. DeFazio," *The Hill,* December 18, 2009, http://thehill.com/homenews/house/72889-pelosi-rahm-do-not-scare-rep-defazio.

23. George Washington, in Upton Sinclair, ed., *The Cry for Justice: An Anthology of the Literature of Social Protest* (Philadelphia: John C. Winston, 1915), p. 305.

24. Senate Report No. 95–1071 (1978).

25. Pub. L. No. 110–409, 122 Stat. 4302 (2008).

26. 5 U.S.C. app. § 3(b).

27. 5 U.S.C. app. § 8G(e).

28. Byron York, "Gerald Walpin Speaks: The Inside Story of the AmeriCorps Firing," *Washington Examiner,* June 14, 2009, http://www.washingtonexaminer.com/opinion/blogs/beltway-confidential/Gerald-Walpin-speaks-the-inside-story-of-the-AmeriCorps-firing-48030697.html.

29. *Walpin v. Corporation for National and Community Service,* 1:09-cv-01343-RWR (D.D.C. filed July 17, 2009).

30. *Citizens United v. FEC,* 130 S. Ct. 876, No. 08–205 (January 21, 2010).

31. *Id.,* slip op. at 35–37.

32. *Id.,* slip op. at 35 (quoting *McConnell v. FEC,* 540 U.S. 93, 283 (2003) (Thomas, J., dissenting)).

33. Video documentary on Kevin Jennings, published by Family Research Council, http://www.stopjennings.org/.

34. John 8:32.

CONCLUSION
A New Birth of Freedom

1. Irving Babbit, *Democracy and Leadership* (1924).

2. George Will, in Panel Discussion with Terry Moran, *This Week,* ABC, February 21, 2010.

3. Ronald W. Reagan, Address on Behalf of Barry Goldwater, October 27, 1964.

4. Ronald W. Reagan, Address to the Annual Meeting of the Phoenix Chamber of Commerce, March 30, 1961.

ACKNOWLEDGMENTS

The authors would like to thank:

Our wives, Rosa Blackwell and Amanda Klukowski, and Klukowski's young children, Chase and Caleb.

Attorney General Ed Meese; Steve Forbes; Tony Perkins, Rob Schwarzwalder, and our colleagues at the Family Research Council; Wayne LaPierre, Sandy Froman, John Sigler, and our colleagues at the National Rifle Association; Susan Carleson and our colleagues at the American Civil Rights Union; Chris Chocola, Thomas ("Dusty") Rhodes, and our colleagues at the Club for Growth; Mathew Staver and our colleagues at Liberty University and Liberty Counsel; Duane Parde, David Stanley, and our colleagues at the National Taxpayers Union; Becky Norton Dunlop and our friends at the Council for National Policy; Foster Friess; Pat Pizzella, and our colleagues at the Conservative Action Project; Colin Hanna and our friends at Let Freedom Ring; Drew Griffis; Jim Lord; Nelson Lund; Carlo LoParo; Bob Morrison; *Fox Forum* editor Lynne Jordal Martin; Jonathan Garthwaite and our colleagues at Townhall.com; Andrew Breitbart and our colleagues at BigGovernment.com; *World Magazine*; Al Regnery and our friends at the *American Spectator*; our friends at the Republican National Committee; our agent Jason Allen Ashlock; our publicist Justin Loeber; and our editing team at Lyons Press, especially our editor Keith Wallman, our marketing and PR director Inger Forland, and our project editor Kristen Mellitt.

This book would not have been possible without you.

INDEX

ABOUT THE AUTHORS

Ken (J. Kenneth) Blackwell is a senior fellow with the Family Research Council and the American Civil Rights Union, and previously worked as a fellow with the Heritage Foundation. For seventeen years, he was a member of the Xavier University faculty and administration.

In 1998, Mr. Blackwell delivered the Becket Lecture on Religious Liberty at Oxford University. He is a member of the Arlington Group, an influential national coalition of pro-life, pro-family, and religious leaders and organizations. He has lectured at Harvard, the University of Newcastle in England, the Moscow State Institute of International Relations in Russia, and the International Academy of Public Administration in Paris. Many of his speeches and lectures have been published in *Vital Speeches of the Day*.

He was a founding partner of the highly successful Blue Chip Broadcasting, Inc., a network of twenty radio stations. At the time of its sale in 2001, Blue Chip Broadcasting had become the second-largest African American–owned radio company in the nation. He and his wife of forty-two years, Rosa, who served as superintendent of Cincinnati Public Schools, have three adult children. In 1994 the Blackwells were honored as one of the National Council of Negro Women's Families of the Year, and, in 1996 Mr. and Mrs. Blackwell together received the Martin Luther King, Jr., Dreamkeeper Award from the Cincinnati Historical Society. In 2006, the Blackwells became shareholders in the Cincinnati Reds, the city's major league baseball team. Mr. Blackwell is a member of the Sigma Pi Phi fraternity, the Ohio Gun Collectors Association, and the Literary Club of Cincinnati.

Ken (Kenneth A.) Klukowski is a Washington, D.C.–based attorney, consultant, and journalist. He is a fellow and senior legal analyst with the American Civil Rights Union. He covers the U.S. Supreme

Court for Townhall.com and is a contributor for BigGovernment. com and for *Fox Forum,* the online opinion page for Fox News. He is also frequently published by numerous other outlets, including the Wall Street Journal, the New York Post, Politico, the Washington Times, and the Washington Examiner. He has worked in several positions in government and for public interest organizations, and currently writes, consults, and speaks on legal, political, and public policy issues, and lectures at law schools across the nation.

Klukowski's work covers the full range of issues but focuses on the Constitution and the federal judiciary. He has represented various conservative organizations in writing amicus briefs in Supreme Court cases involving First Amendment and Second Amendment issues. His scholarly works have been published by Georgetown Journal of Law & Public Policy, New Mexico Law Review, George Mason University Civil Rights Law Journal, and the Yale Law & Policy Review, and have been cited in a number of respected legal journals and in court filings. He holds an undergraduate degree in business from the University of Notre Dame, studied history and political science at Arizona State University, has formally studied theology, and earned his law degree from George Mason University School of Law. A native of Indiana, he currently lives in the Virginia suburbs outside Washington, D.C., with his wife Amanda, who is a practicing emergency room physician, and their two young children, Chase and Caleb.